WITHOUT RAIN
THERE CAN BE NO RAINBOWS

A MULTIMEDIA MEMOIR
BY RYAN CHIN

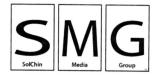

SolChin   Media   Group

SolChin Media Group, Portland, OR
www.solchinmedia.com

20 19 18 17 16 15 14 13 12 11   1 2 3 4 5

ISBN 978-0-9836073-2-8

Although this is a work of nonfiction, certain names have been changed to protect privacy. Unless otherwise stated, all pictures and video accompanying this multimedia memoir are the original creation of the author.

A MULTIMEDIA MEMOIR

THROUGHOUT THIS BOOK, YOU'LL see this symbol 🖥, indicating that a video accompanies the text. Although the book stands alone as its own storytelling device, each of the twenty-four videos adds visual and audio accents to the written story. The footage in the videos was extracted from over sixty hours of tape that I shot in New Zealand and in the years since my return. The videos are meant to be viewed *between the lines* as you are reading—I have taken great care in choosing the videos' content and their placement with the goal of building on the ideas, emotions, or images presented in the text. Some are simply quick clips of raw footage, but most are edited with musical scores, voiceovers, and meticulously crafted sequences. They'll act as a window into New Zealand culture and my experiences as I lived and taught there. All the videos are short—ranging from thirty seconds to three and a half minutes.

Whenever you see this symbol 🖥, simply use the accompanying code to look the video up on Youtube, Vimeo, or www.withoutrain.com.

As a writer I have strived to make every word count, and as a filmmaker I have agonized over every second of video that you will see. I had no idea how the two practices would come together to deliver my story, but as the Kiwis say, I had to "give it a go!"

Youtube Channel: withoutrainmemoir
Vimeo: withoutrainmemoir

BE ⚇ THE MATCH®

A portion of the book's profits are donated to Be The Match.

MY BROTHER PASSED AWAY from leukemia; he was only twenty years old. His doctors told us a bone marrow transplant could save him, so everyone in our family had our blood tested to see if we were a match. When none of us were, we turned to the Be The Match Registry, but still no match was found. During every happy moment in my life that I can't share with my brother, I can't help but think: *What if? What if we'd found him a match?*

At the time, the number of people registered as bone marrow donors was small, with very few minorities, and the only way to be tested was by having blood drawn. Nowadays, medical and technical advances have made it easier than ever to register as a donor. After signing up online, you'll receive an in-home kit to swab your cheek and mail back. There are now nine million potential donors on the Be the Match Registry, but there can never be enough. Minorities are especially needed—because tissue types are inherited, patients are most likely to match someone of their own ethnicity.

Every year, more than ten thousand patients in the United States are diagnosed with life-threatening diseases such as leukemia or lymphoma, and their best hope for survival is a bone marrow transplant from an *unrelated* donor. You can help save a life so somebody else's family doesn't have to ask 'what if?'

Please consider registering with Be the Match. More information can be found at www.BeTheMatch.org.

My sister, brother, and I.

CONTENTS

CHAPTER
1

HOW WRONG I AM

I LOOK FOR MY best friend of six years. His seat is empty, but in some ways he's here: the essence of his soft fur and good-morning face licks, his tail thumping the van door, his liver breath, that deep groove between his eyes that I always rubbed with my fingers. My chest tightens, but my grief must wait; a crisis looms.

My van and I claw up a formidable hill, faint headlamps parting the blackness. The hill steepens, and the van sputters. I straighten up, take a few deep breaths, and grip the steering wheel a little harder. Dented guardrails hug the road on one side, a crumbling cliff on the other. There is nowhere to pull off of this road—the maps call it a highway—in my current location, Middle of Nowhere, New Zealand.

It's easy to find yourself in the middle of nowhere in New Zealand. While roughly the size of California or Japan, New Zealand only has a population of four million people. By comparison, California has thirty-six million, and Japan one hundred fifty million. It's well known that New Zealand has more sheep than people. In fact, the ratio is twelve to one. So if I break down and no one is around, maybe a dozen sheep will help push us. *Us* I should explain, is my old red van named Lonna and me, a Chinese American on a mission to find a primary school teaching position in New Zealand.

Rain batters Lonna's windshield and pounds her roof. Her dented roof can hold enough water to help me survive for days, but our erratic ascent causes the roof water to cascade down the back window. Her worn cylinders lose compression; the RPM needle dances. She's barely holding it together, but her pride—and our safety—is at stake.

"C'mon, girl," I say, rocking back and forth in my seat in an effort to be more involved in our ascent. "You can do it."

The voltage light flickers, so I turn off her wipers. Lonna likes that and revs up a little. I concentrate all remaining power and turn off her lights. I downshift into first gear and squint into the darkness. I've had some adventures, but driving with no lights and no wipers on a pitch-black, rain-soaked night is entirely new for me.

Darkness and more darkness, I'm still inhaling, and still rocking. As we crest the hill, I finally exhale, raising my hands overhead like the speedy kid on the schoolyard who beats everyone to the fence and back. With the hill behind us, I flick the lights back on. If Toughy were here, he'd be giving me the look: *Laughing again? What's so funny now?*

Toughy, my first dog, a chow chow—golden retriever mix, passed four months ago. Even though I'm in a different country, driving a different van, I constantly find myself cracking the windows for him and waiting for his tail-wagging, face-licking greeting whenever I return. But when I look at the seat next to mine, there are nothing but CD cases, notebooks, and overripe bananas—and that's just the tip of the emptiness.

Toughy and I found each other during a drive I took from Chicago to San Francisco. Fresh out of college and on my way to my first career job, I was determined to create my own life. With the cruise control on, my feet on the dash, and the blur of the Arizona desert out my van window, I decided it was time to have a dog. The next day I stopped to see an old friend in San Diego and learned his dog, a golden retriever, had mated with a chow chow. I figured it was no coincidence, and we walked up the street to check out the pups.

Toughy at eight months old.

I unlatched a wooden gate and walked into a small yard. Four puppies and a protective, barking mother swirled around me. The largest puppy reared up, put his oversized paws on my leg, and began licking my hand.

"All the other ones are for sale, but you can *have* him," said the chow chow's owner. "His name is Toughy. You're the first person he hasn't bitten."

I quickly scooped him up and was out the gate with my first dog. For six years he taught me to share my time and the joys of caring and love. He knew that he was holding me back from my dream of living overseas, and I'm certain that's why he passed.

Since my arrival in New Zealand, I repeat a sort of daily mantra: "You'll find a full-time teaching job here. You have to. He left you so you could do this."

Despite my belief in fate, it's not looking too good: broken van, big hills, and hundreds of applicants for every permanent job for which I've applied. It all brings an overwhelming and confusing mix of emotions: worry, fear, depression, determination, excitement, hopelessness, liberation. I want to promise Toughy, "I won't let you down, boy."

Lonna and I pull into a picnic area next to a lake, relieved we've made it to a good nesting spot for the night. We come to a skidding stop in the wet grass next to a sign that reads *No Camping*. I turn off the engine and stare into the darkness, while still holding the steering wheel. When blood returns to my hands and my heart drops out of my throat, I fumble for my headlamp and toothbrush.

Will Lonna start in the morning? Who knows? It's not the best situation, but for the time being I'm totally sorted. *Sorted* is a local term I've picked up recently. Once you make it up and over a hill in an ailing, twenty-year-old van, you turn to your imaginary passenger and shout, "We're sorted, mate!"

The rain lightens up, and I shuffle over to the lakeside to brush my teeth, disrupting the placid surface with a mouthful of spit. Soon, the rain stops altogether, and the stars come into focus. Watching their shimmering reflection, my eyes follow the tiny waves; they disappear into the darkness but I can still see them—like Toughy. I can't help but let a sigh leak out before I trudge back to my home on wheels.

My eyes open to sunlight, and I'm up in an instant. I walk up to the so-called highway expecting to see a car mechanic and tow service business, but all I see are a few country houses. It's Friday and a temporary teaching job I've landed starts on Monday, leaving a couple of days to go about one hundred miles. I'll make it even if I have to abandon Lonna and hitchhike.

I jump in Lonna, ready to go. But is *she* ready?

She is. I give her some gas and release the clutch. Her old engine spins the tires in the loose gravel, sending the small rocks spitting and pinging Lonna's underside.

Looking at the night's campsite in the rearview mirror, I hear my mom's directives to stay in hotels. She definitely wouldn't approve of my sleeping arrangements, but she'll never know. It's in the job description of sons to withhold worry-inducing information from their mothers. For years I rock climbed and never went into any detail about what it actually entailed. I'm sure she thought I was just scrambling around on some rocks, not high on some wall with my legs shaking, wondering how I was going to continue going upward or retreat downward.

Mom and Dad would be cool parents in anyone's book. In the book of Asian parents, however, they are super cool. Both were born in small villages in southern China, and both came to America in their early teens. If you went by stereotypes, you'd think they'd be very traditional with a rigid idea of success. The opposite is true. They never made me play the piano (although I wish they had), and they never pressured me to do anything I didn't want to do. Back when skateboarding was looked down upon and there were no skate parks, my dad helped me build my own ramps and my mom drove me to the next town to buy skate equipment. All the love, support, and gentle guidance they provided must be part of the reason I'm so driven to succeed on this current endeavor of mine.

Despite Lonna's great start, she quickly shows symptoms of the previous night's malady. I gather as much speed as possible on a descent into a canyon, swoosh across a bridge spanning a large river, and grit my teeth for the hopeful climb out of the canyon. Her will, my will—it's just not enough, and the climb halts our northward progress. Lonna's rusted rims and worn tires come to a crunching stop in some gravel on the side of the road.

I stare at the map for a moment and toss it aside. Who knows what's nearby? What difference does it really make? I have no cell phone signal and no idea how far I will have to walk until I get a signal or reach a pay phone. I take a few deep breaths with my forehead on the steering wheel, a few allotted seconds of despair, and then I'm on it.

At least the view is good. We've managed to climb about four hundred feet above the river. Off to my right is a drop-off into a valley and to my left, a short cliff. Although I can't see the ocean itself, I can see where the broad, green river valley and its dotted pastures end. The river has a hint of color, as many rivers in their lower reaches do; it probably runs clear during dry periods, but the sinuous sandbars tell me this river moves a lot of sediment. Down in the valley, the weak morning sun has given way to more intense spring rays. But up here where I'm standing, there's still a hint of the night's chill.

Opening Lonna's back hatch, I shake my head, staring at the mountain of items I've accumulated in such a short time. I've heard more than one story of sticky-fingered locals making slick work of a tourist's car on the side of the road. I don't worry, though. I've got *the* plan.

My laptop, documents, money, cameras, and anything else important fly into my backpack. No cars coming? No sound of cars? Anyone watching? No? All right. Go. I stash my surfboards in the bushes and cover them with a spattering of ferns. I'm ready.

Heading north on foot, I'm ready to crawl over this most recent hurdle in my mission. There will be no jumping hurdles today—my backpack is too heavy. Shouldering all my valuables, and enough provisions to paddle back to California, I begin my chug up the hill that sidelined Lonna. I begin to think of the e-mail I will send my family and friends who are following my adventure: *Lonna grew ill, and I trekked for hours and hours and days and...*

Just minutes into my epic breakdown trek, the road levels out and I'm looking at a few buildings with peeling paint. The sign on one reads *Raupunga Post and Store*, on another, *Te Huki Arts and Craft*. Both have closed doors and cheerless, sagging windows. I seem to be in a small town—or what used to be a small town. Across the street from the buildings is what looks like an outhouse, covered in graffiti. A little farther back lie some railroad tracks, looking shiny enough to be active. Cows, sheep, and birds do what they do best: moo, baa, and tweet. I see no one.

A passing stock truck breaks the silence, sending me scurrying from the road. The stench lingers for a moment before a slight breeze wisps it away. By the time the hum of the truck fades, I'm back on the road, staring blankly at this ghost town. Where is everyone? Do people live here? I imagine a few dust devils and a tumbleweed or two bumping into my leg. No pay phone, no one in sight, but graffiti: what is this place?

But wait. Is that singing? I start to feel at ease. Yes, I can make out the faint sound of children singing. In the distance, a single road branches off from the highway, curving hard to the left and passing a white building atop a hill. It must be a school. My mind races—*They will have a phone, and maybe I can make a connection.* Maybe I was *fated* to break down here. For months I've been trying to land a permanent teaching job for the 2003 school year and maybe, just maybe, this is it.

First, though, an open door in a one-storey brick building catches my eye. I walk toward the house and call out from the porch, but I get no response. Everything seems to be at a standstill. The birds have stopped chirping, as if they're waiting to see what my next move is. There's an old phone with a tangled cord on a table near the door. I think of helping myself, but something about the place tells me to be cautious. Then, the sound of an engine breaks the spell, drawing my gaze away from the phone.

A lone motorcycle makes its way down the road from the school. Even at this distance, I feel the driver's eyes on me—the gaze of a lone rider on a mustang clip-clopping into a lawless town. I dare not move. Best to just stay put on the front porch. A small boy sits on the driver's lap. Unhurried, yet purposefully, they close in on my position. The rider, a Maori man about my height but much stockier, eases the motorcycle to a stop at the building's edge, and I wait for him to cut the engine before I speak.

"Howzit, mate! My van broke down just down the hill. Could I use your phone?"

He lowers the small boy to the ground, never taking his eyes off me, and I grow a little nervous. What if he thinks I'm lying, a thief who was ready to walk in the open door?

"I can give ya a few bucks," I add, taking my backpack off and setting it on the porch.

He sizes me up for a bit, saying nothing. Like many other New Zealanders I've met, he seems momentarily thrown off by an Asian dude with an American accent. Even in Auckland and Wellington, the two largest cities, many people have assumed I don't understand English well. In the smaller towns, I've gotten a few Bruce Lee and Jackie Chan catcalls.

"No problem," he finally replies, swinging off the bike and striding toward the open door. Unlike his father, the boy seems a little unsure of himself, struggling just to keep upright, clinging to whatever he can get his hands on. Still in diapers and not a day over two, the little boy will learn to be a tough guy soon enough.

As the man lumbers past me, I realize he isn't large. He doesn't have the tree-trunk stockiness typical of many Maoris—the indigenous people of New Zealand. That said, his forearms bulge and a rugged air surrounds him. His shaved head accentuates his face, and a tank top shows his lean yet formidable shoulders.

I'm glad he brings the phone outside, as caution keeps whispering to me and I don't want to be cornered. I call AAA, and it turns out I'm only about a twenty-five minute drive from a full-service town. A tow truck will be here as soon as possible. The tough motorcycle man, meanwhile, tells me I'm in a town called Raupunga, and the singing is indeed coming from a primary school. I'd like to drop off a mini-portfolio and résumé at the school, but the last thing I need is for the tow truck driver to get to my van before I do. I give the little boy some *lollies*—candy—and thank the man with a thumbs-up and, "Sweet as, mate."

In the short time I've been here, I've become a proficient user of the term *sweet as*. It can mean "Thank you," "It's all

good," "Goodbye," "See ya later," or—most useful for me—
"Chill out, man. I don't want to fight!" I was in a bar in Auckland one night when a monster Maori man sarcastically mim-
icked an Asian language, attempting to get a rise out of me.
I looked up—and up—at him, unflinchingly, straight in the
eye because I knew he'd respect that, and replied, "*Kia ora,
koe Ryan ahou!*"—Maori for "Hello, my name is Ryan!" Then,
in the instant before he would have pummeled me, I smiled,
extended my hand, and said, "Sweet as, mate!"

Now, the motorcycle man simply nods at my thanks. As the
little boy rips into the lollies, I race back down the hill to load
my surfboards into Lonna. Total time spent packing my stuff
for the walk and hiding all my belongings: about an hour. Total time I was away from Lonna: about twenty minutes.

Soon I'm headed north again, only this time in the tow
truck. I still want to drop a mini-portfolio off at the school just
in case I was *meant* to break down in Raupunga, but my conversation with the driver distracts me and the town is quickly
behind us.

"Yeah, mate." The driver chuckles. "Ya picked a staunch place
to break down. There'd be nothin' left of your van tomorrow."

Staunch is another word I'd never heard before coming to
New Zealand. In this case it means Raupunga is the real deal,
a tough place, an area full of men like the one I just met—and
probably not the best place for a lone Chinese dude to break
down.

As the town fades in the rearview mirror, the driver tells me
stories of gang warfare, and all I can do is sit there with my
lower jaw hanging. As he describes it, that peaceful little town
has an underlying madness. The stories confirm the sense of
wariness I felt, but none of it really makes sense: Aren't gangs
a big city thing? Had I been in danger? I look at the rolling
green out the window and think, *Oh well, I'll never set foot in
that place again.*

How wrong I am.

CHAPTER
2

FULL ON

WHEN I FIRST EXITED the plane in New Zealand, the morning sun slanted across the tarmac, and I fell into a military gait, adrenaline flowing through my veins. This wasn't just an adventure or a vacation, a surf trip or a fishing trip—this was a mission, and it was just beginning. I grabbed my sweat-stained old backpack from the conveyor belt and situated it on my back. The pressure from its straps felt good—like I was going somewhere. Dragging my surfboard bag to a pay phone, I thumbed through a guidebook to find a place to stay. *Stay focused*, I told myself. *That'll keep you one step ahead of the sadness.* Soon, I found a shuttle to downtown Auckland.

The airport, like many airports, was located in an industrial area, so there was no scenery to feast on. I leaned my head against the glass and thought, *Well, you've wanted to come here for years now.*

When I first stepped into the classroom, I knew teaching was something I'd take overseas. Teaching instantly intertwines you with a community, immediately puts you in touch with a community's beliefs, struggles, triumphs, and demons. I'd wanted to teach overseas for three years, but I never would've left Toughy.

During Toughy's last two months, I fixed just about everything to try to get him to eat. One night, I called him over to an empty plate and spooned out a new kind of food, hoping he'd try a few bites. A few licks off the spoon, a couple of chomps off the plate—my insides unknotted a little.

"Good boy, you have to eat…"

Toughy's illness led me to brush the dust from old memories, mental photos I hadn't examined since they were taken. I stared at the plates of uneaten dog food, thinking of my brother. He couldn't eat, either, after his chemotherapy treatments. His real name was Raymond, but I called him *I-Gaw*—Chinese for "oldest brother." I-Gaw, who was four years older than me, contracted leukemia during my second year of high school. I remembered him shaking and vomiting while my family looked on, helpless and too afraid to cry.

I-Gaw hadn't gone easily. When he was nineteen, he went to the doctor for a persistent cough, and they found a tumor on his lung, caused by testicular cancer. Surgery and chemo had him back at college just a year later—a true miracle. For a while, his checkups were perfect. No news was good news. Each checkup was cause for celebration because the doctors said that after a year of being cancer-free, it was unlikely that the testicular cancer would return. The doctors were just as surprised as we were when a rare form of leukemia showed up in his blood over a year after he had beaten his first cancer.

Toughy's liver was full of holes. I tried to keep doing things that made us happy, though. He still begged to play ball, and we continued our regular trips to our secluded spot in the Sierra Nevadas. At times like that, it was hard to believe anything was wrong with him. With his thick coat, he didn't even look like skin and bones.

In the mountains one morning, I pulled out pots and pans, bacon and eggs. Hearing the pans, Toughy looked up, cocking his head. *Ya cookin' bacon and eggs?* I boiled chicken for his meal, and Toughy turned his nose up at it. So I minced it with some bacon, cracked an egg in it, added a little canned dog food, and rested it on the ground in front of me while I sat down to eat my own food. No dog—not even a sick one—could resist this mountain special. Toughy took a few tentative bites then dived in until it was half gone. Good boy! I tossed the leftover special into the fire pit, since I knew he wouldn't touch it again. The vet told me Toughy would probably try new foods for a while but would associate each new food with nausea. Eventually, he'd just stop eating altogether.

A flash of anger coursed through me, but it was short-lived. I could ask why all I wanted, but there were no answers, just piles of uneaten dog food.

When it was clear that Toughy would be leaving me, I decided it was time to push off from familiar shores. New Zealand was the primary target—for its physical beauty, indigenous culture, and surfing and fishing.

Fishing! I was born with the angling seed in me. When I was seven, my parents bought me a fishing magazine that contained an article about New Zealand. A full-page picture of snowcapped mountains and a meandering stream stuck with me, and more than one creative writing assignment during my schooling detailed giant fish caught in New Zealand—no matter that I hadn't been there.

You can call it being free, following your dreams, or simple recklessness. Whatever it is, I'd just spent thousands of dollars to get to New Zealand with no teaching position waiting for me. All I had were some official papers showing I was a teacher and the belief that I was supposed to be there.

Hitting the ground running, I found a place to stay for the week, went for a jog, bought a cell phone, and sent off dozens of e-mails to schools with available positions. By lunchtime I'd already ripped through a couple phone cards speaking with principals. Some were very receptive to the idea of me visiting their schools, but I could tell many of them didn't want to go through the trouble of hiring a foreigner. Why should they with so many local applicants?

I reminded myself to slow down. It wouldn't all happen in a day, no matter how much I wanted it to, so some sightseeing was in order. *Just change the blade, man,* I told myself. This had been my motto since Toughy was in his final months.

When I learned we only had a few months together, I decided to make a grave marker out of wood. One evening I pulled up to my house with a load of wood that needed to be milled to the proper thickness. It had been a hectic day with the kids at school, and I had attended a friend's birthday dinner. I ripped the van doors open and jammed my finger in the process. As I stood there rubbing my joints, Toughy looked at me as though he were asking, *What's your problem?* And I thought, *What is my problem? Everything takes time. Just relax.* Once I unloaded the wood, I realized the blade on the band saw needed to be switched in order to make the proper cuts. Milling the wood just wasn't going to happen in my exhausted state, but I forced myself to change the blade so the saw would be ready the next night.

The next night I set out to mill and cut the wood. I twirled the piece of walnut in my hands, admiring the grain patterns, and wondered if it remembered when it was just a sapling. Did it know how much meaning it would have when I was done with it? Perhaps it felt a sense of pride at its selection for such an important job. Putting it on the table, I started to sketch a large bone on it. I wanted to cut the bone shape out right away, but I didn't want to rush the project. I set it down and told myself, *Little by little. Just change the blade, man. Just change the blade....*

Even with this reminder to be patient, I hurried back to the hostel after a quick tour of downtown. Dad had always told me to get my workspace in order for efficiency, so I quickly transformed the lobby of my hole-in-the-wall hostel into an

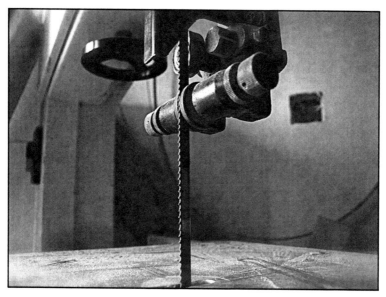

Just change the blade … you'll get there.

office. The place, down a dark central Auckland side street, wasn't that bad, really, but when most of the businesses on the street are strip clubs, you can assume any accommodations in the vicinity may very well be holes in the wall. Mom wouldn't approve, but she'd never know.

To save money, I reserved my cell phone for return calls only, so I spent many hours on my office chair—actually a bar stool with a torn vinyl top—in front of the lobby pay phone. Organization has never been my strong suit, but the mission conjured something new in me: I was taking meticulous notes.

Part of my strategy was to show my face at different schools and to volunteer at any school I could. First, I made a spreadsheet with columns labeled: Name, Location, Phone Number, Contact, Notes. Soon, I'd find a van and hit the road; by then, the schools would be expecting me. It was the perfect plan— I'd familiarize myself with the New Zealand curriculum, catch a few waves and trout along the way, and hopefully get a foot in the door.

It was tempting to work nonstop. Three days passed in a blur; I hardly slept. Suddenly, it was Friday. Not a single minute had been wasted, but it still felt like I hadn't done enough. *Little by little*, I told myself. That afternoon, I forced myself to sit on a park bench and relax. I watched business folks walk by, a Friday evening bounce in their steps. Right then, I decided that my work week had ended too. I was going to have a night out. After a hefty nap, I strolled out of the hostel wearing my party duds. I'm not one to dress up, but I enjoy the contrast of being the kind of person who can go for weeks wearing the same clothes and not showering to the kind who gets dressed for a night on the town.

As I wandered the streets, a certain sort of loneliness crept over me. There were people all around me, I realized, but I was alone. Everything inside me tightened a little, and for the first time since I'd landed, I thought back to my Friday nights in San Francisco.

If Toughy and I didn't head to the mountains and remained in the city for the weekend, I'd often find myself stumbling back to my van after a night out with good friends. Toughy would be waiting. I'd open the door and, imagining Chewbacca flying the Millenium Falcon, say, "Hey, boy, can you drive me home?" He'd give me a few licks, not minding the beer breath, and I'd curl up in a sleeping bag and pass out. Hours later I'd figure out where I was, pop a few ibuprofen, slug some water, and charge to the beach for some surf.

Having washed away the hangover with a few waves, I'd claw my way onto the beach, and Toughy would gallop toward me. How he knew it was me from so far away, I don't know, but his wagging tail and kisses seemed to say, *Glad you're all right. Now will you throw a stick, already?*

That night in Auckland, there would be no Toughy, no familiar van, no good friends.

Toughy died while I was driving to Chicago for my cousin's wedding. The vet had given him two months to live, and just over two months had passed. I couldn't leave Toughy in California, so I forfeited my plane ticket, and we climbed in the van. In Montana, he started to fade. On his last night I felt his heart racing and he never closed his eyes; I think he wanted us to spend every last minute together. The next day he was stumbling on land and falling over in the back of the van. I strained my neck to look at him, and my gaze met his jaundiced eyes, glassy and soulless. My furry son no longer knew who I was. It was midnight, and we were on a lonely stretch of highway in South Dakota.

"It'll be over soon, boy," I said reassuringly over my shoulder as my beloved first dog panted mucous through his nose, his chest heaving erratically.

Toughy slammed into the side of the van as I drove, so I eased to the side of the road, walked around to the sliding door, took a deep breath, and opened it. Mucous dripped from the large window as I buried my face in the side of Toughy's body. I heaved long, red-eyed sobs, and then released. I had a job to do.

It was still about forty-five minutes to a major city. I couldn't have him bouncing around in the back of the van, so I made a barricade with sleeping bags, backpacks, and crates in order to keep him in the front seat. He settled in with my hand on his back. Finally, I pulled into a typical High Plains gas station. Some of the numbers on the gas price sign were missing, a few of the fluorescent lights under the canopy flickered, and a large woman sat behind the counter, staring at a fuzzy black-and-white TV.

"Could I use your phone book, please? My dog is really sick and I need to find an emergency vet," I asked, trying not to sound too tragic.

She broke from the snowy screen long enough to hand off the phone book.

The emergency vet, fortunately, was just minutes away. As I pulled into the parking lot, I called my mom, who sobbed on the phone, sharing in my grief. I could tell she was reliving some of the pain of losing my brother. I thought of her caring for him in his dying days and was overwhelmed by compassion for her.

The vet looked quickly through Toughy's records while I held him on the examining table. "Whenever you are ready," she said, and I asked for a minute.

Kneeling in front of Toughy, I lowered my head against his and whispered, "Thanks, boy. Thanks for being such a good boy and making me so happy." This was finally it. The being that had picked me to be his dad was leaving me. I hadn't even felt this shattered at my brother's bedside. Maybe I hadn't properly mourned I-Gaw's death. Sure, I cried a lot. But had I really absorbed it? Or was it because Toughy was *my* responsibility, the one who showed me that some things were more important than myself? I opened the door for the vet and put my head on Toughy's again. I kept it there until his heaving stopped. We had traveled our last mile together.

My loneliness was palpable as I entered the Auckland bar and ordered a margarita. Almost immediately, I could tell it was going to be a banner first Friday Down Under. I got to talking with a few born-and-bred New Zealanders—or Kiwis, as they're called—at the bar, and we became fast friends. My story spilled out: my dog dying, my decision to come to New Zealand, my dumpy hostel, the hundreds of e-mails and phone calls, and the red tape involved in finding a teaching job.

Most disturbingly, primary teaching positions were not listed on the official skill shortage list. This meant that even if I made a good impression on a principal or hiring committee, they would need to write a letter to New Zealand Immigration explaining why they were hiring me instead of a New Zealand citizen. Immigration could still deny me a work permit even if a school wanted to hire me.

Not wanting to dwell on my challenges, I topped off my rant with a swig of margarita.

The Kiwis dug the story from the Chinese dude with an American accent. The most common response: "Mate! That's full on!"

"Full on!" I repeated, raising my glass.

Full on?

While gulping my third, fourth, and maybe fifth margaritas—it was one of those nights—I inquired about this local term.

"Ah, mate, it's like this," one guy explained. "If the All Blacks (the New Zealand national rugby team) are about to play the Aussies, then it's full on, mate!"

"If someone gets cheeky and you start swinging, then it's full on!"

"Mate! You are on a full-on mission!"

One swaying gent recounted a story about his car's transmission acting up in the middle of nowhere, forcing him to drive home backward. "Mate!" he shouted, sending just a little spit my way. "It was full on! It was dark so my mate shined a torch out the back window!"

My full-on night turned to day. Walking the main street in any city in the early morning, it's impossible not to marvel at humanity: the calm and silence even though tens of thousands of people are within shouting distance, the massive, sleeping structures designed and built by the hands of man. It's a time when nature reasserts itself, stealing the stage from the clicking high heels and rumbling combustion engines. The birds were beginning their morning song, and I grasped my cell phone, my mind fixated on Lori.

I met Lori on my first day of my first real teaching job. She was helping the kids on the playground, her hair pulled back in pigtails, and I'd just run from my classroom, eager to meet my new students. I froze, transfixed by her petite frame, brown skin, and cute upturned nose—until one of my students pulled me out of my reverie. Over the course of the next three years, Lori and I shared date-like moments and lingering, heartfelt hugs, but she already had a live-in boyfriend.

I told her how I felt earlier that year, in my classroom's reading center. It was the longest sentence I had ever uttered in my life. "I know you are with someone, and I don't want to create an uncomfortable situation, and I know we work together, and I know this could be unprofessional, but I just have to tell you that I think you are awesome."

She didn't slap me. She didn't tell me to stop. Her smile was genuine, and she hugged me hard and fast. Those date-like moments, beautiful but maddening, continued.

One of our "dates" was a quick lunch getaway during school hours. San Francisco, with its steep hills and surrounding water, offers a multitude of postcard picnic spots. Luckily, one such place was just minutes from the school where we worked.

We settled onto the bare grass with Toughy nearby. Lori took out a container and said softly, "I made this last night."

I peeked inside at a large rectangle of lasagna and wondered if I should cut a piece off or simply dig in as though we were a happy couple sharing food in bliss. Isn't sharing utensils considered a prelude to a kiss? Lori held the container for a few seconds and then set it on the ground near my leg. Toughy cocked his head and looked on; I'm sure he was thinking, *If you guys are going to get all weird about eating, pass it along this way.* I opted for a big scoop onto the lid of the container and set it back down without looking at Lori. My contribution to the picnic consisted of some different cheeses, olives, a baguette, and fresh strawberries. I made her a little sandwich, and we locked eyes.

I had to say something.

"Listen, I want you to know I'm enjoying every minute of getting to know you better, but I also want you to know I would never put you in an uncomfortable situation by trying anything physical."

She gazed out at the water. "I know, I know you wouldn't..." Her voice trailed off as though she were disappointed.

I squeezed a bite of lasagna to the roof of my mouth, allowing the sauce and vegetables to ooze from between the layers of pasta. Delicious by all means, but I could have been just as happy with a peanut butter and jelly sandwich. Lori's face looked even cuter with a bite of my sandwich in her mouth and Toughy behind her. She commented on the elaborate Victorian houses in the neighborhood and, once again, we couldn't look at each other as we discussed the idea of owning a house and settling in. San Francisco Bay glistened in the distance, the sounds of Toughy destroying a tennis ball filled the gaping holes in conversation, and all too soon it was time to rush back to school. I meant what I said about not making her uncomfortable, but I still couldn't help thinking a roll in the grass would've given me more patience with the kids that afternoon.

She was still with her boyfriend when I left for New Zealand, but judging by the hug she gave me at the going away party, it was no mistake to call her from Down Under. I had her number memorized, and on the first ring I started thinking about what to say—she wasn't even my girlfriend, never had been, maybe never would be.

The second ring brought a little anxiety. What would she think?

Third ring, fourth ring, and her voicemail picked up.

"Hey, Lori! This is Ryan. New Zealand is pretty cool. It's going to be hard to find a teaching job, but I'll make it happen. Hope you are well. See ya!"

Perfect. Nothing too deep or over the top. Just saying hi, keeping a line in the water from the bottom of the earth—after all, I do pride myself on being an angler.

Arriving back at the hostel, there was no time for sleep. I shouldered my pack, slipped my surfboard under my arm, and headed out to meet the beach shuttle. I crawled in and passed out immediately.

The driver woke me when we arrived at the beach. I peeled

my body from the seat and peered around. *Where am I? Oh yeah. I'm at Piha, in New Zealand.*

Just twenty-five miles west of Auckland, Piha boasts the closest and most consistent waves. A campground and trailer park have prime real estate just minutes from the water; houses, some large and some small, dot the surrounding hills. Even from a distance, I could tell which ones were local homes and which were for the weekenders with bulging pocketbooks. The rural vibe, so close to the city, surprised me. Telling myself I'd set up camp later, I hurried down to the beach.

For the first time, I laid eyes on the Pacific south of the equator. A large monolith split the long beach in two, and I could make out a few human specks climbing it. I imagined more than a few rookies had fallen from its steep face. It towered over me, as if to say, "You aren't from these parts." I would later learn its name is Lion Rock. Behind me the coastal range rose steeply, boosting more houses towards the sky. I spotted the shuttle inching up the steep, winding road and wondered how I'd slept through all the twists and turns. Plopping my pack and surfboard into a heap, I collapsed beside them.

Now that I was finally at rest, the last few weeks—the going-away parties, my anxiety, my sadness, the all-nighter—caught up to me. High spirits, low spirits, broken spirits, right then, I was too numb for any type of spirit at all.

The sun and sand grabbed me and wouldn't let go. I napped the day away, never suiting up to surf. A surf session would have been nice, but the waves were huge and I was in no condition for drowning. So maybe the next day. It all seemed familiar: the beach, the sun, and my surfboard next to me. *Where's Toughy?* I wondered in my drowsiness. *Oh yeah, he's gone.*

But that's not just a wave crashing—it's a wave crashing in New Zealand!

It's weird, feeling trapped between elation and devastation.

CHAPTER
3

LOOKING IN THE MIRROR

NOTHING FEELS MORE LIKE freedom than the first day of a road trip. I was only a few miles past Auckland's city limits, but my hands already felt at home on the deeply worn grooves of the steering wheel. It was the van's maiden voyage and—not to get too anthropomorphic or anything—she seemed happy that I'd picked her. I could almost feel her tail wagging, like the old dog with a white snout who gets picked over the younger pups at the animal shelter. There was a hole where the radio should've been, so I'd rigged a portable CD player with headphones on the passenger seat.

Vans have a way of not just getting you there but of being there *with* you. Having owned vans for over a decade and being a pro at living out of them, I purchased an old Mitsubishi. I had e-mailed a picture of it to some friends, asking what I should name it, and one friend replied that the red made him think of a lady in a red dress named Lonna. So there it was: Lonna.

Lonna was loaded with food, water, surfboards, fly rods, and a long list of schools with available positions filed safely away on the dashboard. Showing my face at schools and getting away from the hustle of Auckland was just what I needed. Instead of waiting around for something to happen, I was going to make something happen.

I'd set up meetings at a number of schools for the next day, and I was close to my destination with plenty of sun left, so I figured I might as well catch a wave or two. A few dirt roads later, I parked above the high-tide line of a beach. Behind me, sand dunes surrounded a brackish lagoon; a few tire tracks faded away into the shifting sands. There was a farmhouse in the distance, and rock outcrops at either end of the beach cut the view to just short of as far as the eye could see. The waves weren't much, but the exercise would do me good. I pulled my black neoprene suit over my body and plunged into the Pacific. Before long, I was ready for a *feed*—a general term for a meal in New Zealand. I love the expression since I tend to eat very fast—a cheetah tearing at a fresh kill while yipping hyenas close in for the steal. After dancing with the mighty Pacific, I didn't want a snack, I didn't want dinner. I needed a feed, mate. This, my first night on the road, was also the first test of my mobile kitchen.

Mom instilled in me a love of cooking and food. Her love for us shined in many ways, but her dedication to feeding us good, wholesome fare is what I appreciated the most. She'd painstakingly handpick each cherry we ate while other customers shoved handfuls in their bags; the extra attention added sweetness. Strawberries would get special treatment too. She'd core each one, carefully rinsing it before putting it into a faded aluminum colander. One time, I put my hand on the edge of our Formica countertop, stood on my tippy toes, and reached blindly into the colander. If it hadn't been full, I wouldn't have been able to reach anything, but it was filled to the rim with ripe red strawberries. Mom smiled and pushed the colander closer as if she knew a secret. My tiny hand grasped something so big, it couldn't possibly be a strawberry—but it was.

"Wow!" I proclaimed.

"That's a big one," she replied as her knife flashed back and forth on the cutting board.

She would've been impressed with my setup and the meal I was about to cook. I had a Swiss-made chef's knife; a cast-iron wok; various used pots, pans, and utensils; a few bowls and plates from the two-dollar store (similar to a dollar store back home); and a blue cooler I'd found on a street in Auckland. Everything was stored neatly in a small cabinet I'd made to fit in the back of the van.

The cabinet ran the width of the van and sat right behind the front seats. A platform with hinged flip-tops, of the same height as the cabinet, fit snugly in the back. Both the cabinet and platform had small ledges, so when I was ready for bed, I simply pulled out a few planks and bridged the gap between them, making for a perfect bed. It was the same setup I had in my van in the States.

With the wind howling and the tide lapping within a few yards of Lonna's tires, I started simmering a soup of mung beans, preserved turnips, and Chinese vegetables. Soon, Lonna's windows were dripping as the beans started to break down, causing the soup to thicken a little. I added tofu, gave it a quick stir, and turned the burners off. The twin-burner stove, set atop the wooden cabinet, worked perfectly.

I'm not a vegetarian by any means, but after five weeks of restaurant food, some pure roughage was in order—it'd give the body a good cleaning. I'd made enough soup for weeks, and it tasted great. Satisfied, I slipped into my sleeping bag.

The day broke clear and cold. As I scrubbed the condensation from the window, I realized that I could surf the sunrise. It wasn't something I was used to, as San Francisco is on the West Coast, where sunset surfs are the weekly specials. The waves weren't very good, but a cold splash was the best shower I could think of.

Out of habit, I searched for a towel or blanket for Toughy. Because he was part chow chow, he was extremely loyal—a one-man dog. He wouldn't even play with other dogs unless I was around to watch. Sometimes I wished he was more social, but this trait made for a dog I could trust. When I went surfing I'd simply bring a towel or one of his blankets down to the beach. He'd plant himself there and never move, no matter how many dogs egged him on to play.

Standing there zipping up my suit in the morning's first rays of sun, the elation and devastation sandwiched me again. That feeling started shortly after Toughy's months-to-live diagnosis. As part of my mourning and acceptance that he was leaving, I'd made a special trip to our favorite place in the mountains to dig his grave when he was still alive.

With a shovel and pick in hand, I left our camp with my feet crunching last year's dead grass. The ground underneath was still very soft, so each step made a *crunch-squish* sound. As I walked, I stared at the new shoots of grass poking up through the brown mats of last year's growth.

Crunch-squish. I'm going to New Zealand. Crunch-squish. My dog is dying. Crunch. His liver is Swiss cheese. Squish. A land of huge trout and peeling waves is waiting for me. I'm digging a hole for my dog's grave. His liver function is failing, and the food he eats will slowly poison him. He'll be gone soon, just a memory... no longer a part of my life, just like I-Gaw.

As I stood there in the dry grass, my hands shook, my chest heaved, and my face twitched. I saw I-Gaw storm up the stairs to his bedroom, crying and screaming after our parents informed him that his cancer had returned. He was on his bed hugging his pillow while we looked on, not sure what to do. What could we do? Then I heard my vet saying Toughy had liver disease.

I didn't remember going down on one knee, but the wet ground soaking through my pants awakened me. I wanted to scream, but instead I cinched my backpack, retied my boots, and found the balance point of the pick and shovel in each hand. Then I started running: running toward something, running from something, and running to catch the thing that kept trying to get away.

Toughy sped past, darting back and forth in front of me. We raced downhill, gaining speed, and the familiar song of the stream, swollen with snowmelt, filled my ears. It grew progressively louder, swelling into a chorus, the song of every stream and river Toughy and I had ever seen, heard, or touched spurred me on to catch what I had lost.

My *smile.*

Like always, the ocean splashed a smile onto my face, and soon I was ready for my day. Laughing at my dusty reflection in Lonna's side window, I wondered how many people had slept in an old van on a deserted beach in a foreign land, surfed an expertly painted sunrise, and then thrown on nice clothes to go try to land the best job in the world. Not many, I'd guess.

So empty was the land that it wasn't until I'd reached the main road that I realized I'd been driving on the wrong side. Mental note: don't space out on deserted roads. I discovered Lonna's blower was broken, so no heat. Luckily, we were headed into summer.

Crunch-squish.

That day was my first visit to a high decile school. New Zealand's school funding is determined by the decile system. The official definition by the Ministry of Education reads, "A school's decile indicates the extent to which it draws its students from low socioeconomic communities. Decile 1 schools are the 10% of schools with the highest proportion of students from low socioeconomic communities. Decile 10 schools are the 10% of schools with the lowest proportion of these students." The idea is to provide low-decile schools with more funding to overcome the barriers of educating a low socioeconomic population. As I pulled up to the school, I could see the parents had money.

The parking lot was full of clean luxury SUVs and various other shiny, dent-free vehicles. When I pulled up, the principal had her hands on her hips, shooting me disapproving looks. It felt like I was in a scene out of some eighties teen comedy, where a guy from the wrong side of the tracks drives onto a manicured lawn to pick up a prissy girl. What did she expect me to pull up in? A Jag? "C'mon, lady," I wanted to say. "See this pressed shirt and these nice khakis? I won't rob your school. I promise."

Despite the chilly welcome, I was determined to soak up the local teaching style, so I threw myself into helping teach a kindergarten and first grade class for a day. And, really, how could I not? Teaching a kid to read, one-on-one, is such a fresh and filling joy. There are things you enjoy, and there are things that fill you. When a first grader works through a story and retells it as though she's an Academy Award winner, that isn't just enjoyable; it's filling.

Still, the school suffered from one of the worst cases of white elitism I'd ever experienced. Although I enjoyed every minute of my interaction with the kids, most of the older children thought I was lucky to be alive after I told them where I slept the night before. When I told them where my next stop was, they asked me, "Why?! Why would you ever want to go there?" Then, without waiting for an answer, they'd strut away, declaring, "*This* is the best place." Despite the high percentage of Maoris in those parts, practically the entire school was *Pakeha*—New Zealanders of European descent. Somehow, this publicly funded school had figured out how to keep most Maoris out. They had chosen to build fences instead of knocking them down.

Even though I knew the school wasn't the right fit for me, I finished the day with a chat with the principal. As she returned my résumé, she said they were looking for someone permanent and not just for the year. We both knew, of course, that the school's help wanted ad explicitly said the position was for replacing a teacher on maternity leave for the 2003 school year—just what I was looking for. I wouldn't lie and say I was looking to live in New Zealand permanently. I knew how important staff continuity is for a school. So why was she lying to me?

I'm not sure any other profession demands that you confront your own hypocrisies so regularly. When I step on a piece of litter, I always think I should pick it up because that's what I tell my students to do. Whenever I'm displeased with someone, I immediately think: *This is a put-down.* So much of my life comes under the scrutiny of my teacher's eye—except for my lack of tidiness and organization. I justify those as simply attributes of man. Knowing it would do no good to confront the principal, I smiled, took my résumé back, and thanked her for having me at the school.

Back in my dented, low-life vehicle, I wondered how many people never look in the mirror. How many people never consider their actions, the ways in which they could be more honest with themselves and others? A brief moment of anger charged through me as I thought of the principal and the attitudes at the school. It wasn't worth getting myself worked up over, but I should have at least called the principal's parents—let them know she'd told a fib.

As I began crossing the Northland—a region on the North Island—from east to west, the dense, old-growth forest whizzed by my windows, assuaging my doubts about humanity's shortcomings. Much of the coastline is sparsely populated, lined with open beaches ideal for driving on at low tide. Together, Lonna and I cruised the hard-packed beach, heading toward the equator as the sun set.

The waves were too small to surf, so I decided to look for clams. The water, just cold enough to make me squirm when a wave hit me waist high, soon soaked me, and it no longer mattered. I curled my bare toes, sliding them along the sand underwater, searching for the sharp tips of clams—my dinner, I hoped. After five minutes I had only two clams to show for my efforts, so I moved to shallower water. The small waves and calm shore break allowed me to look for the clams instead of simply feeling for them, and I quickly saw a small puff of sand near my right foot. I plunged my hand into the water, digging with my fingertips. Victory! I raised my dripping arm in triumph. When I'd collected a dozen or so clams, I waded ashore to prepare dinner.

It'd been a good day: a sunrise surf session, a sunset, a filling day with children, a dinner of clams on the half-shell topped with minced ginger and green onions dribbled with sesame seed oil and soy sauce. Plus, the feeling that I was making progress on my mission.

After twenty-some school visits, traveling over five hundred miles, no news, bad news, and a rebuilt alternator for Lonna— she broke down once, near some small town called Raupunga, *the place I'd never step foot in again*—it was too good and too sad at the same time. If only Toughy were here with me.

And that's the way it went for a few weeks. October is a month of seasonal transition for New Zealand, much like April in the United States. I lost count of the number of times gray clouds of despair yielded to double rainbows of teary-eyed jubilation.

It's early November, and the official end of the 2002 school year is approaching. I still haven't found a job for 2003, but I've landed a five-week substitute position at Elgin School in Gisborne. Gisborne or "Gizzy" is a city of forty-four thousand on the east coast of New Zealand. The job will last until Christmas, which marks the end of the 2002 school year and the beginning of summer break. A teacher named Ms. B has back troubles, apparently, so I'll take over for her.

The stakes are high. I won't just have to be good; I'll have to be a rock star. The job will give me a local reference, some much-needed cash, and a solid place to call home for a while. Pulling up to a bungalow, I begin unloading my belongings.

For the next month or so, I'll be living with Andy, a painter, sculptor, and photographer of naked girls that pose under waterfalls, the kind of guy who paints his toilet instead of cleaning it. He lives in a three-bedroom bungalow on a sliver of land sandwiched by sheep paddocks. His New Zealand pride gives him a chip on his shoulder when it comes to Americans, but apparently he figures the Chinese teacher dude will help with the rent.

A small potbelly stove sits in the corner of the family room next to a worn, but serviceable couch. French doors lead to the backyard, where barbed wire separates us from the sheep that wander the land here. The potbelly stove is a novelty for me; I light it every night during the first week even though the cold nights are long gone. It makes the place feel like home. And given the challenge I'm facing, I need some stability. Not only will I be teaching a new grade level, I'll be coming in at the end of the school year. As any teacher knows, that usually means trouble.

Regardless, I'm excited to dive back into the classroom. It's been over four months since my last day of teaching in San

Francisco. I open the French doors to the backyard, stuff the potbelly stove full of wood, and plop onto the couch thinking about my old students.

On the last day of the school year, I always gather the children together for one last word. Spending an entire year with low-socioeconomic children is intense to say the least. Sometimes I was the only adult in their lives who cared for them. On the last day of school, I'd always leave them with one of my most important lessons.

"Class, I'm so proud of all of you! Think back to when we first came together. You guys were only this big," I'd say, holding my hand near the ground. "Now look at all of you! You're all this big!" I'd say holding my hand over my head. They'd roll around laughing, and I'd wait for them to calm down before continuing. "No matter what, just keep trying your best and—remember what do I always say?"

"Learning to work with different kinds of people is just as important as reading, math, and writing," they'd chime in unison.

I find myself saying my lesson out loud as the potbelly stove hisses and its metal exhaust pipe creaks. I stare out the open door, losing myself in the long wispy clouds. I smile and repeat, "Aotearoa," several times. It's the Maori name for New Zealand and it means "Land of the Long White Cloud." The clouds turn from white to yellow-gold, and the fire in the stove reduces to ashes. A distant barking dog prompts me to sit up quickly. Time to plan for the week. I flip open my notebook and ask myself, "What the heck am I going to do with these kiddos?"

As expected, my fourth-and-fifth-grade class tries to eat me, their new Yank teacher. I try to make myself taste bad by taking no crap. Lori helps out from across the globe too. A comic book lover, she does a successful superhero unit with her class. With her guidance, I implement a superhero writing project to drive the activities for the final five weeks of school. Thematic teaching is powerful. We read superhero books, develop and draw them, and I even make up math word problems involving superheroes. If I had more time, we could get into the easy physics of flying.

The fifth graders are kings and queens of the school right now, but their anxiety about going to middle school is never far from the surface. They go from tough to toddlers in the same breath. In response, I frown, I smile, I revel in the madness of fifth graders. I was once one of these kids. In fact, I was worse.

"You aren't our teacher!"

"Ms. B doesn't do it that way!"

"That's not how you say my name!"

One day, one of the girls plops her sobbing head on my desk. "Hallie said she's not my friend anymore!" she cries.

"Well, maybe Hallie is just mad about something else," I say, trying to comfort her. "I'm sure she's still your friend."

"You don't know!" she screams.

Which makes me think, *She's right. I don't know. What do we teachers know?* Meanwhile, she's cussing away, something about how stupid teachers are. Maybe I'm a stupid teacher, but damned if I'm not a caring teacher too—in making her hate me, I made her forget her sadness.

It all gets me thinking, though. So what do we know? Not much, in truth. We are far from perfect. In fact, teachers can be very critical, especially at schools like this one, with tough populations of children. The litany goes like this: The principal isn't doing enough. Ms. So-and-So doesn't discipline the kids. Mr. Such-and-Such is stuck in old ways. Why don't the kids perform? Why doesn't Maggie bring her homework? Why is Josh still in class after his behavior on the field trip? It's all the principal's fault! It's a poisonous atmosphere.

It makes me want to get on my soapbox and scold the teachers: "Learning to work with different types of people is just as important as reading, writing, and math. Teaching is hard enough without us blaming and attacking one another. Now shake hands, make up, and let's go have a nice game of Duck Duck Goose."

Mike, the principal, is under fire for pretty much every problem at the school: for Ms. B being ill, for not finding a teacher to replace Ms. B right away, and now for hiring me instead of a local teacher familiar with the curriculum. He's blamed for the children's bad behavior, so he tries to bond with them during the lunch hour. For his troubles, he gets drilled for playing on the yard with them when he should be doing administrative work in the office. The rift between the teachers and Mike is so serious that the New Zealand Ministry of Education sends out a suit-and-tie fella, Tony, to investigate.

I meet Tony during morning tea one day. The teachers have seen my work, the parents on the board of trustees have seen my passion, and Mike can't stop praising me. Tony seems to like me too, but I've promised the kids I'll toss the football with them, so I don't have much time to chat. I slam a couple cups of black tea and pay my respects.

I run to the yard thinking, *I'll never see that guy again.*

The boys are waiting with the football. They haven't played much American football—or *gridiron*, as they call it. Instead, they play rugby which, as I discover, is more of a religion than a mere sport in New Zealand. During one of my school visits, I noticed ABC charts with rugby themes: *K* is for *kick*, *B* is for *ball*, and *S* is for *scrum*—that brutal action in which the two teams face off and nearly kill each other for control of the ball. Unlike American football, rugby players do not wear pads, and there is no such thing as being down. Today, though, we're playing American style. Even though the boys are athletic, they are not used to catching over their shoulder, as forward passes are illegal in rugby. I teach them some basic passing routes and toss crisp passes to them under the New Zealand sun, possibly having more fun than they do in the process.

Life in the sheep shack with Andy is stellar. His lighthearted way of living is contagious, and the only attribute more impressive than his creativity is his willingness to act upon it. He's thrilled to have an extra eighty bucks a week for rent, and even more thrilled to have something in the fridge besides milk and butter. I've always kept a well-stocked kitchen, a habit my mom says will help me land a nice lady someday. Who knows? Maybe I'll land Lori when I get back.

Our fridge and cupboards have just about everything: different cheeses, veggies, fruits, cookies, rice, and pasta. One item I keep forgetting to buy, however, is cat food. Andy's cat had a litter of kittens in my room. I like cats but I'm allergic to them, so we had to move them to the shed out back. Still, it feels good to buy cat food and give the little furballs some attention. It's not like I'm betraying Toughy by getting attached to another type of animal. After all, they're just cats.

Besides the cats, there's plenty of other entertainment around. We've named a rogue rooster Clint, as in Clint Eastwood. He struts around looking as though he's ready to draw a gun at any moment. And the sheep, normally in the paddock behind us, found an opening in the fence one day. For a few days we had sheep in the driveway, sheep coming into the house, and sheep chewing the bushes outside my bedroom window. After a while I grow accustomed to the melodic chewing of the sheep and their nighttime chats with one another. In fact, I begin to find it comforting, like I'm sharing the space—living in harmony. Then one morning, I hear a man outside shouting and whistling directions to a pack of herding dogs. Within minutes the sheep are gone, leaving trimmed landscaping and piles of "fertilizer" in their wake.

Week by week, November disappears and summer arrives. The kittens are gaining confidence and testing their feline abilities. The smallest of the litter, a tabby with light ginger markings, is my favorite. When we play, she fishtails around the kitchen floor and darts out the front door while I give chase. I've gotten comfortable here, but my short-term teaching gig has come to an end. Meanwhile, the application deadlines for 2003 teaching positions have mostly passed.

As far as I can tell, my mantra of *just change the blade* hasn't worked. How patient can a man be? Little by little, I had gotten all my paperwork in order, shown my face at schools, met dozens of principals, written hundreds of e-mails, spent hours of wrist-bending time on the phone, and completed this temporary job—and I've got nothing to show for it.

I have a few lines in the water for jobs, but I'm not expecting much. No matter how well I did at Elgin School—the parents and principal presented me with a piece of New Zealand greenstone for thanks and good luck when I left—the fact remains that it's just a big risk to hire a foreigner when there are so many local applicants. I say goodbye to Andy, not knowing when I'll see him again, and peel away in Lonna.

I've got a six-week summer break and nothing to do but check the teacher ads every now and then. A friend from the States happens to visit, so we make our way to the South Island along with the rest of the Lonely Planet crew. A screw-it attitude descends, making me feel worse than ever. If I'm not in the immediate act of surfing, fishing, or partying, I'm thinking about Toughy, thinking that I've failed in my mission.

The South Island offers the quintessential postcard scenery, snowcapped peaks and rugged coastline to the horizon, but all the waves, fishing, and touristy eye candy can't keep a smile on my face.

One day, though, after I've all but given up the search, I come across a new job posting. Sitting at an old computer terminal with a painfully slow Internet connection at a dusty South Island video store, I click on the teaching ads. Raupunga School needs a teacher.

Hey, I know that place. That's where I broke down.

I run to the van to grab a coffee-stained, sun-bleached mini-portfolio from Lonna's dashboard, scribble a letter on a torn-out piece of notebook paper, and mail the whole thoroughly unprofessional mess to Mr. Tay of the Raupunga School Board of Trustees. The video store doesn't have a printer, and I'm sick of trying so hard and getting no response. Typed letters, expensive portfolios with color pictures, ironed khakis, and pressed shirts have led nowhere, so to hell with it. I'm going surfing.

Ɂ

When the phone rings, I'm looking at a map of South Island, trying to decide where to fly-fish. I don't answer it on the first ring; I let it ring again just to savor the moment. No one ever calls me, except maybe my parents. This could very well be something good.

"This is Manu from Raupunga School. We would like to interview you."

I can't believe it. After all this time and all this work, finally, another interview. To celebrate, I take myself out to dinner and order a bottle of wine. It's tough to feel celebratory, however. What I mostly feel is desperate. Please, please let this be it. I have to find a full-time position. The school year starts in less than a week, so if this isn't it, then it's not going to happen.

It all hits me as I make my way back to Lonna to bed down for the night. These last weeks of surfing and fishing have been glorious, but I realize that, for the first time in my life, I've been depressed. I'm not having good days and bad days; it's more like good minutes and bad minutes. It was my first Christmas and New Year away from family and friends. Every dog I see takes me back to the days when I could open my van door and bury my face in the soft fur of Toughy. Increasingly, I'm questioning whether my brother would be proud of me.

Toughy left so I could do this, but so far I'm failing. This has to be it. I set the alarm on my phone and curl up into the fetal position. In the morning, I catch a ferry back to the North Island and Raupunga.

To spruce up for the interview, I pull off on a dirt road and find a small stream. I bathe myself using a relatively clean T-shirt, wondering what I should wear. My khakis are wrinkled, and the collared shirts are stuffed away somewhere deep in Lonna's guts. But I couldn't care less about the collared shirts. Instead, I look for my twenty-year-old good luck weapon: my lucky skateboarding T-shirt from middle school, which always adorned my back during skateboard competitions. It was supposed to be on my back for the other interview, but I forgot to wear it. I slip it on and throw a Hawaiian surf shirt over the paper-thin, skintight fabric. I round out the interview outfit with bare feet and surf shorts. It's a country school, I reason, so they should know I have some country in me. Self-defeating, maybe, but I'm beyond caring. What has professionalism gotten me so far? Raupunga, here I come—again.

When I arrive, the members of the school board stare at my bare feet. I have second thoughts—maybe I should have worn shoes after all—but it's too late. Nothing to do now but smile, meet their doubting looks with enthusiasm.

"I'm so glad to be here," I begin. "I broke down here back in October, heard the children singing, and wanted to visit this school."

Unbelievably, Tony from the Ministry of Education, who had reviewed Elgin School's troubles, is here but without the tie. It's January, summertime, and too hot for a tie. He backs me up the way a good wingman should, chiming in at key moments with praise from the parents at Gisborne.

The Ministry of Education also sent an emergency principal, a woman named Angie, to Raupunga. Emergency principals are the special forces of the school world. If two teachers leave a school because they were threatened by an irate parent and the board of trustees is barely functioning, well, it's time to send in Angie, an emergency principal and teacher, to get things rolling.

I talk of giving the children diversity in their lives, of thematic-based teaching, of my flexibility, and about my love of science. Basically, I summon every bit of kiss-ass I can muster.

Angie leans forward, a serious look on her face. "Now, the important question," she says, her grave look betraying a hint of a smirk. "When's your birthday?"

"February 11, 1973."

"There you go!" she exclaims, slapping her hands on the table. "The man's an Aquarian!"

I had never paid too much attention to my sign until arriving in New Zealand. During my early travels, people I met would know I was an Aquarian within minutes. Something about my mission, Lonna, my demeanor, just fit into the Aquarian mold. Now, this lady at my second teaching interview seems to think that all people born between January 20 and February 18 are a gift from heaven to Raupunga School. What should I say? For the first time during the interview, I'm at a loss for words.

"I'm a Libra," Angie explains. "Libras, Geminis, and Aquarians all work well together."

I respond, as profoundly as I can under the circumstances, "Yeahhh."

The other members of the interviewing committee shift in their seats, the same way they did upon seeing my bare toes. They are unconvinced, possibly, that astrological charts are the best way to pick their children's educator.

I can tell, however, that Angie isn't kidding. She's a woman to be taken seriously, a woman who commands respect. And if the stars say that Libras and Aquarians jive, well, who am I to question the stars?

An hour later, my phone rings. I'm a little afraid to pick it up, but I figure that it must be good news if they are calling back so soon. I listen, I smile, I cry, and then I drive to a market for a six-pack of beer to celebrate. I haven't let Toughy down. He left so I could live and teach in New Zealand, and that's exactly what I'm going to do.

Just change the blade was the key to success after all. I can't relax yet, though. School starts in five days. I need to sort out my work permits, gather my belongings from Andy's shack, and prep my classroom.

A couple days later, I'm on my way back to Raupunga. This time, I'm not alone. My passenger is about three pounds, makes me sneeze, and loves to co-pilot from the dashboard. She's my favorite kitten, the tabby with ginger accents, and she was literally thrown into my life. As I pulled away from Andy's shack, he tossed her into the front seat. "Here, you need a cat."

With her feet spread wide, she glided through the open window and landed on the worn passenger seat. She straightened her hind legs and cleaned herself as though she were home. I've decided I'll cure my cat allergies by rubbing her on my face. I name her Baetis, after a family of insects important to us fly-fisher folks. If I took in a dog, I'd feel like a traitor to Toughy—but Baetis is just a cat.

Caring for her will add another dimension to my daily life that I've missed. I remember the day I dedicated myself to being a dad, not just someone who owned a dog. Three weeks or so into my first job, I came home to new-puppy urine on the carpet and a leaking washing machine. The combination of adjusting to my first professional job, settling into a new place, and the logistics of caring for a puppy by myself had pushed me to the brink. I snatched an unpacked moving box, screamed some obscenities, and hurled the box down the stairs. Then, I turned to see Toughy cowering in the corner. I imagined myself an impatient father, unhappy with his job, unfulfilled, and taking it out on his family—and I wondered, *Is this who I want to be?*

I collapsed at the top of the stairs, burying my face in my kid's soft fur. I realized right then that it wasn't just about

Feline Copilot.

me anymore. Soon, I gave up rock climbing because Toughy couldn't join me, and I started hiking, fly-fishing, and planning Sierra Nevada expeditions with NASA-like precision. The joys of being a doggy-dad offset the pains I felt from my office job.

No longer would a five-minute morning walk be good enough. Rain or shine, I set my alarm for long sessions of tennis-ball-throwing splendor with my *kid*. I bypassed beautiful beaches with signs that read *No Dogs* or *Leashed Dogs Only*, looking for the unregulated places where dogs could be dogs. I shunned Yosemite Valley, a California icon, because it didn't allow unleashed dogs anywhere. On my hour-long lunch breaks, I'd scarf down my sandwich during the twenty-minute drive home, spend twenty minutes playing with Toughy, and then rush back to work.

Luckily, I'm now passionate about my job, and lunchtime head rubs won't be a problem. Baetis is one lucky cat, and I'm a lucky man; we will keep each other company.

Eyes watering and nose running from my allergy-curing

experiment, I crest the hill I broke down on months earlier. Chugging into Raupunga, I pass the row houses and the graffiti-riddled outhouse, and it doesn't feel real. I can't believe that this back-of-beyond place will be my home for the next year. I stop halfway up the driveway of the school to allow a family of pigs to waddle past the van. A few kids are hot on the swines' heels, and they glare at me for a split second before resuming their chase. The house I'll be living in, I've learned, is just two or three good rugby ball kicks away from the motorcycle guy's place, where I used the phone. I bet he never thought he'd see me again, but here I am.

I open the office door and retrieve the key to my classroom. I've never used a skeleton key, and I struggle to make it fit. Finally, the door makes a heavy click, and I sigh.

I look into the glass on the door and smile at my reflection, "Good job, Mr. Chin. You did it."

CHAPTER
4

THE MORNING NEWS

I T'S THE SUNDAY NIGHT before my first day of teaching, and I'm cutting ginger. With a quick sweep, I push a small pile of thin slivers onto the edge of the knife and then onto a plate. Sesame oil, rice wine, soy sauce, chili paste, and a sprinkle of cornstarch—I stir it all into a bowl of beef slices and set it aside to marinate for a few minutes. Then, after pouring a little vegetable oil into my cast-iron wok, I set it on the stove.

I can sense Angie watching me prepare our day-before-school dinner, which makes me move faster, more purposefully. I'm not showing off, exactly, but Angie is going to be my boss; she needs to know that I'm someone who can get things done.

The dinner is also my way of thanking her. The interviewing committee was unimpressed with my bare feet, she later told me, but she insisted on hiring me, insisted that I hadn't come here to Raupunga by accident. I couldn't agree with her more.

Apparently, my coffee-stained résumé, accompanied by the handwritten note on scraggly notebook paper, was tossed into the garbage by Tony, the man from the Ministry of Education. He thought it thoroughly ridiculous and didn't even look at it. Mr. Tay, a member on the board of trustees, found it humorous and plucked it from the garbage. Once Tony looked at it, he said, "Hey! I know that guy. The parents at Elgin School loved him." Funny how things work out.

My house won't be ready to move into for another few weeks, so I'm living with Angie for the time being. In my house, the stove and water pump are missing, stolen after the other teachers left—or should I say fled—Raupunga. Well, at least the crooks waited for the teachers to leave before grabbing some essentials. I can only hope they'll show me the same courtesy. Most rural households collect rainwater in concrete or plastic tanks; an electric pump provides water pressure. It's very efficient, and forces you to really think about conserving water, especially during the dry season. If you run out of water, you have to pay a tanker truck for water delivery. More than one native has scolded me for flushing the toilet too soon. "Mate!" they'd yell. "Wait for something solid before flushing!"

Angie lives in one of the nicer houses in the area, a large country house, but she doesn't have any children, so it feels a little empty. She's been a principal and a teacher for decades, she tells me. Her partner, Huck, is a shepherd. In New Zealand, shepherds aren't a thing of the past. In exchange for managing the land and the animals, the landowner gives the shepherd a house and all the equipment needed to do the job. Huck currently shepherds a few hours south of Raupunga, so Angie heads out most weekends to be with him.

With the ginger sizzling away, and the beef already marinated, I reach for a few cloves of garlic. "You know, Angie, I couldn't care less about what my plates and bowls look like. I can make due with cheap pots and pans, but there's nothing like a good, sharp knife. I really enjoy chopping and preparing a good meal," I remark casually as my knife flashes, the garlic victimized.

"Looks like I'll be eating well living with you," she says. "Everything looks great. Where'd you learn to cook?"

"I watched my mom, and I did a lot of cooking in college when I should have been going to class," I reply, dropping the beef into the smoking oil in the wok. For a moment I want to kick myself. Why did I admit to slacking off in college? But Angie just smiles. For whatever reason, she doesn't seem too surprised. She smiles more like an old friend than a new one, seems to know me even though we met just a week ago. Maybe it's that Aquarian-Libra connection.

She exudes more than a hint of worldliness, so I'm not surprised when she tells me that she lived and taught in Saudi Arabia for a few years. Her penetrating hazel eyes make me glad that I'm a straight-up character. She would instantly detect any hint of insincerity or halfheartedness. I add a mixture of cornstarch and water to thicken the gravy and, voilà, our meal of stir-fried beef and broccoli is ready.

Blowing on my first bite, I finally ask the question that's been weighing on my mind. "So what's the deal with the gangs?"

I'm a little worried. After all, I'm a half hour from the nearest town with a police station, and my cell phone doesn't pick up a signal. Will I be safe living here as an outsider? As a Chinese American? What if something happens to me? More than once, I've thought of what that tow truck driver told me after I broke down here months ago, of his terrifying stories of gang warfare.

But then again, gangs? C'mon. How bad can it be?

Danger and safety, of course, are relative things. I find it especially important not to overreact at the prospect of danger. Every night, millions of Americans double-lock their doors in safe suburbs, guarding themselves against terrorism, bad guys, SARS, and West Nile outbreaks, only to be run over by a speeding, oversized SUV the next day.

The school I worked at in San Francisco was safe but not without its risks. I was threatened twice, both times over the phone; although neither amounting to anything, it was sobering nonetheless. Concerned about a student's progress, I called her house and was delighted at first because the phone was actually working. When I asked to speak to the girl's mother, though, an angry, slurring man's voice replied, "Who is this calling for my *bitch*?!" I identified myself numerous times and got the same response each time, so I apologized for the misunderstanding and hung up. The man, whom I later learned had just gotten out of jail, called back via caller ID and told me he'd be coming to school with a gun the next day.

Another time a mother called and accused me of giving her African-American daughter's red hoodie away to a Samoan boy. I explained that the boy's name was on the tag, but she insisted I gave it away—implying that I was racist. Her husband (a very large man, she assured me) was going to come to school to settle things with me. The whole episode depressed me; obviously, the wounds of oppression haven't entirely healed. Do they ever heal entirely?

Angie finishes chewing, pauses to collect her thoughts, then replies, "Damn, that's good. Well, Raupunga is Black Power territory. Wairoa to the northeast, and Napier, to the south, are mostly Mongrel Mob. Frasertown just outside Wairoa has a Black Power pad. Some of the parents of the children here are Black Power. Hmmmm...well, let's see, what else should I tell you? Black Power's color is blue, and Mongrel Mob's is red," she says. "That's pretty much it. They've been at it for years and years."

A worried look comes over her face. "You'll have to be very careful around here," she adds. "I'm not going to tell you what to do. Just be careful."

I inhale deeply, straighten my posture, and reply, "I know, Angie. I plan on being social enough so people know me, but I don't want people stopping in to drink beer on a daily basis."

She winks at me. "Smart man."

As I bed down for the night in one of Angie's guest bedrooms, I reflect on the sequence of events that brought me to Raupunga. I can't think of any other place I'd like to be. Baetis, scratching at the front door, interrupts my deep moment.

Moths, dozens of them, are hurling themselves against the

white siding of the house. The poor things are trying to use the outdoor light for navigation, I guess, and knocking themselves silly. Some of them recover quickly and fly off; some hit so hard that they die. Others, having bounced off the siding, are twitching just enough to draw Baetis's attention. She's playing pinball with them, showing off her hunting abilities, and jumping into the air in pursuit of the low-flying ones. Not wanting to disrupt the performance, I quietly sit down on the front step, like I'm late to the ballet and the doors are already closed. Once she's had her fill of moths, she sets her sights on me, head butting my shins with as much force as her little body can muster. I scoop her up—it's bedtime for Mr. Chin and his first cat.

She curls up next to me, her purring growing louder by the second, while I rub a small ginger spot on her forehead. Baetis will never know her dad who's responsible for the ginger markings, but I'm sure it's the big ginger tomcat Andy saw lurking around the bungalow a few months before Baetis was born. None of this would have been possible if Toughy hadn't left me. He knew he was holding me back. A few tears slip out like loose change falling through a hole in a pocket. When that hole will mend, I don't know.

I wake with gangs on my mind. It's ironic and sort of makes me laugh: I came to New Zealand because I wanted a change from teaching kids who often came from violent and poverty-stricken backgrounds. And now here I am, in a place where gangs sometimes clash. Who would have thought?

Dew lies heavily on the ground, and gravel from Angie's driveway sticks to my bare feet. A few months ago, the gravel might have hurt, but my now-calloused feet take it in stride. Once I hit the pavement of the schoolyard, I sprint to my classroom for some last-minute prep work. I spent the weekend setting up the classroom, and it looks good. The desks are in order, the morning message is written on the whiteboard, I have a read-aloud (a book to read aloud to the whole class) picked out, and my butterflies are in check. I met some of the students too, but they were mostly older kids, not the little guys I'll be teaching. They were at the school skateboarding because the schoolyard boasts the smoothest pavement around. For old times' sake, I had a go on one of their boards. I know I should be careful about becoming friends with the children before I'm respected as a teacher, but I can't resist showing them how it's done.

I've organized crayons and markers (or *felts*, as they are called here) neatly into plastic baskets. Pencils—regular skinny pencils and fat beginner pencils for the little ones—have been sharpened to perfection. To start, I have three groups of tables, with one basket for each group. Sharing is a social skill, and it's important to reinforce it with the children—thus the communal baskets of supplies. I step back and admire my work. The tidy baskets, the perfect spacing between the grouped desks, the clean whiteboard, the doodle-free desktops—overall, this is the best the classroom will ever look. In the corner of the whiteboard, I have written the day's schedule. I'm all about spontaneity, but predictability helps put a child's mind at ease. We'll work on flexibility later.

When the kids start to show up, fresh from their six-week break, the butterflies really get to me—so much so that my memory suddenly goes bad. How does the "Days of the Week" song go again? *There's Sunday, Monday, Tuesday...* damn! That's not it. What time is it in San Francisco? Will Lori be up? She'll be at school. I charge across the schoolyard, plunge through Angie's front door, and dig my phone card out of my backpack.

The secretary answers, and I ask frantically, "Hello, may I speak to Ms. Lori, please?"

I have a teenage moment of nervousness and think about hanging up. But then I hear her voice. The words spill out: "Hey, Lori. I'm about to start my first day of class, and can't remember how the "Days of the Week" song goes."

She laughs, and I can picture her smile. God, she has a nice smile. I can tell she thinks it's cute that I'm calling her from across the globe about a kiddie song. She sings it for me. "All right, are you ready? It's like this…"

As soon as she starts, I remember and chime in with her. After we're done, there's an awkward silence a little like dropping off a girl after a first date and the uncertainty about whether to kiss her or not. Six thousand miles away and we're still having these moments!

I run back to my classroom, singing and gesturing with my hands and humming the tune. As I sing, I can see Lori telling the other teachers I just called her; she's a little giddy, I imagine. My mind wanders as I daydream for a second about her visiting me here in New Zealand. A second is all the time I have, though, as the school bell rings.

And it's literally a bell here in Raupunga—a rusted cast-iron blast-from-the-past hanging off a wooden post in the schoolyard—instead of a wail choked out of a dusty upholstered box with a blown-out speaker. It can be heard all over the school grounds, even by those kids who're busy laughing and chasing their friend. On Angie's orders, one of the older kids is ringing it this morning. He does his duty unceremoniously, with the air of someone who's just been told to go to bed during a good movie. He knows what it means: Summer is over. Now get to work.

Some of the little kids can't quite reach the bell; some can just barely reach it from their best running leap. I'm positive it's a benchmark for becoming a big boy or big girl. I wonder how many kids have bolted home from this very spot, vaulting barbed wire fences with newfound confidence, yelling, "Mum, I rung the bell all by myself today!"

The kids form several loose lines while Angie and I stand before them. During my introduction, I make a point of telling the kids that while I may be new to New Zealand, I'm not new to teaching. Translation: I will take no crap. (At least not

Now that's a school bell.

too much of it—if you're going to be a teacher, then you'd better be able to take some.) As the older kids slowly make their way to their classroom, I line my kids up, all six of them. Sure, lining them up may come off a little militaristic, but I can always lighten up later. That's one of the iron laws of teaching.

We file into the classroom, meandering between the desks for the first time as a unit, a class—a family. We gather in what I call the "morning circle." That's when I notice the eyes. First-day eyes are lovely: the innocence, the fear, and best of all, the individuality. I can see it all in their pupils. It's a real change from San Francisco. There are no African-American eyes, no Bosnian-refugee eyes, no Latino eyes, no Filipino eyes; they're all Maori. There are nowhere near twenty pairs of eyes, either. There are just six, all staring at me, Mr. Chin, their teacher for the year. They're waiting for me to speak. I inhale. So far, so good.

"Good morning, class. Thank you for coming in so quietly and sitting just like I've asked. Now. Every morning we'll sit here and go through our morning news and—"

"What's morning news?" interrupts Kea, one of the two boys in the class.

"Excuse me," I shoot back. "In this class you must raise your hand if you want to speak. Do you understand? Yes? Okay. I like that you asked a question, though. Always ask a question if you have one." Kea slumps over and clasps his hands together. I feel a little bad about coming down on him, but I have to set some standards. "Morning news is where we'll share. You know, share some news about ourselves."

Keri, a six-year-old with lighter skin than the rest of the girls, raises her hand. "What's news?"

"Well, it's like what's happening in your life. You know? Okay. You should start off with your names today so I can learn them. Here, I'll start today's morning news. My name is Mr. Chin," I say, meeting every one of their eyes. "I'm very excited to be here with all of you. I moved here to live and teach, and here I am with you guys in Raupunga. Yesterday, I worked really hard to get the classroom ready for you guys."

"Oh, I get it—it's like what you did yesterday!" proudly exclaims Arataki, another six-year-old girl.

"Yeah, it can be, but if you were getting a new dog or if you were going on holiday to Australia, then that would be news too," I say. Their looks aren't exactly blank, but I'm not seeing any light bulbs shining over their heads either. One girl looks a little terrified, so I modify the directions to be more specific. "Maybe for today you can just say your name, and tell me what you did yesterday. You must at least say your name, and then if you'd like to pass, then you can, but just for today. Learning to talk in front of people is important, you know."

Over the next few minutes, I learn that Hiri felt itchy from playing in the wool her dad had sheared; Brad has a big bull mastiff; Arataki read some books and went to Wairoa, or "town," as everyone around here calls it; and Shay is a little shy (she's the only one to pass). I love it.

We move on to the morning message, a handwritten personal note to the class that can be a great teaching tool for learning the difference between letters and words, say, or punctuation and spelling patterns. Today I ask for volunteers to point out where I should start reading when I get to the end of a line. I also ask them to point to a letter and to a word. By now, the kids have been sitting about twelve minutes, an eternity for six-year-olds (and their equally hyperactive teacher), so it's time for a quick get-off-our-butts exercise.

We stretch a little, run in place, walk in place and do an award-winning interpretation of ice cream melting in the hot summer sun. Now we're ready to sit again and go through our calendar routine. I'm not much of a singer myself, nor do I claim any musical talent. I am, however, a good teacher of songs involving the seven days of the week:

Days of the Week Song
(Sung to the tune of *The Addams Family*)
There's Sunday and there's Monday!
There's Tuesday and there's Wednesday!
There's Thursday and there's Friday!
And then ... there's Saturday!
Days of the week!
(Clap! Clap!)
Days of the week!
"Again! Again!" they yell.
"We'll be doing that *every* day!" I assure them.

And that's exactly what we do until the end of our first week. We sing, we write, we read, we learn lots—including about each other—and I assess their skills. I'm not sure if the kids have me pinned down yet, but I've formulated some loose profiles of them. I say *loose* because I've learned not to let first impressions cement my opinions of people.

Kea, the interrupter, lives next to the school. The rest of the kids, though, live down the street. Pretty much, it's fair to say that anyone who lives in Raupunga lives down the street from the school.

Kea, who is seven, was one of the kids chasing the pigs when I first arrived in town. The sow belongs to his family, I learn,

The Big White One invades the school play structure.

and the children call it the Big White One. They weren't just trying to chase it, he tells me: they were trying to ride it.

Every child society has its own standards—the feats of bravery or strength by which one is measured. They give you local bragging rights, make you king of the hill. Maybe it's the length of time you can hang out in the dark drainage pipe next to the local park before fear overtakes you, or how fast or far you can ride your bike. (Sadly, in today's consumerist world, it may just be who has the most expensive shoes.) Back in the day, it was who could pluck a hair off the woolly mammoth's butt. Here in Raupunga, if you can ride the Big White One, you can strut around as top dog.

The pig has had a litter, and she probably has to eat a lot in order to nurse her little ones, so she's constantly escaping from her pen in search of food. Inevitably, she ends up in people's gardens, and Kea's mom is always apologizing for it.

Kea's mom, Maata, a woman with a mullet-like haircut and a profoundly unhurried air, is the school's janitor. No matter the circumstances, she walks likes she's got all the time in the world. I'm sure it would be the same if she were headed out to a gang fight. Her lanky build, subtle side-to-side sway, and slight head bounce all add up to one thing: chillin'. To round out the picture, she's always got a hand-rolled, half-burned cigarette complete with gravity-defying ash sticking out of the corner of her mouth. That cigarette never seems to budge, even when she greets me each afternoon. "Howzit, Mistah Chnn?" she'll ask.

At this point, I'm getting used to the New Zealand accent, especially the way it's applied to my name. Back in San Francisco, the African-American kids always drew out the *er* and replaced the *in* with a long *e* that eventually tapered into an *n*. Something like *Misterr Cheeen*. Here, the *er* becomes a highly accentuated *ah!* and the *Chin* is so abrupt that it squeezes all the life out of the vowel. I am now Mistah Chnn.

Kea is forever asking questions and chatting about his life, so he alone says my name one hundred times a day.

Mistah Chnn, you know Eminem?

Mistah Chnn, you know Jerry Springer?

Mistah Chnn, have you ever had lamb tails?

Mistah Chnn, I saw a huge goat yesterday!

Mistah Chnn, our pig had babies again.

Kea is right at my favorite teaching age. He's old enough to understand some reasoning and adult humor, but not yet old enough to give me a whole lot of trouble. While he's a bit of a slow reader, he tries really hard, so it doesn't worry me. With plenty of writing and literature activities (plays, for instance) he should be up to par by the time he's had a year with me. He seems to enjoy having a male teacher for a change. I'm not saying female or male teachers are better one way or another—they're just different—it's always good to mix it up.

Another boy in my class, Brad, has hazel eyes that look unsettled, almost angry. While I wouldn't mind having a few more boys in my class, one Brad is plenty. Basically, he's five going on a very tough fifteen. He spends most of our first few days with his arms folded, chin tucked against his chest, eyes angled up to let me know he's watching. His body language says he's aware of what I want him to do, but damn if he's going to do it. He usually wears a ragged T-shirt, a pair of dirty shorts, and *gumboots* that come up to about his knees. Those gumboots—PVC boots made by the millions for the wet trenches of the world wars—combined with his bull-legged walk and fiery glare, give him a certain menacing presence. I'm glad he's not fifteen and bigger than me. Later, when Angie tells me that Brad's father is a Mongrel Mob member, the pieces fall into place. If Raupunga is a Black Power stronghold, Mongrel Mob members and their families who live here had better be tough.

Luckily, Arataki balances him out. My model student, Arataki is a self-learner, witty, and smart. She's going to be a joy to teach—and will make me look good in the process. Her confidence is lagging behind her abilities, but she'll come around once she discovers how cool she is. She's going to be my neighbor, once I move into my own house, and apparently checking out the teacher next door is one of her preferred afterschool activities. As a result, sometimes her morning news details what *I* was doing the previous afternoon. (It's not a bad thing, however, to be reminded that I was humming a tune as I worked in my garden.)

Shay, Hiri, and Keri are the remaining girls. Shay, though painfully shy, breezes through all her assessments. As a teacher, it's scary to watch children try really hard and not get anywhere. Some of the children I taught in San Francisco had obvious neurological problems—maybe their moms used alcohol or drugs during pregnancy—and the glassy-eyed stares of those kids still haunt me. Fortunately, none of the children here have that stare. Keri is painstakingly quiet most of the time but can explode into a tirade instantly. I'll have to keep an eye on her.

It would be easy to cast judgment on the parents of my students. Like, what the hell are they thinking being in a gang? If they love their kids, why would they invite that kind of danger into their lives? I try my best to let these thoughts go, however, because I've learned to recognize how *my* upbringing and *my* beliefs affect me as a teacher.

The graduate program I attended urged us to turn over every stone in our consciousness, to root out beliefs so hidden, so deeply embedded in our thinking that we couldn't see how they affected our interactions with the students. It's easy to recognize issues on the surface, but what about those subtle thoughts you grew up with, the ones that inform every facet of your everyday life? How do those affect your teaching? I took to this process eagerly, questioning the hell out of my upbringing and examining the barrage of powerful but unstated messages that accompanied it: my buried feelings about race, for example—feelings I hadn't even realized I possessed.

One evening during my first year of teaching, Toughy and I headed out for one of our walks, our normal loop that took us by a park. As usual, I couldn't find my keys to lock the door behind me—I must spend days each year looking for my keys and wallet—so I just left the door unlocked. As we returned to the house, my overimaginative mind set in, picturing an intruder. *He* had been watching, I decided, had seen me leave my house with the dog and had slipped in after we left. Moving from room to room, he sizes up my valuables, finally settling on the DVD player. But wait: *What's that noise? It's the owner. He's back from walking his dog already!*

I let Toughy off the leash—the better to deal with a robber—and opened the door. I slunk around corners and peeked through slits in-between the door jambs but, of course, there wasn't anybody there. *I've lost it*, I decided—I've been spending too much time by myself for sure. While I was chuckling at my apparently boundless imagination, though, a sick feeling came over me. My imaginary intruder was a black man. My next thought: *Oh my God, my class is predominantly African American, and I was thinking one of their fathers or relatives was robbing my house.*

So it would be all too easy to attach *my* values, ideas, and measures of success to the people of Raupunga. My weapon against this foe is humor. Instead of thinking, *What the hell kind of person would steal the stove from the teacher's house?* I just shrug and think, *I don't blame them—everybody needs something to heat up their water for tea, right?* The stove-stealer could be (and probably is, in truth) the relative of a student. Much better for all concerned, then, to find humor in the situation, to laugh and shrug it off, than to walk around wondering whose mom or dad is the thief.

I spend a lot of time on the schoolyard during playtime trying to get to know the older kids. Some of them try to show me how tough they are.

"You know the Crips in America, Mistah Chnn?"

"No, but a lot of the kids I taught in the U.S. had family who were in gangs or knew people who had been hurt or killed from gang stuff."

Some of the boys would often respond with a fist, the sign for Black Power. "Black Power rules around here, Mistah Chnn," they'd say.

I want to ask questions, but I don't want to seem like I'm condemning gangs or supporting them. So I just listen and ponder. What is the difference between a gang and a tribe? Are the gangs in Raupunga (or RPG, as people call it) a result of poverty, tribal roots, localism, pride, or a little of everything? Doesn't it give the children something to be proud of? What would I be like if I grew up here?

One of the older boys, a twelve-year-old named Kahu, reminds me of some of the boys I had in San Francisco. I can tell he wants to like me and to do well in school, but something is stopping him. I can practically see the potential leaking out of his pores. Someone's got to let the kid know there's more than Raupunga and that he's meant to be more than simply a gang member. I'm purposefully not using the word *better*. There's just so much *more*. Is it possible for a person to be a responsible and emotionally aware gang member? Kahu is an incredible illustrator. Couldn't he be a gang member *and* go to a university to study art? I would love to know the answers to these questions.

Out of curiosity, I do a Web search one evening. I find dozens of articles on Black Power and the Mongrel Mob, both of which are predominantly Maori. There are stories on their histories—and on their extensive record of violence. The Mongrel Mob was born when a judge called a bunch of incarcerated men a pack of mongrels. Or so the legend goes. For its part, Black Power was formed as a sort of self-defense group, in response to the Mongrel Mob's habit of kidnapping and raping women. One story sticks with me: when a huge fight erupted in the middle of a town square, it got so out of hand that people thought it was staged, some kind of theatrical show. I'm still wondering about Black Power's name, though: there isn't a single black man for hundreds of miles.

Baetis is getting on too and gaining confidence in her new home. Yesterday, a much larger cat tested her skills. Baetis kept the huge ginger cat square in her sights as she backed up paw over paw into a defensive position beside one of Lonna's tires. Each time the cat stepped forward, Baetis would lunge and hiss before retreating into a different but similar position. She seemed to understand the dangers of staying in one spot too long. Looks like I won't have to worry about my little girl taking care of herself.

Angie won't let Baetis have free rein of the house. I respect that, but I like having Baetis nearby while I'm sleeping, so I've leaned a piece of wood up to my bedroom window to allow her to come and go in my room as she pleases. If I hear her clawing her way up the steep wooden ramp when I'm on my side, I'll turn over onto my back. Purring her approval, she'll clamber onto my chest to knead the sleeping bag. Even though she's *just* a cat, she's pretty cool.

I've been told there are no animals allowed on the school grounds, so Baetis cannot come into the classroom. It strikes me as a funny rule, given the fact most of the children have more than a few flea bites, escaped cows do their business on the schoolyard, and a big white pig rumbles through frequently. It helps me out one day, however, when a yellow Lab puppy comes tripping up the hill. His paws are too big for his body, and he's got a short length of chewed rope attached to his neck. His obvious elation at having escaped has him chasing his tail, bees, and another puppy that has also appeared out of nowhere. Rules are rules, so Angie makes the kids chase the puppies off the school grounds

"Big Head, go home!" screams one of the older boys. The dog charges off, yelping as he goes, the chewed rope bouncing around his ears. I don't notice that I'm crying until I have to wipe tears away. Big Head is about thirty pounds, the same size as Toughy when I got him. Big Head. What a funny name for a dog.

One day that first week, I notice a "tough" boy trying to light either a cigarette or a joint in the bushes during playtime. I inform Angie, who calls the long-haired young man into her office, makes him confess that he's got a joint, and in short order has him crying for forgiveness. So routine are these feats of authority for her, it seems, that she might as well be signing off on some boring paperwork for all the attention she gives it. The episode confirms my hunch that Angie is someone I don't want to cross.

We're all dragging by the time the end of the first week hits. The air is still, sweat beads on our foreheads, and we all wish the school's pool was in working order. Even Kea and Arataki, the easy kids, are getting on my nerves a little. While I'm now in my fourth year of teaching, this is my first time teaching a mixed grade level. And anyone who's spent any time around young kids knows there's an ocean of difference between a five-year-old and a seven-year-old. Adjusting the curriculum and keeping activities within each kid's individual learning level is twisting my brain into knots.

But as one of my mentors once told me, "It won't be fun all the time, but always remember to have some fun with the kids." With that in mind, I tell the children to clean up the room, pack up their stuff, and head out to the schoolyard for some games. Having only six kids is a challenge because you can barely form two teams for a relay, so I just let them chase me for the first few minutes. Shay, determined as ever, pursues me doggedly, her expression growing more confident as I let her get really close before I dodge out of her grasp. Brad, meanwhile, looks particularly disgruntled, mumbling dire threats in between huffs and puffs, something about getting his bull mastiff to *get* me.

The grass is in need of mowing, and its seedy tips burn my calves as I bob and weave through the children. The cows in the distant pasture, the view from my classroom, the sinuous clouds of the *Aotearoa* sky, and knowing I'm home for the year—these thoughts fill me. I collapse, finally, allowing six Maori children to swarm happily over me.

So far, it's been nothing but peaceful country living.

CHAPTER
5

THREE RICOCHETS

P ARTING A WORN CANVAS curtain, I duck into a covered area behind my neighbor's house. This is where Arataki, my star student, lives with her sisters and parents, Rangi and Cherise. Technically, they're not my neighbors yet; I'm still living at Angie's, waiting for a new water pump and stove.

I use the term *covered area* because I'm not sure what else to call it. It's not a deck because there's no wood decking. It's not a patio because it's only dirt. It's simply an area off the back of the house that's been covered for protection from the elements. Wood carvings, an old couch, a refrigerator, engine blocks, and various other car parts huddle beneath the tin roof. Rangi spends a lot of time back here, I'm guessing; this must be his man-hutch.

Rangi, a striking forty-year-old with high cheekbones, is long-limbed but not skinny, and I'm sure he can pack a punch. He's a member of both the Black Power and the Raupunga School Board of Trustees, which confuses the hell out of me. I've only been here a few weeks, but it's already obvious that he's a respected man in the community, and totally committed to his *whanau* (the Maori term for "family"). He just doesn't fit my definition of a gang member: Since when do gang members volunteer? How many of them read to their children every night? It's all very odd to me.

And here I am on a Wednesday night in Rangi's covered area, along with thirty or so other people, with more showing up every minute. Many of the men wear black leather jackets or vests, decorated with sewn-on patches that say *Mangu Kaha*, Maori for "Black Power." Some of the younger boys, who aren't yet patched members, just wear blue bandanas—Black Power colors. They're swilling their beer, laughing with the ladies, swelling their chests, and standing burly-stiff. Typical teenage stuff—*acting* tough and cool instead of simply *being* tough and cool, like their elders. I notice that one good-sized young guy is clearly assessing my worth and doing it with a fairly convincing ass-kicking look. Maybe he thinks it would be cool to give the new guy a thrashing. Or maybe he wants to see if I know kung fu—which is understandable. I am Chinese, after all.

When I was in third grade, my dad was transferred, so we left our home in Chicago's Chinatown and headed for suburban Connecticut. My brother, sister, and I attended a small Catholic school where we were the only Asian kids. The most common question we were asked was, "Do you know karate?" I always replied, "No, but I know kung fu!" I didn't know any martial arts at the time, but I could do a pretty good Bruce Lee imitation. I still don't know kung fu, but I'm sure I could improvise something convincing if the kid starts swinging.

Instead of confronting me, though, the kid loses interest, walking off in search of another hit of weed or slug of beer. I turn my attention to another group of men whose ages are between the teenagers and Rangi. Their demeanor, too, lies somewhere in the middle—though not as brash as the teens, they still have a dash of "Check me out..." and a pinch of "What are you looking at?"

Abruptly, one of them approaches me, extending his hand. "What's up, bro?" he blurts. "I'm Balls." Before I can reply, he pulls me in like he's going to head-butt me. Whether I want to or not, I'm locked in my first *hongi*.

When I came to New Zealand, I knew there'd be plenty of new experiences, and I looked forward to them. This is not something I expected: to be standing toe to toe with a Maori gang member who calls himself Balls, his sweaty forehead pressed to mine, the tips of our noses touching. If I didn't know better, I might think he was trying to kiss me. But no. This is my neighbor's Waitangi Day party, and I am getting my first taste of the "breath of life," or hongi, the traditional Maori greeting.

This is just beer breath, though: Balls, it's pretty clear, started his Waitangi Day celebration much earlier. Releasing his grip, he gives me a crooked-tooth grin and a swaying shoulder slap before he staggers away. He is soon replaced by another patched, barrel-chested Maori man with whom I repeat the whole forehead-touching process. I'm a bit nervous, but I'm sure my eyes show respect and no fear. Not for the first time, I'm glad I'm a what-you-see-is-what-you-get kind of guy, someone with nothing to hide. It would be tough to hide anything from an XXL Maori man whose eyes are just inches from yours. All it would take is one swat from this guy to pound me into the dirt.

What would happen if one of the younger punks started a fight with me? Would Arataki's mother make them stop? Would Rangi simply raise his hand between gulps of beer and utter, "Enough"? Would Angie get up and start swinging? Should I fight back? What would Arataki think? As I sip my beer, I ponder my options. Right as I'm concluding that I'd have to try my hardest to kick some ass because that's what they'd respect, a man taps me out of my daydream. It's the tough motorcycle guy, the one who let me borrow his phone when I broke down in Raupunga.

A smile of disbelief fills his face. We lock in a hongi, tap our glasses, and gulp some beer. He can't fathom our meeting again, either. His name is Maka, I learn, and we form an unspoken but powerful bond. If anybody messes with me, I suspect, Maka would have something to say about it.

Partying on a Wednesday night isn't something I'd normally do, but tomorrow is Waitangi Day, a national holiday. Besides, it'd also be extremely un-neighborly of me to turn down a perfectly good party. As I had told Angie during the dinner I made her, I want to make myself available to the locals. The last thing I'd want is for anyone to think I'm above sharing a few beers and laughs.

Dating from 1839, the Treaty of Waitangi coerced Maori chiefs into accepting British sovereignty. At the time, there were over two thousand settlers and no central government, and the land-grabbing had spun out of control—even by colonial standards. The Treaty of Waitangi re-established British rule. Under the treaty, the Maoris retained possession of their land and fishing areas, but they had to accept the new government's preemptive right to purchase land. All land sales, by Maoris or Europeans, were transacted via the government. In return for acceding to British rule, the Maoris were, at least in theory, guaranteed the same rights and privileges as people of British descent.

While most Maoris, I learn, think the treaty was a scam, any reason for a day off will do. Even if it's a day honoring an agreement, the Pakeha (Maori for "white man") cooked up to make themselves feel better about the raping and pillaging of a culture. Harsh words, I know, but after reading stories detailing atrocious acts against the Native Americans, and seeing firsthand the sad state of life on many Native American reservations, my compassion for the Maoris comes easily. Although, judging from the short time I've been here, I'd say the Maoris have maintained a good deal of their identity and culture.

It's all a bit overwhelming, so I ooze into a dark corner, just a few steps from the action. It's hot under the covered area right now, but I'm sure there's a space heater or a woodstove tucked away somewhere for the cold months. Winter is months away, however, and it occurs to me that those heavy black leather jackets must be really hot. I guess it's better to look cool than to dress for the weather. It's not exactly like women wearing pointy high heels and then complaining about how much their feet hurt, but it's similar.

Naturally, everyone I meet asks me how I ended up in Raupunga. My reply is pretty much the same each time:

"Well, I had this dog named Toughy...been a teacher for three years...I love teaching...thought about teaching overseas...but would never leave ol' Tough'...he died of liver disease...I was gutted..."

Gutted. I've used the word while cleaning fish but never to describe my feelings. The local term fits perfectly. I wasn't just sad, I was gutted—and I still am, to a measurable degree. The crying doesn't happen every day anymore, but it's still a weekly event.

Typically, I finish my story with a mention of Lonna's breakdown and my chance encounter with Maka. The reactions were usually of a piece too:

"Mate, I reckon you were meant to be here."

"Welcome to RPG—there's no place like it!"

Angie is at the party too. We came down from her house together, having agreed to go early, share a few cold ones, and bug out before the night gets too crazy. I can only imagine what *crazy* means in this context, but apparently it's not a matter of if the party will get there, but when. Now, beer and cigarette in hand, Angie is whooping it up with Cherise and a few other women. She certainly doesn't seem to be holding back on account of me. All too soon, the volume increases to a point where conversation is impossible, shoulders bump and rub, more beer ends up on the ground than in people's mouths, and a tense discussion erupts. Angie and I look at each other; time to go.

Mangu Kaha (Maori for "Black Power") graffiti on a rural shearing shed. This mural was probably created during a break from buzzing sheep.

The next morning, I happen on Rangi's house while running errands. The music is still going, but the scene outside the house looks like a bomb went off: Men in black leather jackets dangle out of cars and sprawl in the dirt. The few still standing are staggering around, proudly tossing back another cold one at nine in the morning.

Behind the debauchery, meanwhile, is a white house with blue trim—my house. Finally, the move-in day arrives, and I'm officially *living* in New Zealand. My house has three bedrooms, one bath, and a large living room with French doors that open to a dining area and kitchen. Since it's just Baetis and me, and the only heat source is the woodstove in the living room, I plan to make the living room *our* room. The glass door on the stove will allow another dimension of coziness—firelight. One bedroom will be my closet, a toss-everything-and-close-the-door-behind-me room, while the other two will remain vacant. I give it my personal touch by painting the living room blue and the kitchen cabinets yellow and orange. The drawers get their very own driftwood handle pulls. After sleeping on a camping mattress for close to half a year, I break down and buy a futon. So, to tally up: a home, a bed, and a cat.

I also have a small garden, which should yield its first crop soon. Along the narrow path in front of the house, I've planted bok choy, mint for fresh tea and for mojitos, basil, Swiss chard, green onions, and lettuce. I chose this spot because of the sun it gets but, most importantly, it's right out front, where I can admire it even in passing. I've read that plants grow better with admiration. Whether it's true or not, I don't know, but I think we all do better with a little admiration. I've always wanted to see how green my thumb is, but I've never had the opportunity until now.

The front of the house basks in the morning sun, and I develop a pleasing breakfast ritual: eating cereal on the front step, rubbing Baetis's ginger spot, and checking out the garden's overnight growth. Having had enough, Baetis hops off my lap and strolls over to a patch of Swiss chard. She straightens up, then suddenly dives into a tunnel leading underneath our house. Our house is elevated about two feet, leaving a tight crawlspace, a perfect place for Baetis to call her own. But there were only a couple tight spots to access the crawlspace, so I excavated a network of personal tunnels for Baetis to travel from the garden and into her own realm. Lined with pebbles and sand, the tunnels are big enough for her to dive into quickly if one of the many feral cats in the area chases her. I finish my cereal and sneak up to a metal vent to spy on my little girl; Baetis is unaware of her dad watching. I sigh, knowing how a father must feel while watching his child play in a treehouse that he built. Baetis bounds through the crawlspace as though she's informing all rodents the queen has arrived. If the prance in her step is anything to go by, she seems to know she's home. And so do I.

One morning on the way to work, as I near the winding driveway leading to the school, I run into Kahu. He looks lost. Not literally lost—he's walking in a straight line, and he's obviously on his way to school—but figuratively lost.

Kahu is thirteen and has a light complexion and curly black hair. He's not a big kid by any means—at least not as big as he acts and surely not as big as he'd like to be. I've heard his brother is a serious Black Power prospect and will probably be patched soon. Undoubtedly, Kahu must look up to his older brother. I'm not sure where Kahu's dad is, or if he's a significant person in his kids' lives. Kahu, it seems, has no one cheering for him. As we trudge up the driveway, the rugby field with its rusting goal posts reminds me how much I owe to my parents. Rain or shine, I can always look to them for support.

About the time my voice started to change, I began to appreciate the efforts of my parents and to take their well-being into account. On a rainy Saturday morning, I peeked through my parents' bedroom door. The pile of sheets lifted and dropped in rhythm with a grizzly-like snore. Dad told me to wake him for my soccer game, but he looked so comfortable that I decided to let him be. My game was close enough to ride my bike, so I wrote a note and slipped out feeling good about the decision. Dad had worked long hours all week; he deserved to sleep.

Mist and fog blanketed the field almost to the point that the game should have been canceled. I remember feeling grown-up: learning to treat your parents with compassion will do that to a kid. My game reflected those newfound feelings as all the other kids seemed really slow compared to me. As I streaked down the sidelines toward the goal, I heard someone yell, "Go Ryan!" Through the mist, and beyond the netting of the goal, I could make out the figure of a man standing with an umbrella—my dad. Nothing could stop me from scoring that goal. As the net kicked back from the force of the ball, Dad let out a roar that I can still hear to this day. Now, I can share that roar with my students. Although I can't replace what Kahu is missing, I can cheer from the sidelines, be a fan of his.

Kahu kicks a stone, and we both watch it rattle along the road and into a ditch. My interaction and understanding of Kahu is growing since I began teaching science to the older kids. We have a funny relationship: one second, he's going to great lengths to piss me off; the next, I'm filling a gaping hole in his spirit and he couldn't be happier. Today, though, we're simply two people headed to the same place, both caught in an early morning haze.

"Hey, Kahu. Howzit goin'?"

"All right."

"Cool."

His face is blank during this exchange. I'm sure it'll be just as blank at the end of the day. He'll still look as if he's missing something. This is different from looking for something, because when you're searching there is anticipation and expectation. Kahu isn't looking for anything, though, which worries me. Maybe he needs to know what's missing before he goes looking. Can I help him discover what is missing? Can anyone?

It makes me wonder how much difference a teacher can ultimately make. If children are shaped by genetics, parents, extended family, media, and the communities in which they live, what can a single teacher do? Kahu may be the unreachable kind of kid who haunts the dreams of teachers. In my short career, I've had many.

There was six-year-old Dean, who had been molested. His young mom had alcohol and drug abuse problems, and she locked Dean in the closet repeatedly while she had sex. He had apparently seen his mom raped and beaten many times as well. By the time I met him, Dean lived with his grandma, who had gotten a restraining order against Dean's mom—her own daughter. I spent a year teaching Dean, and one image kept coming back to me: He's two or three years old, in a dark place; long coattails brush his back. The floor dusty with a scattering of shoes. One side of his face is pressed to the floor, and the dust sticks to his curly hair. His position gives him a one-eyed view through the crack under the closet door. He's shaking but doesn't know to cry or to be scared. There are no questions in his mind. His mom's screams, the man's loud voice—these are normal. Right?

Dean's world was so foreign to me, but I wanted to help. It was my first year of teaching and my energy was boundless, so I kept him after school for bonding time. His therapist and I had extensive conversations about his behavior, and we were hopeful about his future. On the last day of school, I knelt down in front of him with tears in my eyes and told him I tried my best to be a good teacher and friend, but I wouldn't be able to be there for him all the time. The years passed. Right before I left for New Zealand, I heard he had been admitted to an institution. I wonder if he's still got his face to the floor, looking through that crack under the door.

Then there was Audrey. At six years old, she was riding the city bus by herself to school. She would stuff her face and pockets with whatever food she could find, including sandwiches that belonged to other kids. During journal time one morning, she drew a picture of a bullet flying over a sleeping girl. It was a self-portrait. How could she possibly learn anything, I wondered, while she was worrying about gathering her next meal and staying alive? She was eventually placed in special education, though I don't know if she was really a slow learner. Maybe she just had survival on her mind.

So I wonder about Kahu too as we make our speechless walk up the hill, past a grassy hill that leads down to a rugby field and a crumbling netball court. Across from the rugby field sit a handful of houses, one of which is Big Head's home. I'm not keeping track of his whereabouts nor do I look for him, but when he comes my way, it makes my day and crushes me all at the same time. Once we arrive at school, Kahu asks to use my skateboard, which I keep in the classroom. I hand him the scuffed board along with a bike helmet and resist the urge to join him.

When the rest of the kids arrive, we file into the classroom the same as we would any other day. Morning news is all typical stuff: billy goat sightings, billy goat escapes, Shay went "all the way" to town, and Brad still has a bull mastiff that might *get* me.

Because I have so few students, I can read leveled books individually. With my bigger classes in San Francisco, I grouped my students into four to five levels and read with small groups. While I'm reading with one kid, the rest of them work on special assignments and go to activity centers I've set up. It's a beautiful sight: Kea reading a book with my guidance, Arataki and Hiri making words with magnetic letters, Shay reading and memorizing high-frequency words at the Word Wall, and Keri reading on her own.

Teaching literacy is one of the most rewarding—and most heavily debated—subjects in education. As I like to write, *My prsnal techng blf is there is no slver bullet. Dffrnt things wrk for dffrnt kds.* Phonics is important, but it's also not the only way we read. People are still able to decipher my first grade spelling because they grasp the *meaning* behind it. Meaning and comprehension, I believe, are the two most important points. Take Shay. She knows her letters and sounds, but I don't want phonics to be her only reading tool, so we read a lot of easy books with predictable sentence patterns. It's great to watch her pick up the repeating sequences, look at the pictures and then "read" with confidence. Kids can't read with fluency and expression if they're always stopping to sound out every other word.

As for Kea, I can tell that his previous teacher may have overemphasized phonics, as he concentrates too intensely on the words in the books we read. When he's stuck, his brown eyes seem to swell as he leans in closer to the text, his finger pushing harder and harder into the page.

I say, "Hey, Kea, just relax and *think* about the story," which in this case is about a farm. "What do you think the farmer is riding?"

Kea pulls his head away, looks at the picture, makes the *t* sound a couple times, then, with a smile, emphatically says, "Tractor." No tunnel vision this time.

"Nice job," I say to him. Then, in a murmur to myself, "Tunnel vision—happens to the best of us."

As morning tea approaches, I look around the room and find myself wishing that Lori could meet the kids. What if she came here? She could visit the school for a few days, and then we could tour around New Zealand for a few weeks. It's not an aching-heart daydream, exactly; more of a hopeful one. Why can't I stop thinking about her? Right about the time Lori and I are running toward each other across a deserted New Zealand beach with arms wide open, the gong of the school bell sends the kids running out onto the yard. Morning tea has arrived.

I make for the basketball hoop. Lately, I've been playing Around the World with the older students. A lot of them are pretty good shots—especially the girls—because most of them play on the local netball team. I had never seen netball until I came to New Zealand. A fast-paced game where passing holds the key to victory, it's played on an NBA-sized court but there's no dribbling. The net doesn't have a backboard, either.

As I'm running down a loose ball, Angie emerges from the office and asks to speak with me.

There's a hint of urgency in her voice. Something must be wrong if there is even the slightest ripple in her usually placid demeanor. A student hurt? Gang trouble? My job in jeopardy? What can it be? I hope it has nothing to do with my job. I've only been here a few weeks, but it's really feeling like home.

Inside the office, Cherise, Arataki's mom, is talking on the phone. Her words come in a rush, fast and excited, so I can't really make out what she's saying. Angie, though, sits with her lips pressed tight. At first I think she's mad, but there is no anger in her eyes, just concern.

Some Mongrel Mob members were robbing a Black Power house in Wairoa. The Black Power guy came home and just started shooting, and word is that one Mob member is dead. "We just got a call that Mob members are on their way from Napier to Wairoa," Angie adds.

I knew that madness would make an appearance at some point, but when and to what degree, I had no idea. Looks like I'll have some answers soon.

Outside, I can hear the kids laughing and playing while Angie gives us emergency instructions. They're pretty simple: No children are to leave the school grounds for lunch, the pre-school at the bottom of the hill will move in with us at the top of the hill, and we should continue on with our day as normal. No sense alarming the kids.

Just then, Maata, Kea's mom, enters the office. I notice her usual arm-swinging walk is just a little stiffer, like the air has gotten thicker and she's trying to push through it. She looks at me and exclaims, "It's all on!"—meaning, "You're going to see what the Black Power and RPG are all about."

As if reading my thoughts, she says, "Don't worry, Mr. Chin. She'll be sweet as, but you might not want to sleep at your house tonight."

Dragging a chair over to the window, she climbs onto it and peers out at the road. "Yeah, your house is on the main road. They probably wouldn't get out of their cars, but they might fire a few. Bloody Mongrels!"

The scariest part of the whole scene is that Maata is talking about the prospect of bloodshed as if she's delivering the weather report. Her tone is so matter-of-fact. I suppose I shouldn't be surprised. In San Francisco, if something heavy went down in the low-income housing projects where a lot of my students lived—a drug bust, say, or a shoot-out—the children would have smiles on their faces as they discussed it the next day. Still, shouldn't Maata be a little more scared? This can't be normal, even for RPG.

It takes me awhile to grasp the situation. Here I am, six thousand miles away from the "tough" city kids I used to teach in America, and someone is telling me that I shouldn't sleep at my house because there might be a drive-by.

The nearest stoplight is fifty miles away, and this lady is telling me someone might spray bullets at my house. The headlines back home are often filled with the thugs who missed their intended targets and hit an innocent bystander instead. It's one of the most cowardly acts I can think of. What happened to squaring off against your foe with your fists? Or ten paces at dawn?

Obviously, nobody has a monopoly on senseless violence. One idle night in an Auckland hostel lobby, I found myself sitting around a coffee table with some Palestinians. It was an eye-opener. They refused to admit that Israel even existed. As luck would have it, I found myself at that same coffee table with an Israeli a few days later. With a shrug, he defended his country's actions: "There is no right and wrong. There is only point of view." And, of course, even as I was hunting down a teaching job in New Zealand, my country was gearing up to invade Iraq.

The school sits on the site of an old Maori fortress known as a *pa*. Standing on a chair, I've got a full view of the empty streets leading up to the school. It's easy to see why the Maori chose this hilltop location: it's got great sightlines and is easily defensible. If you're a good shot, you could probably hold off a small army from the roof of the school. I don't ask, but it's likely that some of the men in the community are somewhere on top of this same hill, armed and ready. I can't wait to hear the children's morning news tomorrow.

Suddenly, I'm reminded of my first time in Raupunga, when I broke down. There's no sheriff here. If you want safety, then you have to provide it. Best to leave this story out the next time I talk to my mom.

More news trickles in. One Mob member is definitely dead, run over by his buddies during the botched robbery. The police have been alerted and are setting up a roadblock south of Raupunga to intercept the Mob members heading to Wairoa. There's only one north-south road along the coast, so it should be easy to cut the Mob off. That sounds encouraging, but I have questions. Are there backroads they could take around the roadblock? Will the police maintain the roadblock all night? They'll have to let up at some point. What will happen then? Will Raupunga be attacked? Should I leave? My house is, after all, on that north-south road.

A lone police car enters Raupunga. What affect can it possibly have against carloads of Mongrel Mob members? Someone told me most New Zealand police don't even have guns. That's the job of the Armed Offenders Squad, local versions of America's SWAT teams, more or less. The car circles the empty streets a few times and then slowly pulls away.

Morning tea has stretched almost to lunchtime by now. I round up the class for a quick story and a few math tune-ups. School isn't canceled, so we might as well do something other than stare out the window. The rest of the day passes without incident. I turn down invitations to sleep at Angie's house, Kea's house, and Arataki's house, figuring that if Raupunga is attacked I'd prefer not to be around at all. So I pack up my valuables, water the garden, feed Baetis, pick some fresh bok choy, and head down to Mohaka Beach. I love having a bedroom on wheels—time for a sleepover in Lonna.

In the three short weeks I've lived in RPG, I've been to the beach at least a dozen times to check on the surf conditions, fish, collect sticks and rocks for the garden, and simply feel the dark, coarse sand on my feet. The Maori believe that the places where waters meet are sacred, and I agree. The powerful tides and the constant influx of sediment from the river shape a new beach for me to walk on with every visit. Sometimes the actual mouth of the river shifts by thirty yards or more. Giant logs are buried and then reappear days later—just another reminder of how change is the only constant. The only thing missing when I hit the sand is a dog. I consider asking if I can take Big Head with me, but decide against it. I'm not ready for that yet.

As it nears the ocean, the Mohaka River is more than one-hundred feet across. In addition to the normal sticks, logs, and stumps you usually find at a river mouth, there is pumice as far as the eye can see. A rock of volcanic origin, pumice is the only rock that floats. Being an inquisitive man—and a geology major—I do a bit of research. At least some of that rock, I conclude, could date back to a volcanic eruption from fourteen thousand years ago—before New Zealand was even inhabited by humans.

It was one of the largest eruptions in recorded human history; the Chinese, who were meticulous record-keepers, noted that the skies were red at about that time. There have been more recent eruptions too, so I could be wrong, but it's fun to watch the pumice gather in the turbulent waters at the mouth of the river while pondering its origins. By the time most people reach adulthood, they've lost their sense of wonder. I'm glad I've never lost mine.

Walking the beach in the last light, I try to sort through it all. As the last bit of the sun's warmth fades, I stare eastward, out at the ocean. Despite the physical beauty that surrounds me, I can't free myself from mankind's complexities. Just a few minutes' drive away, my home for the year may be under attack. There are people up there whom I've already grown to care about. What will I find when I wake up? I thought gangs were only found in the cities—not here in the countryside.

The night passes, punctuated by crashing waves, crickets chirping, jet planes high overhead, loud *baaa*s in the

Bedroom on wheels.

distance—basically, anything that might, to my slightly spooked ears, sound like gang members on the warpath.

But morning comes. There are no clouds in the sky, so it's a pretty uneventful sunrise, color-wise. Nothing dramatic.

For me, though, it's not really just another sunrise. The people who live here may be used to the idea of gang wars and drive-bys, but I'm not. Maybe some people would just get the hell out of town and never return. But as a former rock climber, I know that safety is relative. People would look at my pictures and declare how dangerous it was, but every day they'd drive eighty miles per hour, bumper-to-bumper, down a four-lane freeway. That hurtling mass of moving metal—not to mention all the other drivers—makes driving far more dangerous than hanging off a rock face hundreds of feet in the air with your trusted climbing partner. The same goes for surfing large waves. It may look scary, but as long as you keep your head together, it'll be okay—as long as you don't run into a great white shark.

Some surf right now might do me good, but there are no

rideable waves today. Instead, I pack up my stuff and shift Lonna into gear. Let's see what happened overnight. I'm worried, but I tell myself, *She'll be right, mate*, as the locals say.

The local expressions have a certain ring that makes them fun to say. As Lonna grinds up the steep road, I consider how the word *she* is used as a non-gendered pronoun and replaces *it*. "She'll be right, mate!" I repeat.

She is. There were no bullets or Mongrel Mob invaders during the night. I learn that a few of the men have made a run to Auckland for more ammo, just in case. Rangi, meanwhile, has raised the level of his roadside fence from about hip-high to head-high. Walls of corrugated metal and other bullet-slowing material were erected in haste. Now people are securing them. I have a chat over the fence with Rangi and some of the other Black Power men, telling them I slept at the beach. After they're done chuckling, I ask them if they would please bulletproof the front of my house too. This gets a big laugh—further evidence that well-placed sarcasm and laughter can be a bonding accelerant.

As I make my way to school still chuckling, I consider the beauty and versatility of laughter. Giggling, bellowing, and cackling create friendships, are good for our health, and help us to cope during uncertain times. Those are obvious benefits, but laughter has a place even during sad times.

Of course, I didn't laugh at I-Gaw's bedside or at his funeral, but I still giggle every time I think of the bubble episode. I can picture it perfectly: my family cruising through the white-capped mountains of Colorado for the first time—my sister, brother, and I stuffed in the backseat. As we crested a steep mountain pass, my brother's face began to disappear behind a large bubble-gum bubble. Somehow, it kept growing, eclipsing his entire face, and our hysterics grew with it, filling the car with peals of laughter. And that was just one of many laughs I shared with I-Gaw. The death of loved ones hurts so much because of the laughter you shared with them. Laughter never dies.

The kids obviously slept about as well as I did—this morning, they're wide-eyed, adrenaline pumping nuts. Half the town, it seems, slept up at Kea's house. A few of the older boys, including Kahu, show up with blue bandanas, and Angie promptly tells them to take them off. I can understand their motives. This is a chance to strut your stuff, a time to stand up for who you are and what you believe in. What those beliefs are, I still haven't figured out.

By evening, everyone is packed with ammo, and the tension still seems high, so I decide to sleep on the beach for another night. This time, however, I sleep well. Next day, same story: No news is good news. It was just another night in Raupunga.

As I pull up to my house that night, I decide to do a little bulletproofing of my own. My living room has three windows facing the front of the house. My futon is in the back corner, the farthest possible place from the front wall. My fence is a simple, corral-type barricade with cable rails—not much in the way of bulletproofing. After digging around for my keys, I move Lonna about ten feet forward from her usual parking spot in front of the door. I tuck her under the eaves, just a foot or so out from the wall. Then I hop the fence to check out my work. As I stand across the road from my white house with blue trim, I picture myself in the car of a drive-by shooter. Checking out the angles, I can see that the bullets will have to go through Lonna to get to me. If one makes it through both of Lonna's sides and the front wall of the house to hit me, I figure, then it must be my time. Three ricochets are what it would take to do me in.

In the meantime, life goes on. Across the way, I can see some of the boys kicking a rugby ball around. Arataki, who must be done with her homework by now, is hanging out in front of her dad's newly reinforced fence, trying to act like she's doing something else besides watching me. I wave at her; she waves back. Baetis calmly cleans herself on the front steps of our home. She has no idea how crazy we humans are. I sigh, shake my head, and walk to join her for a fine evening in our mostly peaceful country home.

CHAPTER
6

THE ONES THAT GET AWAY

I N THE WEEKS SINCE the drive-by scare, life in RPG has gotten back to normal. Maata's walk is back to its old chillin' self, everyone is stocked with bullets, Arataki's yard has taken on the look of a fortress, and the Mongrel Mob have declared that they won't retaliate—they were the ones doing the robbing, after all, and their fallen soldier died at the hands of one of their own members.

My life is settling down too. The work has gotten a little bit easier, but it's not quite on cruise control yet: I'm still trying to wrap my mind around multi-age teaching. It's tricky to have kids of different ages in the same class. Nevertheless, my garden is growing, and it's impossible to go anywhere in town without running into someone I know.

One afternoon, a few of the boys invite me to tag along on one of their favorite pastimes: chasing wild goats. Sure. Why not?

Leaving the afterschool cleanup for later, I trot out to the edge of the rugby field, where they're waiting for me. I'm barefoot just like the boys are, but my feet are nowhere near as tough as theirs. Running on grass with no shoes is one thing; running through the bush chasing wild goats is another. I start to go back for my shoes, but the boys take off at full speed, hooting and hollering, toward the barbed wire fence at the edge of the field. It's too late.

Ah, screw it! I can't have them thinking I'm soft, can I? So I pop my internal clutch, and I'm off. I'm a naturally competitive person, so it gives me a little thrill when I realize I can actually keep up with them, creaky thirty-year-old bones and all. I could overtake even the fastest ones if I wanted, I realize, but I choose to stay in formation and bring up the rear. We jump the low point of the barbed wire fence that is supposed to keep the cows in check. Then, suddenly, we double back. A dare has been made.

"No way, mate!"

"How much you wanna bet?"

"Dunno, but no way you can jump that section."

Nik, a skinny sixth grader who attends Mohaka School, trots back toward the fence, jumps the low spot, speeds up and then U-turns suddenly toward a section of fence at least as high as his chest. Uh-oh. Nothing good can come of this. I want to close my eyes.

I can hear it now: "How could you let Nik do this? What kind of example are you setting, Mr. Chin? Jumping fences and chasing goats with the children? He needed forty stitches. You're fired!"

Nik's feet leave the ground.

Apparently, though, Maoris can fly. I'll keep my job after all.

Soon we're back in formation. I imagine Toughy running beside me, his fine, long fur streaming behind him, his eyes and nose searching for a target. No matter what I did, I could never stop him from chasing deer. He would love to be here chasing goats with his dad. My chest begins to heave, but I don't have the breath to cry. In any case, the tears have been different lately, more frequently ending with a smile.

Next, we come upon a few hundred of the country's 4.6 million cow population. They scatter just enough to let us through. One of these days, it occurs to me as we dodge heifers, there will be a mutiny, an uprising, an *Animal Farm* event of global proportions. An image of being stomped to death by bovine hooves fuels my pace. For a moment, I cease to be an adult. Instead, I'm a teenager outrunning cops. The speed is liberating as I try to keep up with the pack and my feet leave the ground.

The Maoris are the most coordinated bunch I've ever met. I taught a few kids to juggle, for instance, in just a few minutes. As we run, some of the boys settle into a straight jog, but most of them use the banks and dips like a half-pipe, displaying a familiarity with the moves even though they've never really skated. Together, we pull one-eighties, cross-body tweaks, fakies to reverts, and three-sixties across ditches and ponds as we move into prime goat territory.

Most people think of the brain as the keeper of our memories, but our muscles, joints, and ligaments have memory too. Everyone has a little kid buried deep inside; today, mine is in his full glory. I relive close to a decade of skateboarding tricks as the cows watch me, chewing their cud.

As we approach the canyon that marks the end of the fields, the boys fall into a silent line. Their breathing becomes more deliberate; the tricks and zigzagging fade into a hunched and light-footed lope. Now they are mighty hunters. Their intensity of focus, their utter joy, gets me thinking.

Teaching is a profession of common sense. Children learn best when they can relate to material from their daily lives. Such a realization is obvious, but after you pay thousands of dollars and complete a teacher's program, you will be able to put it this way: you must teach to the children's "embedded context." Now I understand why little Brad's morning news was about goats for two weeks straight. From here on, I resolve, we'll read every goat book I can find; we'll write about goats; we'll count goats by the ones, tens, and hundreds; and we'll begin production of our first play, *Three Billy Goats Gruff.*

The story is a children's classic about a family of goats that encounters a troll at a bridge. One by one the goats meet the troll until the biggest billy goat pushes the troll off the bridge.

The plan unspools as I trot. How will we make the horns? If we're going to do this play right, we'll have to make some horns. We'll do some phonics with the *gr* blend and the *oa* word pattern. Maybe we'll count by threes to hone our memories and instill a little number sense. And then we'll decide who plays the troll and who plays the biggest billy.

Twenty-three years ago in Chicago's Chinatown, two seven-year-old Chinese boys squared off atop a makeshift bridge (it was really two Formica tables pushed together). A boy named Albert played the troll; I played the biggest Billy Goat Gruff. A seventh grade class cheered as I toppled Albert. The applause was thunderous. I'm sure Big Billy Goat Gruff still lives within me, ready to lower his horns at "trollish" challenges.

All of which is to say: portraying the biggest billy is a responsibility. I'm sure all three boys in the class will want to play him, so we'll have to draw lots. I'd love to just give the part to Kea or to one of the girls, actually, but that wouldn't be fair. I bet Arataki will be thrilled to narrate—even if she isn't, it'll be good for her confidence.

"Ehhh-mmmbedded Cohhhntext," says Billy in my mind.

Our pack slows, and all goes silent as we track our prey. "Can you smell 'em?" one of the boys asks me, breathing heavily through his nose.

Always willing to play along, I crouch a little lower, shake out my hands a few times, and grunt back, "Must be a big 'un."

Scanning the horizon, I peek over the rim of a series of canyons. I look intensely at nothing, an idea I picked up in a bird-watching book. Picking out birds among clusters of leaves and branches, targeting a large camouflaged trout on a stream bottom, or in this case, spotting a big ornery goat in dense foliage is not done by searching for the target so much as by scanning the area—absorbing every detail and picking out tiny movements, a slight shadow, anything that breaks the pattern.

I can't believe how vast the canyons behind the school are. A trickle of a stream winds through the soft sandstone canyon floor, and I find myself wishing for a bit more flow—just enough to support a few trout. Continuing to scan the hillside, I think I see a deer in a stand of fern trees, but it's just a stump.

Even though we're goat busting, I'm sure the boys wouldn't pass up the chance to chase a wild pig or a deer. Basically, anything they can chase would be game. If there is one good thing that came from the introduction of mammals to New Zealand, it's that it provides hunting opportunities—or should I say *busting* opportunities?

New Zealand didn't have goats, deer, pigs, cows, sheep—even humans—until a thousand years ago. In fact, before humans settled here, there were no mammals at all except for a few species of bats and marine mammals. The ecosystem didn't miss them either; birds evolved to fill those niches. The most famous of those homegrown birds is the kiwi, the flightless bird that has become the country's national symbol. Its name is used to describe the popular green furry fruit grown here and distributed worldwide, but it's much more than that. Pictures of kiwis are printed on packages of cheese, beer, bacon, lottery tickets, and are used as corporate logos. So intense is their identification with this vaguely goofy-looking animal that New Zealanders even call themselves Kiwis. Like so many iconic animals, though, it's now an endangered species. Both habitat loss and invader species (rats, stoats, ferrets, cats, and dogs), that arrived on boats with man, have taken a heavy toll on the kiwi.

The moa is another flightless bird once native to New Zealand. It could reach a height of twelve feet, and it weighed five hundred fifty pounds. These days it qualifies as the Loch Ness

Monster or Yeti of New Zealand. Although it's been extinct for hundreds of years due to overhunting, there remains a steady stream of reported sightings to this day.

Abandoning my search for a bear-sized bird, I train my gaze on the boys. It's good to see them just being *boys*. Right now, they aren't thinking about acting tough, they aren't thinking about joining Black Power—they really aren't concerned about anything besides catching wild goats. I've only known them about a month, but I already feel a parental concern for them. I worry that they may not recognize their fears and that they won't get the support they need to keep from going astray. In short, I'm just concerned about the decisions they'll make in their lives, whether they'll fall short of their full potential.

Suddenly, a hushed clamor interrupts my thoughts. A target has been spotted, a white nanny in the distance. "Mistah Chnn," whispers one of the boys. "You want to give it a go?"

Would I like to run as fast as I can? That's a silly question.

Running in the halls and down stairs is a huge no-no in schools, and it can be a hard rule to enforce. Why walk when you can run? The open spaces of an empty schoolyard, a newly carpeted room with no furniture, or a vacant gymnasium practically beg for a stampede of small, charging feet. When I lead children to playtime, I can feel their excitement at the imminent release of tension, the anticipation of letting loose. I love it. A ten-second burst of carefree play at recess can erase a horrible morning in the classroom. Playing with Toughy, who vibrated with happiness whenever I unleashed him at the beach, had the same effect. Children and dogs remind you to charge ahead, even if you can't go as hard or as long as you used to.

So I peel out, laughing my ass off, my grown-up feet bolting across the crunchy summer grass. Deep inside, though, I'm still a little boy in the schoolyard, running from the kid I just squirted with a ketchup packet. I'm still amazed at how accurate I was with that ketchup, painting the back of his shirt with red. To chase and be chased—simple, ageless glee.

I cover about ten of the twenty-five yards between the nanny and me before she turns and flees. I kick in the turbo, despite having no idea of the proper take-down technique. I'll worry about that when I get there, I guess. She charges down a steep path that leads down to the canyon floor, her rump disappearing around a blind corner, the RPG boys and I in hot pursuit, leaning into the corner like Formula One cars on a banked track. When we turn the corner, though, we come face to face with a huge billy with horns to match. He watches the nanny streak by, then cocks his head back in our direction. He doesn't budge.

The dust from the fleeing nanny hangs heavily in the air, mixing with the musky smell of goat droppings. Quickly, I run an unblinking risk assessment: How much damage could this large, surly animal with long horns do to me? Much to my relief, the big billy pivots clumsily on the narrow path and follows the nanny at full speed.

"Git'm, Mistah Chnn!" the boys shout.

The last thing I want to do is get closer to the oldest and biggest Billy Goat Gruff. But egged on by the boys and full of adrenaline, I charge after the king and maneuver into grabbing distance. He is surprisingly slow and, as I reach out for a handful of skin and fur on his rump, graphic images of my demise—"Chinese Man Skewered!" the headlines will scream—shoot through my mind. I extend my right arm but fear paralyzes me. I *pretend* to grab at his rump several times, slowing down just a tad. He finds a break in the foliage and plunges down a steep chute to the canyon floor.

So my first goat bust ends in failure. But isn't that normal for first-timers? Had I been a seasoned goat buster, I would have gotten him for sure. In truth, I'm happy with the outcome. I'll take failure over puncture wounds and hooves to the gut any day. I'm not interested in testing out the New Zealand health care system.

After the failed attempt, I bow out honorably. I've got work to do back at school. As I approach the barbed wire fence, I consider trying to jump the high section, but Big Head and Memphis, his Jack Russell terrier mate, come bounding up to me, leaping with flapping tongues. A few more RPG dogs join the ruckus; within seconds, my legs are covered in drool. As quickly as they appeared, they're gone, tearing off toward the horizon. I think about off-leash areas in San Francisco city parks and laugh. A run for many urban dogs consists of a six-foot leash on a sidewalk, or if they are lucky, a fenced area the size of a few classrooms. Big Head and Memphis can run as fast as they can, in one direction, for hours without worrying about dogcatchers or crossing a single road. My gaze follows their progress, and soon they're just dots in the distance. I feel a pang of self-pity—I miss having a dog.

When evening comes, I'm thinking about making horns for the play. I'm on my own here: figuring out child-friendly, cost-effective ways to make props is just part of a teacher's job. I've got prop-maker's block though, so I take a walk over to the lot next door. Baetis scampers along behind me, weaving in and out of the dry grass. As I check on the blackberries, she disappears into the thick brush, reappearing on an old fence post seconds later. She looks at me for approval and cleans herself on the swaying gray post. Obviously, her kingdom extends past the boundaries of our house. I pop a few overripe blackberries into my mouth and ask her, "Who's the queen 'round here?"

I've been pillaging blackberries from the lot for over a month, and they're finally beginning to run out. Fortunately, I notice, the grapes are starting to ripen. They're a little tart and the skin is tough, but the price gives them all the sweetness I need. I'm so absorbed in picking and eating the grapes that I don't see Maka until he's almost next to me.

Most of my encounters with my neighbor consist of simple

hand waves or a "What's up, mate?" head nod. Today, he's pushing his son along on a big tricycle. The boy is pedaling hard, his fingers clenched around the handles for leverage; I'm surprised the handlebars aren't bending under his pressure. When the little guy stops for a rest, he resembles a burly man in riding leathers taking his helmet off at a gas pump. No doubt he thinks the tricycle is the first step toward riding a chopper. I've been hoping to see Maka, actually; I recently heard he'd been shot.

"Mr. Chin, you should ask Maka to see his bullet wound. It's mean as," Cherise, Arataki's mom and the school secretary, declared, as though she were telling me about a good movie.

Adding the word *as* is protocol for Kiwi grammar, and I've grown to like it. It's like a create-your-own-metaphor tool. Things can be *sweet as*, *cool as*, *chill as*, *mean as*, and if you are bummed out you can be *sad as* too. In this case, *mean as* tells me the bullet wound is cool.

I've never seen a bullet wound. Even though I'm dying to see it, I figure it'd be impolite to bring it up. I squeeze my hands and rub the palms together. The evenings are starting to have a bite, but Maka, as usual, is wearing a tank top. Tough guys don't get cold.

"Howzit, Mistah Chnn?"

"Pretty good," I reply. "Just settling in, you know? How's it going with you?"

"Sweet as, but a bloody Mongrel shot me in town."

"No way," I answer, playing dumb but barely able to contain my excitement. Here's the opening I've been waiting for.

"Just walked up when I was sittin' in the car eatin' fish-n-chips with m' mate! In the shoulder and out the back," he says matter-of-factly. And with that, he pulls up his shirt.

Adorning his shoulder blade is a tattoo of a burning, flying skull that looks as though it was separated from its owner at high speed. The skull is screaming, but it doesn't look like it's in pain. It seems to be enjoying itself, actually. I imagine it feels even more badass now that it has this one-of-a-kind scar. "Bullet came right out the mouth," Maka explains. Indeed, in the bottom right corner of the skull's jaw is a round "divot" about the diameter of a pencil.

"That's crazy!" I blurt out, then add, "Well, I'm glad you're okay."

By this time, the little man is done fueling up his chopper. He slips his helmet on and with a kick of the starter, he's off, his gun-shot dad trailing behind. The sun dips behind the school, and I gather my grapes. Nothing like a chat with your neighbors to end the day.

When it comes time to make the play props a few days later, we're ready. The children are eager for some horns and listen attentively to the directions. As I watch my students paint and craft without hesitation, I feel a freeness developing within me. In fact, I've been painting on my own for a few months, inspired by Andy, the shack-living artist I stayed with before I came to RPG. When I arrived, he had just started a new piece. He never seemed to work on it for more than fifteen minutes at a time, but after a few months a beautiful painting of an ocean sunset took form on the canvas. Talk about just changing the blade! While I've never picked up a paintbrush except for art assignments in primary school, I've begun painting on large pieces of cardboard just to see what happens. I'm starting to realize creativity is an inherent trait, and I'm as capable as the next guy. The Kiwis, who are forever saying, "Just give it a go, mate!" might be onto something.

The horn-making project goes well. After a morning of twisting scrap paper onto wire and painting, we've got ourselves some impressively psychedelic-looking goat horns. Now it's time to clean up—not the easiest task to get a bunch of hyperactive little kids to do. So I grab a dry erase marker

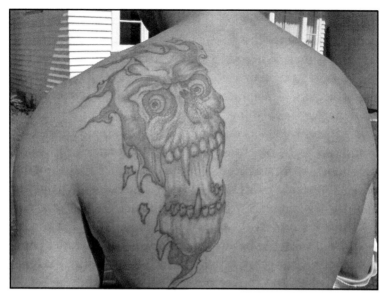

Maka, the first man I met in Raupunga, and his bullet wound.

and say, "All right, you guys are awesome. The horns look awesome. Now, let's do an awesome job cleaning up. If we can have everything cleaned up and be seated at the rug in three minutes, we'll earn a class point. Remember, it's okay to move quickly, but we aren't going to run. All right? Let's go."

The children scatter to complete their various missions. Kea collects the brushes; Hiri and Keri wring out some towels that are dirtier than the tables they intend to clean; Brad just leans against a table and swirls his finger in paint-water, admiring the different colors. He requires some extra motivation.

"Hey, Brad, I know the swirly colors are cool, but why don't you help Kea clean the brushes? He'll show you what to do. Maybe we'll do some swirly paintings soon." Brad glares at me, but he joins Kea. "Now let's move it," I boom out to the class. "Let's earn a point."

The honeymoon period is long over, so I've started class points as a way of motivating the children. It's nothing fancy, just a place in the corner of the whiteboard where I make tick marks in groups of five. At the end of the week, if they've accumulated twenty-five points or more, they'll have extended P.E. and games. When they start getting bored with this tactic, I'll start using a marble jar instead. There's a reason I like the little guys—imagine telling kids in middle school they'll get a marble for cleaning paintbrushes.

What earns you a class point? Acts of supreme effort, tact, kindness, and—my favorite—*doing* without being asked. This morning Arataki, unprompted, organized all the table baskets. Yesterday, Kea helped Shay tie her shoes. It's not just about a few points, of course—with luck, they'll internalize these lessons. My parents understood. "Hey, Ryan," Dad would yell from the bathroom. "Did you see the toilet paper roll empty? Change it!" My chores included keeping the toilet paper stocked and the ice trays filled, and to this day I take those duties seriously.

I've got nothing against a little positive reinforcement, but there's a fine line between rewarding good behavior and outright bribery. Give too many rewards, and they might cease working. When I was asked about my classroom behavior plan during my job interview, I replied, "It's a balance between praise and reward, with just a little punishment thrown in when it's called for."

Punishment, though, is a harsh word. I prefer to think of it as more of a reminder. If a child knows the rules and willingly breaks them, then there has to be some consequences. That's just the way our world has been set up. Punishment shouldn't, however, be used to motivate children. There's a difference between a child thinking, *I'm not going to do that because I'll get punished* and *That might be disrespectful. Maybe I'll do something else instead.* I don't want my students to feel that canceled playtime and detentions are hovering over them like storm clouds—though my childhood was plenty stormy.

Mom and Dad weren't authoritarians by any stretch, and I wasn't a horrible kid. They just wanted us to grow up to be cool people, although sometimes my actions weren't so cool. When I-Gaw and I got into it really bad—usually in the basement, a 1970s special with tan paneled walls and orange semi-shag carpet—my mom would stomp into the room and rip open the brown bifold door of the basement closet. As always, she was looking for an empty hanger. Not just any old hanger, though; she wanted one of the dry cleaner's hangers from Dad's pants, the ones with white cardboard sticks on them—the better to whack us with.

Once she found one of the dreaded white sticks, she would rip it off the wire while I-Gaw and I cowered, blaming each other for the spanking that was coming our way. As Mom stepped forward to whack us, he would usually get a few hits in on me too. We were going to get it anyway, he figured; he might as well fill his little bro-bashing quota. I know a lot of people frown upon hitting children, but I think a little physical reminder isn't so bad.

Ah, the joys of sibling rivalry (and bonding). What I wouldn't give to have I-Gaw around right now for a good brother-on-brother wrestling match.

As I grew older, use of the white stick gave way to writing lines:

"I will not throw rocks."

"I will not antagonize my brother."

"I will not play with matches."

I wrote so many lines that I knew I could get twenty-four or twenty-five lines on each wide-ruled piece of paper, or that I could get about thirty-three on each piece of college-ruled paper. Once, when I was bored at school, I premade a few pages of "I will not_____," so when I screwed up, I'd have less work to do—a brilliant use of my school time. Unfortunately, when I tried to use my prefabricated sheets, the sentence I had to write didn't fit on one line.

Funny, I don't even remember what I did wrong that time. Maybe it was, "I will not forget important lessons."

Mom and Dad called Eileen, Angel—or Little Angel—which was fitting. She never gave them a reason to make her write any lines. Sometimes she helped I-Gaw and me write *our* lines because she felt bad for us; or maybe we made her feel guilty, like the good brothers we were.

So far, there hasn't been any need for line-writing, negative calls home, or detentions. I hope it stays that way. Dealing with behaviorally challenged students in San Francisco was a soul-sapping experience, and those hyper-anxious fifth and sixth graders that I taught here in New Zealand weren't much easier. I'm loving my small class of children. These kids actually listen to me.

Now, with the last brush washed and the tables smeared with diluted paint, the paint-splattered children rush to the rug, eager to earn a point. Maybe I should have given them a few more minutes—those tables are still really messy. Oh, well. We'll go over proper table-cleaning techniques another time.

I smile and slash a few points on the board. And now it's rehearsal time. "*Rehearsal*," I tell them, "is just a fancy word for *practice*. Just like you practice for a rugby game, we have to practice for our play." Now, more rewards: "Everyone is going to get a rehearsal card for stamps. You'll have to listen carefully to my directions to earn stamps. At the end of rehearsal, we'll count up the stamps for a small prize. Got that?"

The stamp card is mostly aimed at Brad, who's portraying the Big Billy Goat Gruff. He's not exactly listening to me these days, but occasionally I can pry a smile out of him before he folds his arms, tucks in his chin, and resumes his glaring.

Plays are amazing educational tools. They cover virtually every subject and touch on every bedrock value I'd want my subjects to learn: the importance of teamwork, for instance, and the idea that the performance is the reward. Back in San Francisco, my first-year production was a nonfiction piece. A Hispanic girl, a Filipino girl, and an African American girl were my narrators. They detailed the life cycle of a butterfly, while teams of caterpillars, chrysalises, and bursting butter-flies wiggled, crawled and flew all around them.

I chose a shy and very special child, Ken, who had muscular dystrophy, for the camouflage role. We made a paper suit for him so he'd match the wall in the back corner of the room. Boys with muscular dystrophy seldom live past their teens. I'm sure Ken will remember jumping out on cue to scare our audience for the rest of his life. I know I will.

Lori generally mounted more music-oriented productions with her class. I had hoped to do a joint class production with her, but after *the letter*, we both backed off. We'd had some great moments together: a bike ride, a picnic lunch during school, a dinner party at my house, and an evening of doing capoeria together. Soon, though, the grayness of it all was too much for the both of us, so I took it upon myself to end it; I wrote a completely over the top letter and presented it to her right before she left for a weekend trip. Giving her the letter gave me a feeling of closure, almost as if I were saying, "Good-bye, but I'll see you later."

Among other embarrassing lines, I wrote, "...I won't go so far as to say you're the one, but I have never had so much vision when I looked at a girl..."

When she returned from the weekend, she said, "I don't think we should hang out anymore."

I nodded and replied, "I know. I know. It's just too much..."

We didn't talk about it then, but we each knew that we shouldn't spend much time in the same room together. For a second, I allow myself to daydream about chasing goats with her. A goat bust, dinner at my place, and a cozy fire—how's that for a perfect first date in New Zealand?

The class's first rehearsal goes well. Brad is a little shy, but he relishes pushing Hiri, the troll, off the bridge and onto a crash mat. As we walk back to class, I get an idea for constructing the river. "Hey, let's go to the woodpile. Pick out the flat pieces and bring them back to the classroom."

"What for?" Hiri asks.

A major production.

"I'll show you tomorrow," I smile.

The next morning I pour blue and white paint into tubs and spread the flat pieces of firewood out on the grass. After explaining the idea of a mosaic to the children, they spread out, happily painting the wood. Bits of windblown grass and leaves stick to the wet paint on the masterpieces, adding to their natural realism. With the mosaic river in place, our set is complete.

The demands of a major production have left me yearning for some of my own time on the water, so after school I hop in Lonna and tear down a dirt road to pick up my new fishing mate, Tim.

An eleven-year-old native-born Kiwi, Tim attended Raupunga School with his brother and sister until his mother, Karen, decided that home schooling would be better for them. He spends a lot of time hunting, so no Australian possum, wild pig, duck, pheasant, or rabbit is safe from his gun. Karen thought it would be good for Tim to learn to fly-fish, so she asked me to let him tag along; in return, I've gotten plenty of delicious meals from Karen, who's something of a cook. She also introduced me to the cup-of-tea interrogation, a technique used by locals to dig up dirt on the new guy in town. I quickly learned that a cup of tea with Karen is a cup of tea with a high-volume bullhorn, and innocent pieces of information can quickly spiral into drama-filled gossip. I made the mistake of admitting my challenges of teaching a multi-age class, and it took all of twelve hours to morph into "Mr. Chin doesn't know what the hell he's doing." I shrug it off, opting to focus on the unique opportunity I have to bond with Tim and his family. After a long day on the river, Tim and I will slog up the loose gravel driveway. Through the window, I'll see the kitchen light burning, making my stomach growl, and I'll think, *Just in time...*

One of the reasons I'm so hungry after an excursion with Tim is his ability to glide effortlessly over the landscape. It doesn't look like he's running, but it always seems as though I'm struggling to keep up. He'll turn his freckled face toward me, wave his arm, and say, "This way." Then I'll shuffle after him until we reach our destination. He's a practical boy, a meat-and-potatoes kid who isn't completely sold on fly-fishing, which is, after all, not the best way to actually catch fish most of the time. It's a process that one must appreciate, but I think it's slowly growing on him. For now, though, Tim spends a lot of time watching me fish and seems content just letting his fly swing around aimlessly instead of casting with purpose. Still, we have a lot of fun together and share some good laughs.

During one trip, we surprised a dozen goats as we drove around a bend in the dirt road. I fishtailed Lonna into the grass and skidded to a stop. We were out the door like car thieves bailing after running into a roadblock. The wide, grassy hills above us allowed the goats to spread out in seconds, easily evading us. I've caught plenty of trout and waves in New Zealand, but never a goat. If only I could practice my takedown technique somehow. One Sunday, the opportunity presents itself.

On the way back from a weekend of surf and cold ones, I stop by Huck's house. Angie's partner has found a new herding gig just north of Raupunga, and I discover he has spent the last few days having his sheep dogs round up wild goats. There is a market for wild goats in Europe and the Middle East. The kids at school share tall tales of getting rich by catching goats. Angie has driven up for the weekend, bringing a request from a friend for a goat to make curry. I'm just in time to practice some goat busting.

With shaky hands, I grab the barbed wire fence to the paddock where Huck is keeping the goats. As he and Angie sit back and watch, I jog toward the herd, a goat-busting greenhorn. There is nowhere for the goats to hide but, like an inexperienced cheetah on the African plains, I have trouble picking a target. As I move through the herd, studying the goats' movements, I gain confidence.

Martial arts teaches you to control your opponent's head by grabbing an ear, a handful of hair, or even the nose. The successful goat buster makes good use of this theory: deftly taking hold of the horns with a quick grab is part of the trick. Even though Angie's friend has requested a nanny, I go after a big billy first—just for sport. Call it testosterone or just recklessness. It's like squirting ketchup on that third grade bully—it's something that must be done. I zero in on the target goat's large rump.

With my right hand, I grip a fistful of fur and skin, sidestepping to avoid the bucking. Patiently, I wait for him to turn his head. With my left hand, I grab his horns, collapsing my body weight onto his head while scooting my legs forward. I finish in the classic goat-buster position: both hands on the horns, my body holding him down, out of reach of his kicking legs. Behind me, I hear Huck and Angie laughing. He's a wild goat, I know, but catching him feels a bit like fishing an overly stocked fishing pond. The satisfaction just isn't there. If only I had caught that big bad billy with the boys!

Sometimes, I can still feel the waves that pummeled me when I hesitated on the take-off while surfing. I remember rock climbs that thwarted my best efforts; I can recall the color and texture of the cliff faces as my muscles and my mind failed me. I remember blowing my dismount at the high school gymnastics meet, and I still cringe at the memory of not talking to the cute girl, who came to watch me compete in (and win) a skateboard contest. And, of course, there are the many fish that broke my line. Now I can add to that the bittersweet memory of the white, dusty rump of a big New Zealand billy goat. I file all these memories away in my mind. The label on the file: The Ones that Get Away.

CHAPTER
7

BEST DAYS

Reading time in my classroom. All eyes are on me, hands folded in laps, faces expectant. *All* is sort of a grandiose word, maybe: the class has shrunk to just five bright young minds. It's weird seeing so few children on the rug, but I still have my hands full with all of them being different ages. Also, I have a new student.

Her name is Oliana, and she's joining us just a little too late for her acting debut. Our *Three Billy Goats Gruff* play was a success even though Brad walked around with his arms folded and refused to speak. His face was so contorted with anger that I feared he might really gore Hiri in her troll costume. As our handpainted river of blue and white firewood frothed behind her, Arataki set the scene for the audience. Just as I suspected she would, she made me look good. The parents were impressed, and I gave myself props. Not bad for our first production.

Oliana will eventually get her chance on stage. In New Zealand you simply start school when you turn five—no cut-off dates, just come to school on the day you hit that magic number. She's a good kid, warm and eager to please, with a desire to learn that makes me wish there were more Olianas in the world. My goal is for her to leave my class at the end of the year knowing the whole alphabet and having the ability to read beyond pure memory reading. I think with Oliana's spunk, she'll reach a level at which she's decoding letters and problem solving—reading. If we don't reach those goals, I'll make sure she at least *thinks* she can read. That way, she'll experience the joys of learning. Curriculum and pedagogy are important, of course, but building confidence—making sure my students love learning—is just as important.

That's one of the reasons I left the United States—to get a break from the pressures and cookie-cutter curriculums forced upon public school teachers. Unfortunately, in America, education on many levels has been reduced to a mere business, in which reading levels are treated like bottom-line dollar amounts. It's a dangerous direction, this numbers game, sure to ruin the essence of primary education and smother the joy of learning. But enough with the righteous daydream. I have a read-aloud to finish.

"No sooner had people begun to tend their gardens or gone fishing and hunting than the sun would set and all would be darkness once more," I read before asking, "Who here thinks it's cool to not have enough daylight to go fishing or to play?"

No one raises a hand. I can see that they all feel sure of their decisions, which is good to see. Sometimes a herd mentality prevails. A child starts off happy with her decision, her belief, her opinion, then slowly realizes she might be the only one who feels that way. Soon, the confident smile fades; she's anxious about her classmates, what they think, afraid to be out of step with the group.

It was my first year of teaching. A Filipino girl, sitting with her legs crossed on our multicolored carpet, was writing on her dry erase board with a blue marker. The question of the day was, What is your favorite food? She sat to the left of me in a circle while everyone shared: pizza, pizza, hamburgers, pizza, hamburgers, cheeseburgers, French fries, pizza, pizza, and McDonald's. When her turn came, I noticed that her hand was blue from the dry erase ink, because she had rubbed out her original choice—fish—and replaced it with pizza. Is it natural to follow the herd? Is it natural to be unsure? Is it natural to want acceptance?

Right now, in my classroom in RPG, there is no peer pressure driving this consensus. Not a single child here thinks it would be cool if the sun only showed itself for a teensy-weensy bit each day. I couldn't agree more.

"Yeah, it wouldn't be any fun if I couldn't surf or go fishing." I frown. "What do you think Maui is going to do about the sun?"

Kea rolls his eyes as if I've just asked him what one plus one equals. "Maui is going to beat the sun up!" he exclaims.

He obviously knows the story, so I hold my finger to my mouth to silence him. I don't think Oliana's heard it.

I'm reading a classic Maori myth called *Maui and the Sun*, or *Maui Tames the Sun*. The sun, you see, used to just shoot across the sky, meaning you had no time to get anything done. Walk out the door at sunrise and by the time you tied your shoes, it'd be dark. By the time you put your wetsuit on to go surfing, the sun would be gone—even if you woke up at dawn. Very frustrating.

Something had to be done, so Maui devised a plan. After rallying his doubtful bros to the cause, he walloped the sun, wailing on the sun with his ancestor's sacred jawbone. Following this thrashing, the sun agreed to slow his sweep across the sky. So we should all thank Maui. He should be the richest man in the world too. Just think of the royalties from sunblock, sunglasses, bikinis, and all sorts of other products we wouldn't need if not for the sun. Leave it to me, an American, to put a capitalistic twist on the story.

Just as I'm turning a page, Hiri screams: "Mistah Chnn! There's a cow!" Sure enough, just beyond our window, a black head is chewing cud and peering in at the classroom. It's an escapee from the pasture beyond the rugby field. Chew, chew, swallow, swallow, regurgitate, regurgitate, chew, chew.... She cocks her head at me, maybe wondering what I'm reading. It's weird. I've never seen a hole in the barbed wire fence, which makes me wonder if they can just materialize on our side, like wizards from a fantasy book.

As cows go, this one is pretty small, but she's still a large animal—with the face of a misbehaving child who, now chastened, is ready to return to the classroom to learn. It's almost as if she's saying: "It's not my fault that I'm a cow. Please let me in." Shay is transfixed. I want to tell her, "It's just a cow, you've seen them your whole long life." But of course, it's not just a cow—it's a cow looking in through our classroom window.

"Should we let her listen to our story?" I ask them.

"She can't come in here!" they respond.

"Why not?"

Laughter and incredulous glares—I must be slow to ask a question like that, their faces say.

I wave my hand at Kea to go scare her off, but before he gets out the door, some of the older boys from the other class tear into the scene like a police raid on a drug house.

Kahu leads the mission. No surprise there: he usually directs the pack on goat-busting expeditions, leads the boys in the school *haka* (the Maori ritual dance), and starts the troublemaking when I teach science to the older class. I worry about Kahu. His only goal at the moment is to make it through the prospect stage of the gang hierarchy and become a fully patched member of Black Power. A fine goal, I reckon, so long as it's not the only one. After successfully shooing the cow away, Kahu and his crew sulk back to class. I empathize with them. Math, writing, or chasing cows? It's no contest.

The cows belong to a woman I've never met named Villy, and I wonder if she knows how savvy her cows are. Every time I see cows that have gotten loose and speak of them, people shake their heads and sigh. "Not again," they'll say, or, "Damn! Villy's cows!" Some mutter dark words under their breath about "fair game" and "meat for the freezer." Then catching

A couple of the boys juggle a soccer ball in the schoolyard. Note the gifts from Villy's cows.

themselves, most of them will laugh, a little nervously, and try to play it off ("I was just kidding ... ").

Despite all the excitement, the class manages to settle back in for the climax of the story—when Maui beats the tar out of the sun. Just as I finish with an emphatic, "The end," someone raps the bell: morning tea has arrived.

The children bound away, their beautiful chatter fading. They are literally walking on their land. They are too young to understand the oppression their ancestors endured and too young to shake their heads at the barriers still evident in the New Zealand population. So I shake my head for them and think of a woman I met during my early travels in New Zealand. On a deserted beach, a woman appeared over a dune, fighting the wind with a couple kids in tow. Considering I was an hour off the main road with barely a house in sight, a Chinese man must have been a different sight to her. We made eye contact, and she trudged as though she needed to pick something up that had blown away. For a moment, I wondered if I was trespassing on her land. The kids charged up a sand dune; the gales snatched their laughter and turned them in carefree circles. The woman grabbed her hat in mid-flight revealing a leathery face that showed decades of stormy days, hard work, and most likely liquor—lots of it. I could practically hear the clank of the bottle.

"Hello," I shouted above the sound of the wind.

"What brings you out here?" she yelled.

"I'm a teacher from the States looking to teach in a place like this," I replied with a wide of sweep of my arm. "Preferably where most of the school's kids are Maori."

"Why does everyone show so much compassion to them?" she snarled.

"Um, well, I just think, uh, it'd be different..."

We shifted in the winds, more for something to do than for balance. I mused over the idea of landing a job in the nearby school and teaching her children. I was certain teaching in rural areas of New Zealand would entail mixing with people whose beliefs I did not share.

I stood saddened by the encounter. She left with a simple goodbye, and I watched them disappear back over the dune, the blowing sand quickly erasing their tracks. If only the scars of oppression could disappear as quickly.

I know few details about New Zealand's history, aside from its colonization roots and the typical oppression and atrocities that went along with it. If this woman lived in the United States, she would definitely be a staunch opponent of affirmative action. I can see both sides: the Maori wanting some form of compensation and white New Zealanders, or Pakeha, thinking, "Stop crying about the past, and let's get on with it."

I can read about prejudice and racism and sympathize for the victims, but in reality, I have no idea what type of person I'd be had I grown up on the receiving end—or the giving end, for that matter. The Israeli-Palestine conflict seems so childishly tit for tat from the comforts of my fire-lit home, but I don't know what it feels like to have lost family members to enemies a stone's throw away. Nor do I know what it feels like to be an African American. Sure, I've examined my beliefs and have compassion for what they as a people have gone through, but I really have no idea.

During my freshman year in college, Dave, an African American who roomed down the hall from me, pinned me against the wall in our dorm hallway. A few friends and I wanted to have a card game in the lounge, but someone had taken the large table as they sometimes did for study groups in their own rooms. I started to look in the adjacent rooms for the lounge table, and Dave's room was the closest one with an open door. Dave thought I'd singled him out and exploded off his chair, then pinned me to the wall, gripped my throat, and screamed, "Why you looking in *my* room?" His large eyes bulged from his face; a fury like none I've ever seen pulsed from them—but he was not mad at *me*. He was mad at something much larger, and maybe that's why I didn't fight back. Something in me told me not to, that I should just let him be. I can't imagine being profiled as a thief simply because of my race, but Dave came from the streets of Chicago. He had experienced profiling of the highest degree, so I didn't blame him for his actions.

I stand and stretch; some tea and a cookie will ease my feelings about humanity's shortcomings. I step outside, thank Maui for the warmth on my face, and peel my jacket off. The air is still cold enough to give me a few goosebumps. With luck, it'll be warm enough by afternoon to make use of the faint hum beyond the fence, Kea's family water pump.

One of Angie's goals at the beginning of the school year was to get the pool—a cracked, neglected thing with a few feet of algae-ridden rainwater in it—in working order. That's how it goes in RPG: even if you have money to buy a new one, most of the time you can't, so you fix what you've got. With New

Zealand being an island near the bottom of the earth and Raupunga located far from the larger port cities, picking up new merchandise—or new parts, for that matter—can be a long ordeal. It's a refreshing mentality when contrasted with the toss-it-and-get-a-new-one attitude in America. Now the pool's ready to use, and the good old-fashioned pool fixin' has shown me how things are done in Raupunga.

During an earlier board meeting, I accompanied Angie and a few members of the board up to the pool to have a look. We walked up to the edge, bent down, and rubbed the cracks, stared at them, stood up, nodded our heads, took a few drags off the smokes we'd rolled, bent down again, picked at the cracks, stared at them some more, commented on the sunset, and relit our smokes. There were a few words about finagling funds to pay someone to fix the leak, but this was strictly for the meeting minutes. Now we could write, *Discussed and reviewed bids for pool repair*. The decision was made. She'd be right, mate!

The RPG solution: rub a little crack sealant in, slowing down the slow leaks, and use a generator (the hum) to divert some water from Kea's home next door to start filling the pool. That way, the water would pour in faster than it leaked out. Never mind the slight tint to the water; everyone was used to swimming in the river anyway. Besides, we'd treat the water with chlorine as we would with any other pool, courtesy of Kea's Uncle Steve, the school's maintenance guy. Swimming lessons would become a regular part of our day.

I can only imagine what we'd need to do in America to use the pool. We'd have to hire a licensed, bonded, and insured contractor (five thousand dollars) to do the repairs; pay a certified inspector (one thousand dollars) to give it the stamp of safety; buy an approved filter (two thousand dollars) to bring the water to standards suitable for human contact; and finally, pay the noise ordinance fine (at least two hundred dollars), because someone complained that the generator we used to divert the water was too loud.

Swimming lessons, I discover, are a great way to end the day or close out the morning before lunch. After all, how many millions of paid office hours are wasted in the thirty minutes before lunch and the thirty minutes before quitting time when it's okay to *pretend* to work? It's no different with children, as the clock ticks, hunger looms, motivation sags, attention drifts. Art and P.E. plug that gap with developmental and confidence-building activities, such as painting and swimming.

It also occurs to me that the pool would be a perfect place to check Lori out in a bathing suit, if she were a teacher here. A perfectly natural man-thought, it steals over me one day in the pool as my kids splash and yell their way through some creek-water combat. But she's six thousand miles away. And we've never kissed. And she's still with someone. Why can't I stop thinking about her? It's been three and a half years since I first saw her across the schoolyard that morning.

That first year, Lori was a student teacher in kindergarten. The second year, she was to teach a kindergarten class of her own, but there weren't enough students. I was just as disappointed at not having her at the school as she was at losing her job. In my third year, I decided to move up to second grade; meanwhile, a second grade teacher's retirement gave Lori a place at our school. Suddenly we were together on the same grade level. Was it a sign? I don't know, but here I am in New Zealand.

I wonder what she's doing with her class right now. Lori loves the little people as much as I do.

She not only has a knack for teaching but also for navigating the frustrating steps needed for getting a child more services. San Francisco, with its high cost of living, still has a public school system with a lot to be desired. Our school had no on-site counselors or therapists, not even a nurse. We even went for a couple weeks without a proper principal. Having a child tested for learning disabilities or procuring a psych evaluation entailed long waiting lists and hours of phone calls and paperwork. But Lori's tenacity benefited many of the students. She secured dental care for one boy, a family therapist for another, and expedited the transfer of another girl into special education. I'm sure Lori will make a fantastic mother someday.

I know she would love Oliana.

In her first week, Oliana spells her name using fat pencils, crayons, and felt pens. She even uses a stick, scratching her name in the sand dozens of times. She skips out of the classroom on Friday so vigorously that her short hair stands on end with every hop. I wonder if she'll still be skipping out of class in high school. The skipping and smiling student, I think, is a paycheck for the teacher's soul.

I'm not sure if I ever skipped out of any classroom except on the last day of school, but I do know most of my teacher relationships were either love or hate. If you can inspire and engage the attention-deficit kid, harness his hyper energy, you can sit back and watch the magic happen. If you try to fight it to make the kid conform, you're in for a long year.

Such was the case with my fifth grade teacher, Ms. Keefer, and me. I spent much of my time amusing myself during boring workbook lessons, a staple, especially in Catholic schools. As she lectured us on the seven sacraments, I rolled a golf ball back and forth with my friend. Of course, she caught me and promptly moved my seat to the farthest possible point from my buddy. I simply pulled another golf ball from my desk and scanned the room for something to deflect the ball. A worn wooden podium in the corner of the room had just the right angle, and seconds later my friend smiled as the golf ball hit his foot.

My teacher and my parents had many talks, but not all of them were about my misbehavior. When our class needed a time machine for a classroom play, I volunteered to make it, spending a whole weekend cutting cardboard boxes, taping, gluing, and painting until well past my bedtime. It was so big Dad had to bungee cord the trunk closed because it didn't fit.

Ms. Keefer couldn't stop shaking her head and smiling when I dragged it into the classroom.

Webster's 11th Collegiate Dictionary defines *deficit* as a "deficiency in amount or quality." Who, though, determines the difference between a teaching deficit and a student's attention deficit? There is a logic question given to both fifth graders and to college graduates. More fifth graders answer the question correctly than grad school wannabes. Why? Because by the time we have gone through high school and college, we are too damn educated to draw a simple picture to solve a problem. So if you're stumped, remember to draw a picture in the sand or make cut-outs to arrange and rearrange. The question, by the way, is one of those important ones like: Chad sits to the right of Maria. Maria sits in front of Tony, and Tony is sitting so that he can touch Bill. Henry is between Maria and Tony, but only when Bill touches Henry. Two more people sit somewhere between Chad and Maria and Tony. Who is sitting to the right of Maria?

It's fall, and the leaves are starting to drop. I've lit my fireplace at home for the first time. The mornings have been hatwearing chilly, and I'm thinking about firing up the woodstove in the classroom. Oliana is already there when I arrive, flipping through a few books.

"Mistah Chnn, am I making my name again?"

"Yes, funny you should ask."

This is how it begins. In the morning, she makes her name out of blades of grass and glues it onto poster boards with beans. Later in the afternoon—drum roll, please!—she begins to recognize other words that have the same letters as her name. I can almost see the synapses firing away in her head as she makes these connections. Meanwhile, her knowledge of shapes and colors is hitting PhD levels; she's memorized a few books for pretend reading, her desk is tidy, and I just know she's going to meet her goal in the swimming pool. She is high-grade lumber and I am the carpenter.

Outside in the chill, the pool is filled to its cracking rim. I had considered bringing my wetsuit to school for swimming lessons but decided against it. The class can't possibly want to swim, right? I am so wrong.

"C'mon, can't we go swimming?"

"It's cold," I answer, "and we have a lot of work to do on our Rainbow Fish display and—"

"C'mon! Please, Mistah Chnn."

"Okay," I say, understanding the logic. Who cares how cold the pool is? A frosty day at the pool beats a toasty day in the classroom. We suit up, line up, and start our short, shivering walk to the pool.

Hiri and Arataki divert for a second to scare off Big Head. I watch him run off, his latest collection of chewed ropes and leashes twirling and bouncing around his neck, and I feel sick. My hole is still there. Will it ever mend? He has almost doubled in size since I met him, but he still runs like he has flapping socks on his feet.

The boy in me wants to chase Big Head until my chest explodes from joy. I want to turn and charge full speed, calling over my shoulder, "C'mon, boy!" I'd let him catch me; and we'd have a wrestle, which I'd let him win for a few seconds before grabbing his paws, flipping him, and rubbing his belly until he barks, "Dad!" I suppress a sniffle and manage to make it to the pool without the kids noticing.

With my hat off, my bare head is at the mercy of the crisp air. For reasons I didn't understand, I impulsively shaved my head when Toughy was ill. A good friend later told me it was a sign of cleansing and new beginnings. I enjoy the no-frills, low-maintenance look, but it's hard on Mom.

I-Gaw's head was without hair for the last months of his life. It fell out in huge clumps as he endured rounds of the most intense chemo a human could stand. Just as his hair would start to grow back—shoots of hope, almost literally, sprouting from his head—it'd be time for another round. The leukemia just wouldn't give up. It's good that Mom can't see me with my bald head now, because I'm sure she can still see I-Gaw as vividly as I can. He'd turn his large, bare head to give me a thumbs-up from behind the isolation glass while his body was literally being nuked.

Amazed at the miles of thoughts that can run through my head in just a few short steps, I gather the children at the pool's edge. There's always time to slip in some vocabulary enrichment, so we discuss how we are on a quest to "dive and dart like dolphins" and "swiftly swim like seals."

"We can dive into a pool," I say. "What else can we dive into?"

"I dived into the river," Kea yells.

"Mistah Chnn," says Hiri with a self-satisfied smile. "I dived into some wool at the shed."

"Oooh!"

As bulbous white clouds split the cold, blue sky above our heads, we review our goals for the day. Oliana will put her head completely underwater. Kea will swim the length of the pool without stopping. Hiri, Shay, and Arataki will kick across the pool, nonstop, with kickboards.

We snap a picture and get ready for our pool session. I won't tolerate squeamish entries. Letting loose my inner drill sergeant, I remind the kids that they're the ones who wanted to go swimming. "In the pool now! Kea, you warm up kicking on the side and then swim across the pool now! Everyone else but Oliana, join Kea on the side, grab your kickboards, and go!"

I turn to Oliana, whose feet are dangling in the monstrously frigid water. When I look her way, her lips crack into a chattering hint of a smile. She cannot hide her thoughts: *Don't make*

A fine fall day at the RPG pool in Aotearoa, Land of the Long White Cloud.

me do it! The water is going to eat me! See? Look, it has my legs right now. Please don't let it get my head!

Very gently, I say, "In the pool, please."

She turns onto her belly and starts to ease in on her own. She's wincing and gasping, legs kicking furiously as she lowers herself into the monster. Four inches down into the pool, frantic kicking, then two inches up out of the pool—her progress stalled, she clings to the side with a death grip. Her tiny little feet are still a long way off the bottom.

From my place in the water, I extend my right arm as far as it will go. Male teachers must always be careful about physical contact with their students. When a little girl hugs a female teacher's leg, everyone says, "Awww!" When a little girl hugs a male teacher's leg, they think the guy might be a pervert. I make a loose fist and keep it above the water—where it can be seen by all—while her tiny arms grasp my forearm. She lets go of the side, and I pull her around slowly then speed up, twisting faster and faster in tighter circles, her body gliding through the water, until she starts laughing. Then I bring her back to the side of the pool.

Kea swims over and dunks his head over and over. "No big deal, Oliana!"

Silence from Oliana.

"See? Watch!" Dunk, dunk, dunk.

Arataki, kicking by, gurgles a, "You can do it!"

I assure Oliana that I'm not going anywhere and she should let go of the side of the pool. Because she's only five, she hasn't learned to disobey the teacher yet. She lets go.

Sinking, kicking, neck stretching, and mouth gasping for air, there she goes into the life-filled watery world of challenge, novelty, and risk. It's just one second in time, but she gains a lifetime of confidence, I hope, before I allow her tiny hands to close on mine. A chattering, dripping, smile of triumph spreads across her face. The class cheers; even the sky's profound blue seems to exult in her accomplishment. I burn her proud face into my memory.

Once, when I was student-teaching in America, I was spinning a little boy on a park merry-go-round. Six years old and one of the more challenging boys in the class, he threw his head back, held on for dear life, and proclaimed, through a smile widened by centripetal force, that it was the best day of his life. Adult life is inherently more complicated and fast paced. It's easy to be overwhelmed and, conversely, we're less likely to be blown away by simple accomplishments. Oliana's smile and the words of the little boy on the merry-go-round remind me to have "best days" and to congratulate myself for simple accomplishments.

Toweling off, it becomes clear to me that our smiles aren't enough to keep us warm anymore. Today, I announce, is the last pool session until springtime. There are long faces but few complaints. I hold the metal gate with the peeling white paint open for the children, giving Oliana another thumbs-up as she bounces through. As the gate slams shut behind me, I realize that I'll actually have to take a real shower now.

Maybe it's a Chinese attribute, but for some reason my sweat doesn't stink. My friends have harassed me for years about how rarely I shower, but I just define the word very liberally. Surfing is a shower. Swimming in the river is a shower. Teaching swimming in the pool is definitely a shower. I have yet to fill the bath in my house—especially since I have the river, ocean, and pool at my disposal.

Apparently, I'm not the only one who considers the pool a source of bathing.

An enormous hit in the community once it was up and running, it seemed as though the whole town showed up at the end of each school day to go swimming. Unfortunately, all it takes is a few people to ruin it for everyone else. A few mornings, I found myself up at the pool gingerly picking up cigarette butts and pieces of tinted-glass from broken Tui (the Kiwi equivalent of Budweiser) bottles. The School Operations book was consulted and a lock was put on the gate. Henceforth, only teachers and parents who were board members were authorized to have a key, and only they could grant access to the pool. These measures, however, proved worthless—a four-foot-high fence was all that separated hot, sweating bodies from the glorious water, and the people holding the keys were sisters, brothers, cousins, and neighbors. At least the school was playing by the book; theoretically, it wouldn't be liable for any injuries. New Zealand is still a long way from the land of the lawsuit, but they're catching up. The absence of "sue-happy" people here is evident. Rivers abound, so most towns have a bridge and an estuary. It's common to see barefoot kids tossing themselves off bridges right in the town center, while in America kids might get to do it once or twice (next to the sign that reads *No Jumping or Diving off Bridge*) before the cops arrive. And if a kid got so much as a scratch, his parents would sue the city for not having enough signs posted, not having a high enough guardrail—and maybe for allowing a river to be there in the first place.

The threat of lawsuits and silly rules, though, can actually *create* fun. Sneaky stuff can be amazingly entertaining as long as there are no repercussions for anyone else.

Here in RPG, the pool poachers made no attempt to be sneaky. This has been hard to deal with as an outsider. During the warm months, I'd look out my classroom window at the end of the day and watch a bunch of RPG's teens jump the fence with Tui bottles. I knew I'd be picking up the pieces in the morning, but wasn't sure how to approach the situation. So far I'd struck a balance between establishing myself as a teacher and person worthy of respect while also showing respect for others. No matter how I turned the situation around in my head, it would always come back to, "Who the f$#k are you, bro! I'll swim in the pool if I want to!" In the end, averting my eyes and picking up a few pieces of glass the next morning proved to be the easier route. (My two immediate predecessors, remember, fled town under threat of bodily harm.)

So picking up glass at the pool became part of my morning routine. After a while I noticed a bar of soap at the pool's edge. Having no recollection of *my* last proper shower, I chuckled and picked it up. Instead of throwing it away and reporting it, I placed it neatly against the pump house where it could be seen. How ticked off would I be, after all, if I snuck up to the town bath—oops, I mean pool—only to discover that someone had pinched my soap.

CHAPTER
8

PRIORITIES

THE FINAL DAY OF the first term. I stare out the classroom door, a steady drizzle in the air. Angie is standing by the office door, hands on hips, head cocked a little to the side. Her look tells me, "This is serious." She cups her hands around her mouth but drops them as I begin to run toward her. Has something happened? Is it all on again? Will tonight be another sleep-at-the-beach night? Should I park Lonna in defensive position?

But no. Nothing like that.

"Cole's cows have busted out," Angie says. "Take Cory and some of the boys and help him."

"What about my—"

"I'll watch your class."

Calendar time, math tune-ups, and prepping for our afternoon field trip can wait. One must have his priorities in line when teaching in Raupunga. Guess it's time to lead a roundup. When I call the boys over, it's pretty obvious what they prefer. Moments ago their hearts were at or below resting rate. Now, their chests are heaving and their wide-eyed faces beam with anticipation. Strategy time: we kneel under the awning, out of the rain, to discuss the mission. I feel like I should draw a schematic diagram with a fat piece of sidewalk chalk.

Okay, men. You're the best of the best. This is what you've been training for all these years. Kahu, you take point. Cory, you flank the west side. And Kea, you cover us from the ridge.

RPG—there's no place like it.

"All right, everyone just take it easy. You guys know more about this stuff than Mr. Chin. Just remember: the cows might be scared of you, but they're a whole lot bigger than you are. So be smart. Head down to Cole's house, and I'll bring the van around to meet you."

They tear down the hill led by Kahu, the hood of his jersey bouncing as he runs. Cole lives a few houses over from Big Head, it occurs to me. Not that I'm purposefully keeping an eye out for his flapping ears and drooling puppy grin or anything.

Having missed my morning snack, I run into the office to grab a cookie and slug some water. There's no telling how long it'll take to get the job done. As I'm leaving, a photograph catches my eye.

It's a picture of Kahu, taken during last year's *kapa haka* performance. Kapa haka is the traditional Maori song and dance, and schools treat the performances very seriously. I'm looking forward to seeing the children train for it in a few months. Examining the picture, I can tell it was a happy day for Kahu. Someone had sketched a traditional *moko* (Maori face tattoo) on the photo, giving him a mythic look with beautiful hand-drawn swirls and flowing lines connecting his nose and cheekbones. Maori art is greatly influenced by the shape of an uncurling fern, known as a *koru*. Kahu is looking down and away from the camera, and his expression is gentle yet confident. It's the Kahu I'd like to see more often.

My original ideas about gangs have been washed away by my time in RPG. Even those initials are starting to take on a different meaning. True, they're carved and etched into every surface in town, spray-painted under the bridge and part of the graffiti on the outhouse near the main road. The kids paint the letters on their heads. It's tattooed on more than a few of the men.

In my thirty years, I've moved from inner-city Chicago to a white suburb in Connecticut, back to an affluent white suburb of Chicago, I headed west to San Francisco, and now I'm in a place known as RPG. What would I be like if I grew up here and this was all I knew? What kind of pride would I have? How strong would my need for an identity be? What would my goals and aspirations be? Who knows? There's no time for answers now. There's a job to be done.

I break away from the picture and charge out the door. I'm surprised it's not Villy's cows we're rounding up, actually. Did Cole leave a gate open, or did the cows simply find a hole in the fence?

Cole is a warm, stocky man with a leathery complexion. His smile is an open invitation to laugh with him, that of a tour guide who likes showing the new teacher how things are done in RPG. I slow down every time I pass his house to admire the fine collection of rusted relics in his yard: an old push mower, something that resembles a primitive missile, and an exhaust contraption. All sit atop sun-bleached stumps in the yard, like refugees from some outside sculpture exhibit.

As I start up Lonna, I think of my last conversation with Cole. I had stopped by his house to collect some sheep droppings for my garden when a chopper flew overhead. Glassy-eyed, he laughed hysterically, tracking the helicopter's progress across the sky.

As in many rural towns, a good portion of RPG's economy may revolve around growing and selling marijuana. During my early travels in New Zealand, I met an ex-police officer who owned a convenience store. You can always tell when the locals had been busted or the crops were raided, he told me, because no one had enough money to buy stuff at his store. Government choppers routinely spray the plants with herbicides, sometimes without even bothering to figure out who is growing it.

"Them pilots are good," Cole said with a chuckle, straining his neck to watch the chopper. "A mate of mine, who was growing plants under the eve of his house, heard a chopper. Looked out his kitchen window and saw a hose swinging around!"

Cole's gestures revealed the height of the kitchen window, the location of the plants in relation to where his mate was standing and the path of the swinging hose. I gave him a smirk of complicity. "A "mate" of yours, eh?"

Today, I see that Cole is again chuckling to himself.

He waves his right arm in a big swooping circle and yells, but the sound of his quad drowns out his voice. That arm wave, however, is all the direction I need.

If I were back at school, I'd be asking my class to show me rough things, smooth things, bumpy things, light things, and heavy things. We'd review colors and smells, and discuss how words we use to describe things are called *attributes*. The five senses has been the name of the game lately, and the end-of-the-term field trip is scheduled for this afternoon. The class agreed on a destination—the beach!—and they've been buzzing about it ever since. (The beach! The beach! We're going to the beach! When are we going to the beach? Can't we go to the beach today?) Today they get their way. Not only are we spending the afternoon away from school, but they've also managed to wheedle a *sausage sizzle* (hot dogs) out of me. I wouldn't have predicted any of this a year ago. Cooking lunch over a driftwood fire with Maori children? Rounding up cows during math time? Life is funny that way.

But before the beach, we have to get the cows, which are grazing on top of a grass bank a few minutes up the road. They look at us for a chew or two, then drop their heads for their last chomps of freedom—thieves grabbing a final handful of cash or jewels as police sirens wail in the distance. I maneuver the van for a good shot with my video camera and feel like I'm a true documentarian. A couple of the boys climb the bank ahead of the cows; a few others, in a flanking maneuver, sneak up behind them to get them moving.

"Hah! Hah! Get! Hah!"

The escaped convicts trot along the top of the bank, but not too urgently; every so often, they stop to take another mouthful before giving in completely. They know they're busted. The dozen or so cows could easily plow through the two boys blocking their way, but instead they slide down to the road. I've parked like a cop, blocking the road, in an effort to force them toward Cole's house. The boys skid safely to the street and form a loose line behind the cows.

Lonna and I provide backup for the boys, a last line of defense should the cows decide to turn and plow through the kids. I pull up alongside Cory, who's winded but refuses a ride. He's coming up on those early teen age years when kids want to prove themselves. He's looking for his place in the world, and he hasn't been easy to deal with at school. He's all smiles now though. For the time being, I share his glee, aiming my video camera at him for a status report. Like most kids his age, he's not incredibly articulate, and the exchange is about as revealing as a post-game interview.

"Cory, how do you feel about the successful operation?"

"It's all right!"

"Good job, man!"

The cows must do this pretty often, because they know exactly where to go. As the last one trots through the open gate, Kahu slams it shut as if he's closing up his laptop after a day's work.

By the time I return to school, it's just about time to leave for our field trip to the beach. Lately, RPG hasn't just felt like home, it's *been* home. The classroom is like an extension of my house. I roll out of bed, give Baetis a few head rubs and, next thing I know, I'm sitting with my family listening to their morning news.

It's simply sweet as, as the Kiwis say.

I retrieve my class from Angie's room, where they were buddy reading with the older kids. There is no stopping them. They've been waiting days for this, and they pepper me with questions.

"Are we leaving now?"

"When are we having the sausages?"

"How are we getting there?"

"We're still going even though it's raining, right, Mistah Chnn?"

"What happened with the cows?"

"Whoa!" I reply. "Yes, we're still going. We're leaving soon, but first we're having a meeting. Your mom is driving us. Don't you know your mom is one of the drivers? I'm hungry too, so we'll light a fire for the sausages as soon as we get to the beach."

"But first! Everyone on the rug and in a circle in ten seconds!" I command with a smile.

Seeing Kea open his lunch bag on the way to the rug, I add, "Let's not eat anything right now. Let's move it. Five more seconds left for a perfect circle on the rug."

I grab a few first-aid items out of my desk drawer and, out of the corner of my eye, I see Kea sneak a few chips into his mouth. Being a fan of harmless sneakiness myself, all I can do is smile.

The dictionary, for all its usefulness, sometimes doesn't tell you the whole story. Take the word *sneaky*, for instance. The dictionary fails to note exactly how much fun it can be. I'm not condoning crime, but a bit of mischief is perfectly healthy—a discovery I made at an early age.

My kindergarten classroom in Chicago had gray vinyl tiles with a glossy industrial finish, a perfect surface for shimmying. Long rectangular tables lined a rug on three sides, opening toward the front of the room and Ms. Kay's desk, which faced us like a judge's bench in a courtroom. She had a full view of the classroom from up there, but there were times when she'd turn around to write on the board. These are the moments I remember most.

Albert was my buddy and Ms. Kay knew it; thus, we were placed on opposite ends of the back row. We had to lean forward or backward and look past ten other children in order to make eye contact. It made throwing objects at each other a project too. Sometimes I wonder if she was trying to teach us the concept of trajectory, but she didn't seem like the scientific type. One day, I tried and tried to lob a few pieces of crayon at Albert but couldn't quite get it right. So I decided to make a direct attack.

When Ms. Kay turned, I slipped out of my chair with all the stealth of a leopard on the African plains. (Well, maybe not so much—I've seen time-lapse video of a leopard taking *all night* to close in on a herd of gazelles.) As I snaked face-first across the floor, I stopped occasionally to turn my head up and hold my index finger to my mouth. I needn't have worried—my fellow students were just as bored as I was, so they weren't going to tattle. On I went. The sight of Ms. Kay's legs came and went in between the legs of students, chairs, and tables. When she turned around, I stopped moving, my face hovering just millimeters off the floor. As every little kid knows, if I couldn't see her, she couldn't see me. I was invisible.

The stalk continued once she turned to the board again. How I knew she wasn't looking anymore I couldn't say; some children are just naturals in the classroom. Albert was leaning forward on the plastic chair, making for a perfect target. From two chairs away, I lunged and found my mark, jabbing him in the rear pocket of his navy blue uniform pants with the point of a pencil. I laughed maniacally as he sprung off his seat with a yelp. Ms. Kay turned, and I knew I was doomed. I was a kamikaze pilot, with no escape plan. But the laughter echoing through the room made it all worthwhile. If the hiring committee at RPG only knew what kind of man they'd hired to teach their children.

Even though Lonna has lots of room, the passenger seat is the only one with a seat belt, so I can only take one person. Naturally, I pick Kea to be my co-pilot. If teachers say they don't have favorites—well, they're lying. Shifting into gear, I fall into line behind Hiri's mom and Rangi, shuttling the other kids.

Down the hill, I see Big Head hanging out with Memphis. The two of them make for a great duo. Big Head is the muscle, and Memphis is the brains, the mastermind behind their escapades. He reminds me of Bilbo Baggins, the hobbit from *The Lord of the Rings*. Memphis's Jack Russell lineage gives him a sophisticated aura that contrasts with the surrounding countryside, so I keep waiting for him to cross his legs and pull out a cigar. As I watch, they confirm my thoughts: Memphis sits back and gingerly licks his front paws as if he's savoring caviar, and Big Head rolls onto his side to lick his *sack*. Big Head's body is filling out, finally beginning to catch up with his oversized paws. Yesterday, he came by the school after the kids had gone, and I mustered the courage to give him a few belly rubs. With his legs spread-eagled and his back on the ground, he grunted his approval. How much longer I can go without a dog, I'm not sure.

Ahead of us, Rangi's pickup spouts thick black smoke as it trundles down to the beach. I can see Arataki staring out the back window. She and her siblings are lucky. Though their parents aren't married, Cherise and Rangi have one of the more stable *whanaus* (Maori for "families") in the area. Rangi's main source of income is shearing. Shearers are paid per sheep, so it pays to be fast. I hear Rangi is one of the fastest around. It's easy to see a deftness to his actions, an economy of motion that I admire. He isn't as standoffish as most the other Black Power guys either. The man exudes *mana*, the Maori word for "respect." Plenty of Black Power members fit the perfect gang stereotypes—no father figure, low socioeconomic backgrounds—but Rangi comes from an older school. For him, mana, brotherhood, and honor aren't just words. They're the foundation for his life.

Soon we pass Nan's house. Arataki's grandma lives just a shout away from the school, and Arataki often writes about her. Nan has been in and out of the hospital ever since I arrived in Raupunga. I empathize with Arataki and would like to say, "Arataki, I know it's hard. But at least you get to really say goodbye. Tell Nan how happy you are with your family, and thank her for all her hard work," but I'm careful to keep my distance. I don't want to overstep my bounds.

Although I-Gaw's suffering went on for far too long and our best efforts couldn't save him, I find myself increasingly grateful for the prolonged goodbye—and the journey it allowed.

A bone marrow transplant with a perfectly matched donor gives leukemia patients a fighting chance. Finding a matching bone marrow donor, however, isn't as simple as matching a blood type. Doctors use genetic markers to test the donor's compatibility with the patient. While siblings usually offer the best chance at a perfect match, neither my sister nor I fit. In fact, when you looked at the charts, you might think I was dropped on the front step. I didn't come close to Eileen, I-Gaw, or either of my parents—a classic middle child makeup, apparently. We were told finding a perfect match in the general population was roughly one in twenty thousand.

To get the word out, Mom and Dad mobilized everyone they knew. We solicited Chinese students from local colleges and covered Chicago's Chinatown with fliers, recruiting potential donors for testing at our expense. There was even talk of expanding the search to southern China, where our roots lie. With time running out, though, the doctors tried a half-match transplant with my dad.

I shed a few tears for Arataki—and for the pain everyone

in my family still carries from I-Gaw's suffering. Luckily, Kea doesn't notice. He's too busy being shy.

As we drop down to the beach, I reminisce about my previous classes. I took my kids in San Francisco to the beach too. Many of them had never been to the beach despite living only a few miles from it. Evidence, I suppose, of how small their world was. Keeping an eye on twenty children outside the classroom was a nerve-wracking experience. When we arrived, I immediately drew lines in the sand and used driftwood to mark the corners of their boundary. Although it's not necessary, I'll do the same here.

It's a gloomy day with a slight mist that comes and goes. The ocean is calm except for the occasional wave big enough to slam the steep beach. We battle the gray with our glow—of smiling students, a proud teacher, and twin girls who aren't quite five years old but are joining us anyway. They'll be joining the class soon, I've learned, and I look forward to increasing the class size.

"All right, everyone! Over here so I can tell you what's going on," I yell. There's really no need to yell, but it adds a little festivity to the proceedings, so I continue. "Quickly! So we can make a fire. Sausage sizzle!"

We squat in the dark sand while I review the plan: First we find firewood. Then we eat. After the sizzle, we'll go over the attributes we've learned and sort objects into a giant Venn diagram in the sand, two huge, overlapping circles that will allow us to compare it all. Maybe I'll talk a little about the origins of sand. If there's time left, we'll play a few games. My number one priority is that everyone associates fun with learning.

Normally not a big fan of hot dogs, I thread one onto a stick just to fit in. Rangi uses a big log to shelter the windward side of the fire and gets a blaze going in short order. We each stand, swaying with the wind, one hand in a pocket, the other holding our stick and sausage, occasionally commenting on the fine food. There's a saying, "Hunger is the best gravy." Now add the beach, the fire, and a group of happy children, and you've got one hell of a sauce.

I solicit pairs of little feet to help me make two intertwining circles in the sand. The first task is to comb the beach, looking for smooth objects and rough objects. After that the kids will place them properly in the circles. When the children return with their treasures, I'm amazed to see how many things fit into both categories. The Venn diagram fills quickly.

"Okay, class. Great job!" Looking at the twins, I ask, "Are you sure you haven't been in school?"

One of them replies, "No! We're only four!"

"Remember what I always say about learning to speak in front of people?" I continue. "It's important, right? Who wants to tell us about what they found?"

Kea steps forward and picks up a large piece of driftwood, "This piece of wood is smooth and rough so I put it here," he says pointing to the middle of the diagram.

One of the twins walks over to a piece of driftwood she had placed in the *smooth only* circle. "This one is rough and smooth too," she declares, placing it next to Kea's piece.

It appears I will have another student besides Arataki that makes me look good.

We spend the rest of the afternoon sorting pale things and dark things, heavy and light, and living and non-living. The last one sparks some debate. Arataki looks at me with suspicion and says, "The wood was a tree and could still be alive. Can't it, Mistah Chnn?"

That's when it starts to rain again, sheets pelting us and our diagrams, ending the trip before I can talk about relativity.

On the way home, though, I explain to Kea, "You know that rock you put in the *heavy* circle?"

"Yeah."

"Well, *I'd* put it in the *light* circle 'cause I'm stronger."

"Oh. Okay."

I smile and say, "It was an okay day, wasn't it?"

"I like the beach. It's cool," Kea says matter-of-factly.

Back home, Baetis darts out from beneath the house to greet me. She rubs against my leg with more force than usual and meows her unhappiness that her food bowl is inside. The problem with keeping her food bowl outside is that it attracts feral cats. What she needs is a private entry, so she can come and go as she pleases. The house is a rental, so cutting a hole for a cat door isn't an option. But she had a ramp to my window at Angie's house, so another ramp seems like a good idea. I rule out the ground-floor windows because I live on the main road, where people steal stoves. I don't want to invite burglary. My bath window, however, is higher up, smaller and in the back of the house. Perfect. It's a shutter window, so I remove a pane of glass and lean a piece of wood up to it, stapling some canvas bags to the wood for traction.

Now that it's time for the test, I can't find her. I walk around the house calling her name, only to see her dart across the street in the wake of a stock truck. "Please be careful," I tell her as I scoop her into my arms. If only my house were on a quieter street, I wouldn't have to worry so much. I place her on the ramp, and up she goes, disappearing into the window. She sticks her head back out and meows her approval. My chest tightens. Who would have thought Mr. Chin would learn to love a cat?

I have a few weeks off between terms, but I've decided to put in a couple days around the house before heading off to Wellington for a city fix. Tim has informed me that he has the inside scoop on a section of river deep in the backcountry. The next morning I'm up at sunrise tearing down the dirt road behind the school, tornadoes of dust swirling in my wake. Tim is waiting for me with a handful of freshly tied flies. I've been teaching him the art of tying flies, and it seems as though no animal on his farm is safe from his plucking hands. As he shows the flies to me, I recognize the animals from which they came: the chickens shuffle off looking over their wings, and the white goat tied to the fence post looks up as if to say, "Don't even think about taking any more fur!"

Tim tells me we have to stop and let the landowner know we'll be fishing on his land. As we pull up to a small house next to a giant barn, I can't help but grin at my luck; fishing a section of river on private land is always a good opportunity. Piles of leaves scatter in the slight breeze, and we leave trails in the morning dew as we trudge up to the house. The man's wife answers the door and tells us to make sure we close the gates behind us and to *get* some turkeys if we have the opportunity. Apparently, there are a lot of wild turkeys around.

What a grand day it is. We share the bliss of stumbling down a steep slope while the gurgling sounds of a trout-filled river slowly fade in. The panoramic views show the history of humankind's manipulation of the land. Much of the North Island was burned and cleared to make way for stock animals. Green hills dive and dip to the horizon with patches of native bush thriving in the deeper canyons and gullies. We're halfway down when we come across a family of gobblers, so we hunker down to discuss our plan and gather stones.

Our plan is a primitive but effective tactic, surprise. We'll leap from the tall grass like our Stone Age ancestors, chucking rock after rock, and there will be enough turkeys to feed the entire village.

Yeah, well... I make the mistake of not singling out a specific target and am left wishing for a shotgun. I'm certain the turkeys have never seen a Chinese dude, and I can hear them gobbling about how we can't rock chuck worth a damn. I've shamed my people. I've half a mind to drive back to Tim's house for a gun—if it weren't for the glistening river and a splash from a heavy trout.

At the river's edge, Tim seems uninterested in any detailed

instructions. When I point out good areas to cast his fly, he shrugs, shifts his feet, and leaves his fly swinging around randomly in the current. I leave him and focus on the river's lively surface. Fly-fishing a river for trout requires constant attention to minute details. To the casual observer it may seem as though an angler is simply swinging the rod back and forth, but we're actually reading the microcurrents on the river's surface and placing the fly in the areas where trout hold and feed. Success, however, is relative. As John Gierach, a fly-fishing author, once wrote, "It's yet another success. We said we were going fishing and that's what we did."

The fish are more than willing to eat my fly as I catch a half-dozen brightly colored rainbow trout in a few hours. Tim looks a little discouraged, so I tell him to listen up.

"Hey, if you want to catch something, come here so I can show you a few things. You can school me on hunting when we head out someday, but let me show you what to do on this, man."

He reels up and sloshes over to where I'm standing. First, I retie his fly to the line so it will hold if he hooks one. His fly is a creation of his own, made of rooster feathers and hair from his goat. For a beginning fly tier, it's not a bad pattern. Next, I help him wade out to a likely area above a deep pool.

"Okay. If you don't feel like casting a lot, just let your fly swing around down in that deep water. Got it? And don't fall in. Your mom will be pissed at me if you drown."

Within minutes, Tim's rod is doubled over with a fish. I lay my rod down and rush out to help him, but the fish flops off before I reach him. Feeling a little like an old grandpa pulling one-liners, I tell Tim one of fishing's age-old sayings: *That's why they call it fishing and not catching!* Tim shrugs and reels his line up, content with a successful day on the river.

After dropping Tim off with a promise to go pig hunting with him, I rush off to town to take care of some business. I can't remember the last time I paid my bills, and I could use a few supplies. I thought one of the biggest challenges of life

Sharing the bliss.

in Raupunga would be the isolation, but that hasn't been a problem. The children, Baetis, and the endless school projects have kept me busy. The toughest aspect of country living, it turns out, is simply getting everyday stuff done—buying groceries, banking, going to the post office. Most of these tasks have to be done in Wairoa, about fifteen winding miles away. And business hours are traditional, meaning virtually everything closes promptly at five. So as always, I'm scrambling.

As Lonna chugs away, I check the minutes on my phone. With twenty-six pre-paid minutes left, I can call my mom, dad, and sister to tell them I made it through my first term. At happy times like this, I always remember how much I miss my brother. I wish I could call him too.

"Hey, I-Gaw!" I'd say. "I finished the first term. What's that? Yeah, the New Zealand school system is on the quarter system. Maybe you can visit during the next break."

There will be more moments like these. Love, marriage, kids—whatever the occasion, I will always wish he was here.

After the half-match transplant failed, I-Gaw's immune

system was destroyed. We had done everything we could—recruiting potential marrow donors, transferring him to a world-renowned leukemia research hospital in Seattle—but to no avail. As he began to fade, Mom and Dad didn't want him to live his last days in Seattle, so they chartered a medical flight back to Chicago. Family and friends came to see him for the last time. The wait was on.

A loud beep signals I have cellular reception and brings me around to the present. Instead of calling my family, I decide to call Lori.

"Hey! How's it going?"

She sighs heavily. "I'm moving out of Randy's house."

"Oh, uh, well that sucks," I reply before adding, "Yeah, well, moving sucks."

"What's up with you?" she asks.

"Just heading into town for some supplies. No stores where I live, you know."

The rest of the conversation is mostly her venting about school and her challenges with her boyfriend. I lend an ear and secretly smile in the rearview mirror, "Did you hear that?" I whisper to my reflection while holding my hand over the phone. "She's moving out!" I wish her luck with the breakup and hang up, a sly grin on my face. Lonna crests the last hill, and we begin our descent into town. It's a decent-sized hill, and I always think of Rangi as I roll into Wairoa.

Apparently, he and Cherise drove here on their first date years ago, but he didn't tell her that his brakes weren't working. Stupid, sure, but in New Zealand it's always sweet as until something happens—that's a sacrament straight out of the *Go Hard, Mate* bible. He flipped the car at the bottom of the hill. Upside down, Cherise punched him repeatedly and called him an idiot. It's been true love ever since.

Downtown Wairoa consists of one street of storefronts facing the Wairoa River. In its entirety, the length of the business district is four good dropkicks of a rugby ball, plus or minus one kick depending on the size of your boot. At the beginning of the first dropkick is Mitre 10, a hardware and household knickknack store, followed by a bank, another knickknack store, a pharmacy, and a barbershop that sells phone cards.

As I enter town, I feel sorry for the town's residents. The people of Wairoa are constantly battling a poor reputation because of the highly publicized gang disputes. It's sad that a few newspaper headlines can overshadow the beauty of the town and the hard work of its peaceful inhabitants.

Time is running out as I pull into a parking spot. I sprint from Lonna to the bank, accomplishing at least one task before everything closes for the day. Maybe I should have taken care of my errands *before* I went fishing with Tim. Five P.M. comes too soon, though, and doors swing shut in my face. Either the store owners have no mercy or they are scared of the strange Chinese man dancing and yelling in front of their double-paned glass, pointing at shelves in their shops.

Back in Lonna, I scan my to-do list. The post office has closed, so paying bills will have to wait, and the grocer's closed before I could get fruit and toothpaste. Dang.

I squint, picturing the flattened toothpaste tube on the sink at home. No worries. I haven't even cut the tube open yet; I'll make it a few more days. I pull some unpaid bills from my back pocket and add them to a stack of important papers, including a form for renewing Lonna's registration. For months I've been sneaking around, hoping the police don't see my expired stickers. As I churn my way up the hill wondering what the surf looks like, a strong Aotearoa breeze catches the papers, threatening to scatter them to the wind. A few fall to the ground, but miraculously, most of them stay put, just inches from the suction of the open window. If only I hadn't insisted on a once-in-a-lifetime experience—hiking to a remote stream with an eleven-year-old New Zealand boy—then maybe that stack of papers would have been taken care of today.

Priorities, it's something to think about.

CHAPTER
9

LOOK BACK, BUT DON'T STARE

N O MATTER WHAT MAY be going on in your life, basic human needs take priority. I've got plenty of water and food, but winter is here and I need heat. While Rangi cut me a little firewood for the first cold days of this June winter, he's got his own family to worry about. So collecting wood is a weekly chore for me. I've found a good piece today; one that will keep me warm through the night. I roll the beast up to Lonna's back door and, with a grunt, wrestle it into her belly. Her suspension creaks under the weight; bark peels away, sending centipedes and sow bugs scurrying for new homes. I could easily buy my wood, but gathering what I need is almost as comforting as walking the dog in the evening—something I sorely miss.

I bet Toughy and Big Head would like it here in the woods right now, with sticks aplenty to chew. Big Head is a big guy now. He'll fill out some more, but his chest muscles already ripple with each powerful step he takes. He doesn't go for walks; accompanied by Memphis, he charges full-tilt to the horizon and back all day long. Lately, he's been staying at Arataki's grandparents' house, near mine, so I can hear him howling at night from loneliness, the cold, or a little of both. Not many people here allow their dogs inside the house. I'd love to take him for a run on the beach, but I'm still too afraid of the pain that might bring.

I'm perusing a tangled pile of debris at the edge of a clear-cut, on the lookout for large tree ends. Many square miles of what is called "working forest" surround the school; lumber and wood products are one of New Zealand's leading exports. Because of the temperate climate, nonnative trees such as Douglas fir grow many times faster than in the United States or Canada. When a tree is felled, a little nub remains at the base of the log, since it's impossible to cut a large tree clean through before it starts to topple. The lumberjacks cut a few inches off the bottom of the fallen tree and leave the round disc with the nub behind. Just one of these, I've discovered, can keep me comfortable all night if I set the oxygen intake on the woodstove properly. Usually, though, I end up trying to see how hot I can make the house. I'll hang out wearing surf shorts in a reclining lawn chair, with either my laptop on my knees or the latest *Harry Potter* book in my hands, a chicken roasting in the oven, and Baetis purring away beside me. On those nights, I'll burn through two or three of the tree ends.

As Lonna and I rumble home, the centipedes and sow bugs settle into Lonna's cracks and crevices. I weave and brake more than usual on the potholed road; I don't want to spill my dinner. Today was the hundredth day of school, so we counted to one hundred with pieces of carrot, celery, lentils, black-eyed peas, and barley before dumping it all into a pot for some Hundreds Soup. Even after sharing the soup with the older children, there was plenty left. We made celebratory posters using dyed pasta, and the children wrote about what they would do with a whopping one hundred dollars. Kea said he would buy a "flash car"; Hiri, some clothes; and Hoera, a new student, a motorbike.

Pulling into the narrow driveway of the place I've called home for half a year, I stop near the orange tree that will serve as my drive-up snack bar once the fruit ripens. There hasn't been any need to park in defensive position lately—too cold and dreary for gang wars—so I park at the back door to unload and chop the firewood. Splitting wood a few minutes a day fuels the man in me, a manly man who has come to love a little gray fur ball with a ginger spot on her head. Baetis, though, is nowhere to be seen. I walk around to the front of the house and call her.

I hear an excited meow across the street, and she starts prancing toward me. She's looking forward to a warm fire too. I've got a big night planned: another chapter of *Harry Potter* and a few hours of head rubs. And then I see the white truck.

It tries to stop, but a screech and a terrible second later, Baetis is writhing, dragging herself across the road with her front paws until she reaches the safety of a drainage pipe. Despite my claustrophobia, I dive in after her. Dusty and cobweb filled, the pipe is just big enough for me to make progress with each exhalation. With each desperate inch, I prepare myself to find Baetis a bloody mess with protruding bones. Nightmarish meows echo along the concrete walls.

"Stay there, girl. Dad is coming to get you." My mind races, worries: Will she have to be euthanized? I can't do it. Who will do it for me? She'll have to be shot; I know it. And a prayer: Please let my first cat live.

The meows grow weaker as I scoop her up and somehow back out of the pipe. At ease in my hands, she allows me to inspect her. Unbelievably, there is no blood, no bones poking through her beautiful coat. Gently, I run my fingers down the length of her spine. It feels normal. Her breathing is erratic, however, and I can tell she's going into shock. She's not going to be euthanized. No one is going to shoot my cat. There's still time to make it to the vet in town.

Lonna, sensing the urgency, powers over the first hill. By this time, Baetis's tongue is hanging out, her chest is heaving, and she's defecated on the passenger seat. Her meows are barely audible. It hits me: my first cat is dying, and the cold memories surface.

April 22, 1990. The waiting room floor was hard, the air

heavy with despair. Sleep was impossible. Someone was sniffling, sobbing, on the other side of the room. Shivering, I tried to close my eyes, forget where I was and why. Some people were waiting for their loved ones to recover, waiting for good news. We were waiting for I-Gaw to die. It was over.

When I stood at his bedside two days earlier, he turned his head to look at me. The tube in his mouth prevented him from speaking. I hated that tube. What he couldn't communicate with his mouth, though, he said with his eyes. He wouldn't be able to buy beer for me when he turned twenty-one. He was leaving us just shy of legal beer-guzzling age. All the childhood fighting, all the differences we had—none of that mattered anymore. His hand was puffy from fluid retention, but he still gave me a good squeeze. Maybe if he'd had the strength, he would have given me one last punch and a smile. It would be the last time I'd see I-Gaw's eyes open.

There he was. A young man who should've been having the time of his life, graduating from college in a few years, meeting a fine lady, raising a family, and being a loving uncle to my future kids. And I'd return the favor. All this should've been and could've been, but for the tube. For days, we simply waited.

Finally, it came to an end. My Uncle Kenneth came running to get us. "Something isn't right," he said.

Mom, Dad, Eileen, and I pressed up to I-Gaw's bedside, along with a dozen or so extended family members. He had a sense of peace about him, and I wiped a tear from the corner of his eye. Maybe it was just from the fluid he had retained during the last few days, but I prefer to think it was a tear—a goodbye tear. Mom, a broken and spent shell, sobbed weakly. Even Dad, normally a brick, wiped away a few tears. The line on the heart machine danced and jiggled for a few minutes before I-Gaw's hands went cold.

Back in the present, I redline Lonna's engine, knowing every minute counts. A deep, drawn-out meow fills my ears. It sounds like a thank-you-for-trying meow. I sigh heavily.

"C'mon, girl. You'll be okay," I say in what I hope is a soothing tone. Her eyes squint, her chest stops heaving, and her mouth hangs open. It looks like it's over.

Turning Lonna onto a gravel shoulder, I put my head on the steering wheel. The tears start. My insides tighten into that familiar position, but for some reason it feels different. The old devastation is there, sure, but there's something else too, despite the pain: balance.

My mind races back to I-Gaw's bedside, then to a touchdown pass he threw me during a game of pickup football. His weakened body, trembling behind the isolation glass, dissolves into his childhood face pressed against the car window as Eileen and I laugh at him.

Baetis's still body is there on the seat next to me, but I can feel her lying on my chest, purring away. The night Toughy went still in my arms and the day I dedicated myself to be the best "dad" I could be churn together. I hear another noise, and for a moment think I'm still lost in the past. But no, I'm not dreaming.

It's a faint "Meow, meooow..."

In an instant we're back in gear, tires screeching across the blacktop. Baetis is still alive!

"Nine lives, baby!"

Incredibly, she repeats the same act twice more before we reach the vet. I keep driving.

The vet puts her on an IV to stabilize her right away. They can't take x-rays, apparently, because the hospital's technicians are gone for the day, and since it's Friday the techs won't be back until Monday—just the facts of life in a small town. I chuckle as I imagine the scene at the hospital on Monday: Baetis will get her x-rays after the horse with a bum leg, following the man with broken ribs. The good news, of course, is that shock hasn't gotten her, so her condition can only get better.

Darkness creeps in as I roll toward home. A streetlight in

town illuminates the small brown stain on the passenger seat, the spot where Baetis died three times over. Something inside me shifted, I realize, when I thought she was dead. As I pass the spot where I pulled off, I've got nothing but happy thoughts—of Baetis, of Toughy, of I-Gaw. Unbidden, memories of my first backpacking trip with Toughy pop into my head.

It was just a week after I neutered him. I was worried he'd hold it against me, so I tried not to look. My vet assured me this would give Toughy a better life, that it was the practical and responsible decision. It would reduce the number of dogs that end up in shelters, prevent him from straying, and keep him from fighting.

All true, I'm sure, but I still felt guilty. It had been only three months since I'd arrived in San Francisco. Toughy and I had explored the city and local beaches, but we hadn't packed into the backcountry. This, our first backpacking trip, was my plea for his forgiveness. We headed down the coast to 17-Mile Drive, the famed section of Highway 1 just south of Carmel. The coastal hills were a perfect destination: warm and sunny, with the chance of surf.

Before Toughy, the front seat of my Astrovan had never seen so much company. He learned to sit up and wedge his body securely into the corner of the seat, his head swaying with each turn. On that day, his tongue flapped a little more, his grin spread a little wider. Most of 17-Mile Drive runs high above the ocean, so the van was a moving balcony seat to Earth's splendor. Out the open window, the Pacific stretched toward the horizon, and I couldn't imagine life without a dog.

Our hike started in the damp coastal forests, and Toughy immediately let loose. I remember being nervous as he ran ahead and out of sight for minutes at a time. But just as I'd start to call him, he'd tear out of nowhere to make sure I was still there. Soon, the moss and ferns gave way to California poppies; wild lupine bowed in the wind as we passed, huffing our end-of-winter bodies up the steep trail.

It was everything a boy could ever want—except I wasn't a boy. I was a man who understood how special the moment was. As we bedded down for the night in a clearing, the sound of a nearby creek, the moonlight, and the towering redwoods at the edge of the meadow gave the night a mystical feel—almost as though I was looking in on a memory. We'd never slept outside, so I was afraid that Toughy would go exploring and get lost. But tying him up while I slept was not an option—he needed to be free, in case a mountain lion came around camp. The moon tracked across the sky, and the gurgle of the creek lulled me to sleep. When my eyes opened in the night, I popped up right away, straining my neck to look for my boy. The moon, low and green, made three shadows on the meadow grass: a man, a dog, and a backpack. I don't know how many moons we slept under in the following years, but it was all I could ever ask for.

As I pull up to my New Zealand country home, I'm crying again. But they're tears of joy. I'll keep the fire blazing all through this solo night, sitting vigil for Baetis. Besides, winter is project time: edit video on the laptop, tie flies for fishing, carve some pumice. My creative side is running full throttle these days, fueled by spare time, a limited social calendar, and the Kiwis' give-it-a-go attitude.

I've been surprised at how much I enjoy carving pumice. One night, Rangi showed me how he carves bone and, fascinated that I could create a new form by taking away material, I began scratching away at some pumice I'd picked up at the beach. Sure, I'd cut wood into shapes before, and I'd inscribed Toughy's grave marker, but that's completely different from starting off with a rough piece of material and without a plan.

The clear-cuts aren't my only source of firewood; I find myself at Mohaka Beach collecting driftwood and checking the waves a few times a week. Recently, a huge storm brought new treasures to the beach, including giant pieces of pumice. At first I collected it for garden decorations, but then pieces began finding their way into the house. Soon I was scratching at it with sandpaper and miniature files, though I never set out to make anything in particular. Wave-like shapes and other organic contours began to materialize. It's a satisfaction I've never felt before.

Although the Maoris are known for their carvings, pumice is not their material of choice. They more commonly use bone, wood, or greenstone, which is one of the oldest rocks on the planet—hard enough to sharpen into knives.

So I make my way through the night accompanied by the sound of sandpaper, a growing pile of white dust, and the opening and closing of the woodstove. I drink red wine, losing myself in the flickering flames.

It's not loneliness, exactly, but lately I've been thinking, *It sure would be nice to share all of this with someone.* The next thought, inevitably, *I wonder what's going on in Lori's mind.*

Maybe she's scared of dating me. She knows I haven't had many girlfriends. I've been called "unapproachable," "unreachable," and "untouchable" by three different girls, after all; it's a wonder I don't have a complex about it. But it's ludicrous to torture myself about this stuff. If the relationship is no fun and I'm not naturally making it a priority, then it's not meant to be. That attitude, so far, has translated into lots of time with my dog, on the river, and in the waves. Do I have a problem? Or do I simply know what I want?

Here's a telling detail: almost all my relationships have started in October, the beginning of the rainy season in San Francisco, with the breakups coming around the end of April, the opening of trout season. I haven't even held hands with Lori, but somehow I'm sure we'd outlast the rainy season. That has to be a sign, right? Without knowing I've done it, I realize I've opened some pictures on my laptop of Lori at a dinner party. Wine, a fire, and solo living in the country will do that to a man.

My friends and I were all seated at the dinner table when

she arrived at my house. Lori strolled through the door wearing a fitted black T-shirt with a sparkly Superman logo on the front. She closed the door slowly, taking extra time to make sure it was locked, stalling for as long as she could before joining us. No one said it, but there might as well have been a flashing billboard above the dinner table: *There's the girl that Ryan is crazy for. She's got a boyfriend, but here she is looking mighty fine in a tight T-shirt!*

I stood up and gave her a quick hug before introductions. Lori fidgeted as people raised a glass to her between mouthfuls of food.

"Wow, did you cook all this?" She scanned the dinner table.

"Yep," I replied, nonchalantly. "Started prepping a few days ago."

As I walked away to get her a plate and a margarita, one of my friends gave me a quick thumbs-up, and his girlfriend flashed me a wink of approval. Soon, Lori was laughing and conversing easily with my friends and my sister. Eileen was in town with her boyfriend, part of the reason for the dinner party. She knew my dating history and that I didn't fall easily for any girl, so she did what any good sister would do—she bombarded Lori with good-guy stories.

"When I went to Mexico with a friend for my birthday, Ryan flew down and surprised me," Eileen explained. "Mom knew, but I had no idea."

Lori's lips pressed hard against each other before she smiled. Later, as I prepared a crêpe from scratch for her, I don't think I was imagining the glint in her eyes.

I close my laptop and sigh, thinking, *I've got to get a life.* Then I curl up in the fetal position in my sleeping bag right in front of the fire, picking my head up periodically to look for Baetis and wishing my brother could visit me. As I drift off to sleep, the words *Look back, but don't stare* repeat in my head.

A few days ago, I picked up a *Newsweek* magazine to read about the current situation in Iraq. There was an interview with Michael J. Durant, the pilot of the Black Hawk helicopter which had gone down in Somalia; his ordeal inspired the movie *Black Hawk Down*. He answered a question about his emotional recovery by quoting a line from a letter he received from a cancer survivor: "Look back, but don't stare."

The prognosis for Baetis is broken hips, ribs, and a ruptured diaphragm. Luckily, I will have a distraction while they operate on her, and she is recovering at the vet. I'm going to have a visitor—my dad.

Even though Dad didn't totally approve of this overseas endeavor, I think he's happy that I've given him a reason to fly across the world. However, his visit coincides with record cold temperatures.

I hear from him shortly after he lands: "I left eighty-degree weather in Chicago and flew twelve hours to wintertime!" Then he adds, "Ryan, we have to rent a car."

He's seen pictures of Lonna and read about her many ailments, including her broken heater. I pause for a split second and think about talking him into an adventure, but I think better of it. If he were my sister, then maybe I'd be more insistent.

"Sure, that sounds like a good idea. We'll rent a car in Auckland."

Dad is almost always game for my antics, but days of road tripping lie ahead of us. There's no reason to turn it into an expedition of survival—though New Zealand driving in general is a bit of that. I, however, still have to make it to Auckland to meet him, so I don my full snowboarding gear and use hot water bags to keep my feet warm. It takes me twice as long to get there, because I keep stopping to heat water on the stove in the back of the van. Once I come up with the idea of stopping at cafés for coffee and a refill on my hot water bags, I make better time. Most of the people in the cafés barely crack a grin when I tell them the reason I need the hot water. It seems I fit in with the get-it-sorted-mate attitude that prevails here.

As I approach Auckland eight hours after departing from home, I call Dad on my cell phone, musing on technology. The call is going to satellites that beam to the States to look for my dad, and then the signal beams back to the satellites and back to New Zealand where my dad is just a few miles away—crazy. Dad loves that kind of stuff; I get my sense of wonder from him. Despite his age, he's kept up with the times, probably understanding more about the Internet and cutting-edge technology than I do. Mom too has kept up with tech-nology; she alone set up the accounting systems for their busi-ness despite having no educational background in accounting or computers.

"Sometimes it took me all day just to figure out how to set up the fax and the printer," she'd say to me. "But I got it done."

Their attitudes have given me a lot of confidence in just about anything I've chosen to do. Lately, it's been honing my writing skills and learning to edit video.

Dad and I explore New Zealand as tourists, but we do spend a night in my house (thank goodness nothing crazy is hap-pening). In my backyard, I show him how I trimmed some trees and tore down a section of corrugated metal fencing to give me a better view. We snap a picture with the Mohaka Riv-er Valley falling away behind us.

"Dad, this is a million dollar view. Never mind the house," I say.

His straight face bursts into laughter as he rubs my head, and replies, "Sure is, son. Sure is!"

In the evening, I stuff the woodstove to capacity, and we feast on green-lipped mussels simmered in olive oil, white wine, and garlic. They're farmed commercially and are an

Million Dollar View.

important export of New Zealand, so they're cheap. Needless to say, I've been making the most of eating affordable seafood. Dad sucks away at the shells, adjusting his position in front of the fire to make sure all sides are of him are warmed properly. It's still way below freezing, which is uncommon for Raupunga, so we'll have to keep the woodstove blazing. As we kick back in my house in the Middle of Nowhere, New Zealand, Dad beams as I tell him how I teach the same stuff he used to preach to me.

"Dad, I tell the older boys that if you do something wrong long enough, you are going to get caught! And I'm constantly telling the kids to recognize what needs to be done and do it before being told."

"Damn, son! No kidding?" He grins.

During the night he seems to relish getting up to stoke the fire but can't help mumbling a few words about buying me a space heater. Watching him in the flickering light, I hope I'll be as good a dad as he is one day. When we part ways in

Stitched up kitty.

Auckland, we hug and he chuckles at my hot water bags and down jacket. Later, my sister tells me that Dad told her, "I don't know why your brother chooses to live the way he does." We have a good laugh over it; my family is used to my lifestyle by now, so I take Dad's comment as a compliment. I can picture him perfectly dressed in a suit and tie relating the story of my heatless van to his colleagues. He's laughing and shaking his head, "That's my Ryan ... "

After dropping Dad off in Auckland, I pick up Baetis from the vet. She twirls around and around, pressing her face to the cage door when she sees me and displays no signs of broken hips or ribs. I comment on her good condition, and the vet replies, "Put two cat bones in the same room and they'll fuse together." Baetis's shaved belly has a line of stitches running down it from the surgery that repaired her diaphragm. I scoop her up and place her in a bin.

Finally we arrive home, and I transfer her to a homemade kennel since the vet's orders are to limit her movement. In typical Raupunga fashion, it's made from a broken pallet and some chicken wire. She stretches and rolls over, waiting for a head rub. I add driftwood to the fire, and the swirling blue and yellow flames lap at the stove's glass door. Flopping into the lawn chair beside her, I open my laptop, intending to do some late-night video editing. Instead, I start adding to an animal fantasy story; a nameless dog-like creature, after wandering a beautiful but foreign land and mourning a good friend, comes to a realization:

The fragility of the spirit was evident to him now. He lost himself in beautiful places and activities he loved, but it was a fraction of the nutrition his spirit needed. Seeing the need for more balance in his life, he began seeking breaths to share, minds to please, and hearts to nurture. He'd been deprived of love, starved for it.

As the fire dims, I read the passage again and again. I know what I must do. There's a yellow Lab I've known for months now, and he will give my spirit what it needs.

CHAPTER
10

DOG BARF

S TRANGE NOISES FILL THE room, waking me from a deep sleep. I lift my head from my pillow. Beside the bed, Baetis paces back and forth, her ginger streaks glowing in the firelight. Slipping the covers off, I reach for my hatchet. Is the noise coming from inside the house? Is it an animal? A burglar? A student messing with me? Or could it be the Mongrel Mob? I grip the hatchet more tightly, holding my breath. There it goes again. This time, I'm able to pinpoint the location and, breathing a sigh of relief, I set the hatchet down. There's an animal under the house, scratching at the floor. A deep, slow *meow* permeates the wooden floor. Baetis rubs at my leg; she wants to go out.

Grabbing my headlamp, I push Baetis from the door and head out into the moonless night to investigate. I've got a hunch that my little girl isn't just feeling better; I think she's ready to be a mom too. I hear scurrying and, sure enough, I catch a fleeing ginger cat in the beam of light. If only it were that easy for me—scratch at the floor under Lori's house and she's mine.

A month has passed since the accident, and Baetis is recovering well. Her limp is gone, and the fur on her belly is starting to grow back. She was born an outdoor cat and loves the freedom. It'd be selfish of me to keep her inside any longer. So the next day, I make two calls to Angie and Andy and ask them if they'd each like a kitten. Their answers are a resounding yes, so I let Baetis out feeling like a gray-haired father handing his daughter off at wedding. But when I don't see her for two days, I begin to wonder if I made the wrong decision.

Finally, one morning I hear her bouncing up the ramp to the bathroom and the thump of her feet landing on the floor. She's walking a bit funny, and her normally well-groomed fur looks mussed. She's doing a feline version of the *walk-of-shame*, that college ritual of stumbling home after a one-nighter.

"Hey, girl! You okay?"

"Don't ask," she purrs. "Just give me some food."

I have a feeling she won't mind being inside for the rest of the day. I'd love to just hang around the house too, but instead I stir the coals and toss a log into the stove before heading out the door. Soon there will be no need for fire. A bag of sheep manure sits on the walkway, ready to fertilize the garden. The bok choy and chard survived the worst of winter, and I notice tiny sprouts of new growth for the first time.

Today is sure to be a tough one. Angie has a bad disk in her back, and it will require surgery. Ms. Kenton, a local Maori woman who just recently earned her teaching license, has taken her place. She is a quiet person, and she always seems to smile—no matter what.

"The weather is a bummer, isn't it, Ms. Kenton?"

Smile.

"Ms. Kenton, come quick! Cory ran away at lunch!"

Smile.

"Look, Ms. Kenton! Someone broke the window in one of the classrooms."

Smile.

I'm not sure if it's a supreme sort of levelheadedness or something else altogether. Either way, with Angie out of commission, the dynamics at the school have changed. The boys, sensing a power vacuum, have gotten much tougher to keep in line. However, I live by my classroom preachings: working with different kinds of people is just as important as reading, writing, and math. It can't be easy stepping in for Angie, so I try to support Ms. Kenton in any way I can.

I break up a ruckus at morning tea. Mick, a large, mostly even-tempered boy with no gang ties, tries his luck standing up to Kahu. Though smaller, Kahu is more at ease with aggression, and he gets in a few good blows before I can break it up. Kahu, laughing at Mick's tears, taunts him as I stand between them, daring him to take another swing. Mick is going to be a big dude one day. If he was any bigger, I'd have trouble holding him back, but he allows me to guide his shaking body into the office.

"Just sit down and relax for a minute," I tell him. "Right now, you are making a good decision. You could have gone after Kahu again. You could have pushed me away. You could have run away from the school, but you didn't. Right now, you are making a good decision. We'll talk after you calm down."

Wiping his tears away with trembling hands, he folds his body and lets his head drop between his legs. I know what he's going through. In the world of middle-school boys, few scenarios are worse than losing a fight in front of your peers. I speak from hard personal experience here. Not only did I fight the only kid in sixth grade with hairy armpits, I did it twice.

"Ryan, what happened?" Mom asked as I came in the door.

"I just got hit by a ball," I lied. "I'm fine."

One of the punches had cut the inside of my cheek. I stood in the bathroom, spitting bloody saliva into the sink and looking into the vanity mirror. Unbelievably, my face wasn't bruised. No cuts. No swelling. I had absorbed dozens of point-blank punches. Brian, the sixth grade giant with a mustache, had completely whipped me in front of everyone. Heavyweight wrestlers—like Brian—weighed in at over one hundred thirty-five pounds. Middle school lightweight football players—like me—were one hundred pounds and under, a real-life David and Goliath story.

Still, as I watched the blood and spit swirl down the drain, I knew what I had to do: go again. I'd pick on Brian some more tomorrow and show everyone that today was a fluke.

The next day I told anybody who would listen that Brian had jumped me and hit me with a cheap shot. Truthfully, my face still hurt and I was scared, but ego and wild hormones wouldn't be denied. This time, I was better prepared: I wore a lighter jacket for mobility and boots for traction in the slushy snow. The last bell rang; I was ready. A huge crowd had assembled for the main event. Friends of mine raised their fists, shouting directions. Teachers, unaware of the impending title fight, lined students up for the bus. Parents in cars waved and honked at their children. I walked out the door and there he was, fists clenched, ready to give it to me *again*.

Parents give a plethora of good advice, but most kids are too dumb to listen. For some reason the words of wisdom don't hit home until you mature. One of my favorites: "Do something wrong long enough, Ryan, and you'll get caught." And another: "Try not to make the same mistake twice."

So I got whupped by Brian not once but twice. I started a fight in front of the school not once but twice, resulting in my suspension. Looking back, I can only say that sometimes you have to offset your flashes of brilliance with occasional acts of raging stupidity. Balance—the key to a healthy life.

In an empty classroom, Ms. Kenton is giving Kahu a talking to. I want to grab him by the ear. His arms are folded; his smirk says, "What are you guys going to do to me?" Taking away privileges hasn't had much effect, so I adopt the disappointed approach instead. I've been praising him for all the little things he does right (his drawing, for instance), and it feels like we've been making some progress. I don't want to push him away.

"You didn't make a good choice," I begin, shaking my head slowly. To drive the point home, I add, "You know I'd planned on calling your mum to tell her how well you've been doing in science. I'll still do that, but now I'll have to tell her about this too."

His smirk droops a little. Maybe I've made a bit of an impact. Increasingly, though, I feel powerless against the currents that are pulling Kahu away from me. I can see where he's headed, and it's depressing. I head back to my class of little kids, hoping for some joy.

I don't find any. Today, the twins, who started school a few weeks ago, are discovering how mean other kids can be. Rachel, another new entrant, pinches Jane, capping it off with a torrent of verbal abuse.

"You can't draw," she spits. "That's ugly!"

Pulling both of them aside, I force Rachel to look at Jane's face. I ask her how she thinks Jane is feeling, then: "Do you like making people feel this way?"

She hesitates for a moment. "No."

I know, however, that it made her feel good in the moment—and that she'd probably do it again. One definition of power is the ability to step on those who are weaker than you. And a lot of people like feeling powerful.

As I get the children started on a writing and drawing assignment in their journals, my thoughts drift back to middle school—and how mean *I* was. That fight between Brian and me didn't come out of nowhere. It was because I made fun of him for using a typewriter in class. He couldn't write legibly because his fine motor skills were lacking.

Brian fought, but Matt simply took my abuse. My behavior is almost too shameful to admit now. I remember dishing it out to him in the cafeteria.

"Poor boy," I snickered, pointing his way.

"Welfare boy!" added another boy in line behind me. "You get your lunch for free!"

Matt squinted; wrinkles creased his forehead, too deep for an eleven-year-old but there they were, carved into his young face by the brutality of middle school. He was the same size as we were, if not a little smaller, so anger wouldn't do him any good. He had no protectors. The lunch lady didn't defend him—she couldn't hear us.

She plopped dry mashed potatoes on his plate and followed that up with ladles of gravy—so viscous that it held its form for a beat before sliding off the side of the potatoes. Matt hung his head, trying to disappear into himself. He'd eat by himself near one of the teachers. Tomorrow he would try to avoid standing near the Chinese bastard. He never cried, as I remember it. He was probably used to the teasing, having come to a bitter understanding of his world: if it's not the Chinese boy, then it will be someone else.

I can still see his face. If I saw him today, I'd take him out to lunch for a week straight. Maybe I'd let him give me a few good licks too, in some futile attempt to even things up. Why did I say such hurtful words? Wasn't I a gentle boy who took care of his hamster like it was his kid? Hadn't I come from loving parents and a stable home? It's hard to conjure, but I believe my actions were an experiment, an intrapersonal version of playing with matches. To learn, I needed to either get burned or burn something down (thankfully, this never happened with real matches). I wasn't aware of it then, but I needed to be mean, to feel its affect on myself and others. It makes me hope that Rachel's actions are just an experiment too.

I remind them of my rules: "Remember, journal time is story time not spelling time, so just write however the word feels. Don't worry about spelling everything perfectly."

All teachers have their ideologies, and there are a million different theories on how best to educate children. I like to separate the writing of a story from the spelling and penmanship that goes into it. Too often, they all get lumped into the same category. I'd much rather see pages full of detail and a strong voice riddled with errors than a few boring lines of perfectly spelled words. Spelling and grammar—that stuff can be taught later. But feeling free enough to tell a story? That's something I don't want to squash with a bunch of rules.

Kea shares first. "I saw the foal yesterday," he begins. "I like the foal. Maybe one day I will ride the foal." He shows us his drawing of the young horse, and we respond with a round of applause.

Jane, who is just learning to write her name, is ready to tell us the story in her picture. I always like to ask, "What is the story in your picture?" instead of, "What did you draw?" I've noticed that children who are allowed to ramble on and on about a picture have an easier time learning to read.

"This is our pig," she says. "He's a big pig. He's getting ready to roll in the mud. He likes rolling in the mud. I like our pig."

Proudly, she holds up a picture of a few circles with stick legs.

"Wow! Is the pig in a pen or does it just run around?" I ask.

"Sometimes he runs around and sometimes we lock him up."

"For homework, I want you to draw the pen and some of the other things around your yard. Class, that's called the setting. Remember how the setting in the book *The Rainbow Fish* is the ocean? The setting in Jane's story is her yard."

We spread our hands as wide as they'll go for Jane; this is called a big hand. Arataki, meanwhile, gets a sea otter clap: make a fist on your chest with one hand and clap it with the other. There are no sea otters at the local shores, so I had to find some pictures of sea otters breaking shellfish open on their chests to explain this one.

At the end of the day, I pull Kea aside.

"I want you to write more tonight about the foal," I tell him. "Remember how we use our senses to write about the things around us? Also, don't you think it would be fun to write about what the *foal* is thinking?"

Kea grimaces, clearly puzzled by this strange request. "How do I know what the foal is thinking?"

"Just make it up!"

"Mistah Chnn, do you want to see the foal with me?"

I promise to see the foal with him one of these days.

Good old Kea. How long will his innocence last? He's a sweet, easygoing kid, but what about when the gang gets hold of him? Will he demand more of life than what Black Power can give? I wish I knew. For now, all I can do is try to get his reading up to par.

As I lock my classroom door, I hear a car coming up the driveway. It's Karen and Tim. The car has barely stopped before Tim jumps out and runs across the yard, his freckled face hidden by the deep hood of his sweatshirt. He pulls his hood back to speak.

"Mr. Chin, I spotted a few pigs down by my house. We should go get 'em!"

Over the years, I've downed a few birds with a shotgun and tried bow hunting for deer, but hunting never has grabbed me the same way fishing has. With no plans for the weekend, though, a hefty hike through the countryside with a chance at fresh bacon sounds like a great way to spend a day. And of course, Tim's gossip-filled stories will no doubt provide another level of enjoyment as we pursue wily boars.

A few days later, I'm in my usual position trying to keep up with Tim. He clips along ahead of me occasionally calling over his shoulder to emphasize a juicy bit of local hearsay.

"You know So-and-So, Mr. Chin?"

"Yeah."

"Well, I reckon he's stew-pid for picking a fight with Such-and-Such. He got whupped! And you know Mr. What's His Name? I heard he bogged his motorbike down and near froze to death trying to walk home. He's thick, that one!"

"Thick means he's a dumbass...eh?" I ask, already knowing, but just wanting to carry on the conversation.

"Yeah ... he's real stew-pid."

"We all do stupid stuff sometimes. You know ... we have to balance out all those moments of brilliance," I reply.

"Yeah. I reckon so. Hey ... you know Dad and I skinned over sixty possums last weekend. Reckon that's a lot, huh, Mr. Chin?"

"Yup," I reply, huffing, puffing, and smiling.

I break out the video camera to get a few shots of us hiking up and over and down and around the meandering hills. The sinuous fence lines stretching to the horizon make for some epic footage. We play it up for the camera by using a fence post to steady the rifle as though we are taking a long sniper shot. As it happens, those camera shots would be the only shots we took all day. No bacon, just a couple friends laughing about the silly things people do.

A few weeks later, I'm dashing through the countryside again. Kea and I are looking for the foal in the golden fields behind the school, scattering cows and scaring horses. Big Head is nowhere to be found, but Memphis joins us for the expedition. In the distance we hear laughter. Then a small motorbike comes into view, bounces along the dips, and rises in the field. Kea's sister and cousins are riding it, all three of them at the same time—helmetless, of course. In New Zealand, remember, everything's sweet as until something happens.

Just then, Kea spots the foal.

There they are, a mother and her small brown foal, grazing just over a rise. Its legs are too long for its body, but it moves with grace. I set the video camera up and sit down with a sigh.

This is what I imagined, *this* peaceful country, when I booked my plane ticket. It's still hard for me to get my head around the gangs, the violence, the family dysfunction.

Nevertheless, a foal has been born, Kea's pig is on its second litter, buds are forming on the trees, and Baetis is eating for a family. The sun slips away on another day in RPG. On my way home, I pass Big Head's temporary home. I hear him crying and howling.

"Soon, boy," I whisper. "Soon. Maybe tomorrow."

When I arrive home, I look for Baetis, finding her balled up in the garden among the chard and bok choy. She rolls and stretches, covered by orange- red- and green-stemmed leaves, deepening the indentation in her favorite spot. Her belly seems to swell in tandem with the new garden sprouts. Now, her tiny head pokes out, waiting for my hand, so I rub her head and prune the old winter-burned leaves off the nearest chard plant.

Much to my relief, now that she's starting to show, she stays close to the house. My heart jumps and I look for her at each passing car. For her sake, I vow to live on a quiet street when I return to California. One thing I've learned, though, is not to call her. I halfway suspect that the excitement sparked by my voice—and the prospect of dinner and a warm fire—might have made her careless in crossing the road.

Being a good papa, I make sure she eats right. With each chicken I roast, she gets the neck, the gizzard, and at least one leg. Occasionally, I also enjoy tossing her an entire steak. (Is there any sound more appealing to a carnivore than the heavy *thwap!* of a slab of raw meat hitting the floor?) Tonight, we will share the last of the kahawai.

When I first arrived in January, a local saltwater fish called kahawai were running up the rivers to spawn, congregating at the mouth of the Mohaka River, where I get my driftwood and pumice. There were so many of them that it was possible sometimes to catch a fish with every cast.

Since then, I've become a kahawai connoisseur of sorts:

Kahawai

Dipped in a beer batter

Steamed and topped with ginger, green onions, and soy sauce (which, no doubt, would have made my grandparents proud)

Pan-fried with sautéed garlic, cherry tomatoes, olives, and capers

Drizzled with olive oil and the juice of a lemon from the tree in my backyard

Seared with a little wasabi, for a taste of Japan

Fillets rubbed in brown sugar and smoked

Baked with salt, pepper, and butter

And always, I round out the meal with a salad, bok choy, or chard from the garden.

Some people here don't like kahawai very much—mostly, I think, because it's so common that they can't believe it's any good. With the right marketing, however, it could be the next salmon—just look at Chilean sea bass. If the food industry can trick the world into believing a powdered concoction is better for babies than what Mother Nature has provided mammals for thousands of years, I'm positive that kahawai can be sold as a delicacy.

Say you're in a fancy restaurant in San Francisco, New York, or London and see "Pan-seared kahawai with a lemon caper vinaigrette" on the specials board. You'd probably ask your server, "What kind of fish is kahawai?"

Your server's recitation might go like this: "Well, kahawai are native to the waters off New Zealand, and they migrate up the rivers in summer much like salmon do. Their flesh is oily yet white and flaky—not quite as oily as, say, mackerel, and not quite as flaky as halibut, but there *are* similarities. It has a slightly meaty texture, though not so much as mahimahi, swordfish, or tuna. I love it. It's my new favorite fish."

Naturally, you'd reply, "Sounds great. I'll try the kahawai."

Tonight I've kept it simple: a little butter, lemon, salt, and pepper in a baking dish. I open the oven and flake-test the fillet with a fork. Baetis rubs at my leg; she's ready for dinner.

Baetis prefers plain fish, so I suck the lemon juice and butter off a few pieces before spitting them out for her. I laugh and choke on my own mouthful, realizing that living alone out in the boondocks is turning me into an animal myself—sitting on old stumps and spitting food onto my living room floor to feed my cat. What's next? Licking myself to keep clean?

Stomach full, I stoke up a big fire, and soon it's a toasty eighty degrees in the room. I recline in my lawn chair and hook my video camera up to the computer to review some footage of my first pig hunt. Huck, Angie's partner, is a fanatical pig hunter; he informed me that my stay in New Zealand wouldn't be complete without sticking a pig. The standard method for hunting swine in these parts is to let loose the dogs, let them corner a hog with mammoth-sized tusks, and then stick it with a knife. I spent a couple of nights practicing stabbing motions with my kitchen knife, but during the real hunt, I wanted to run away from the pig instead of toward it.

By the time the dogs finally locked in on the pig, during the last hour of the hunt, we had completed a grueling four-hour loop, winding through bush so dense I almost lost Huck and his friend Ted. Even with Ted leading the way with a machete, I often had to use my arms to push through the prehistoric-looking ferns. Waving my arms, and unable to see my feet, at times gave me the feeling of swimming rather than walking; the spongy ground, combined with a stream's distant gurgle, swallowed our voices and footsteps. At some point during the hike, I stopped to take pictures of a giant native kauri tree, and when I looked up from the viewfinder, everyone was gone. All I heard were a few birds and the wind in the treetops. So I did what anybody would do—I screamed for my friends like a kid lost in the mall. Dejected and pig-less, Ted suggested we let the dogs run one last time, and they took off toward a small patch of bush up a hill. Huck and I stood and watched them charge up the steep slope while Ted followed them. For a skinny little guy, he sure could move. Must be the diet of wild boar meat.

"Bet we get one here," I said to Huck. "We tramp all over creation and right here, just five minutes from where we started—"

Just then, the dogs started howling.

Huck, who had been trudging like a man in wet sand just seconds ago, suddenly turned light-footed. He darted up the hill, shouting, "That's the one, mate!" while I struggled after him.

Huck topped out before I did, and he raised his hand in a signal to halt. We'd lost the sound of the dogs. I noticed some huge vines swaying suspiciously off to our left and knew that a pig large enough to move those vines was a pig I'd run from. I was contemplating my escape route down the hill when Huck heard the dogs, and we were off again.

Between his huffing and puffing, he yelled over his shoulder, "Those were cows, mate!" his hand pointing wildly at the swaying vines.

The information did little to calm my nerves, for a bear-sized pig could still be around the corner. Then the dogs' barking grew louder; they had stopped moving.

"They got 'im!" Huck screamed, doubling his speed.

Visions of a large, angry animal fighting for its life filled my head as I clipped along behind Huck. His knife swung on his belt, the same one he'd hand me to do the job once we arrived. Unlike my first encounter with Big Billy Goat Gruff, there could be no pretending. I was about to enter the ring, to get in touch with my spear-toting ancestors. I remember thinking, "I'd much rather be fishing the stream behind me—much safer."

As we got closer, squeals and snarls joined the chorus of barks. We rounded the corner of a bluff and, much to my relief, Ted was already raising his gun. A single shot, and it was all over. Thank God for guns.

Huck turned to me and said, in a cheerfully aggressive way, "Ya got lucky, mate!"

He was smiling at the pig and at the thrill of the chase, but he was clearly a little disappointed that I didn't get gored. The funny part is, if I had gotten gored, he'd have carried me out, laughing all the way. Kiwis, you gotta love 'em. He handed me the knife; I was still responsible for cleaning the swine if I wanted to pass this class. I knew enough to bleed it, so I tilted its head back and made a clean swipe across its throat.

"All right, mate, now stick it ," he said, laughing at my awkwardness. "That's it! Slice it all the way down..."

I've always maintained that meat eaters should be able to kill and gut their own meat. We're so disconnected from our food that some of my students in San Francisco didn't know that McDonald's hamburgers came from cows. While I had gutted birds and fish, the sheer amount of entrails made this operation a little messier. This, I told myself, will make me appreciate my morning bacon all the more. Surprisingly, it didn't take much longer than gutting a fish. Just one double-handed scoop through the legs—like hiking a football—and it was good to go.

The tape ends just as I'm running across a stream with the pig on my back—bonus points in my Manliness 420 course. With fishing season coming up, I'll turn down any future hunting invitations. I won't regret leaving New Zealand without "sticking" a pig.

The cooling cast-iron stove calls for more wood and Baetis picks her head up, waking from a nap. What a year I've had, and it's about to get better. Lights out early because tomorrow is a big day. A yellow Lab has been waiting for me.

Finally, I'm ready—the healing was slow and tough—but I'm ready. I'm parked in front of Big Head's house. There's a tree behind the house hung with half a dozen gnawed-off ropes, each documenting one of Big Head's great escapes. Arataki's grandfather has been taking care of Big Head lately. He's a good man, but he lacks the energy for a Lab puppy.

"Kia ora, howzit?" I say, when he answers the door. "I'm heading to the beach and was wondering if I could take Big Head."

"He'd love that," he replies immediately. "We've got him on a chain now. Bugger keeps chewing through ropes and running wild."

With Grandpa's blessings, I bound around the house, a little boy ready for a frolic. Big Head, knowing something is up, leaps to his feet. Tail wagging, he gives me a quick lick as I unclip him, and he leaps into Lonna with no inhibitions. His face says it all: *What took you so long, mate? Let's go!*

He's reluctant to jump into the passenger seat, though, to take on the role of co-pilot. He paces back and forth on my sleeping platform, smashing into the windows with each turn. Finally, he hops into the front seat and rams his snout out the window as far as it will go. He pushes hard into the window opening, obviously nervous about the trip.

"It's all right, boy," I say, trying to calm him. "We're just going to the beach. You'll like it there. Ever been to the beach?"

He sighs and obliges my head rub, which quickly morphs into more of a supporting hold. In fact, soon he starts to look a little ill. I drive faster than usual down the dirt road. Just as the dark-sand beach greets us, a deep guttural sound fills the van. I can't open the sliding door fast enough for him. He squeezes through, leaving a cloud of fur swirling in the door opening. Motion sickness soon forgotten, he's a speck in the distance. I imagine him thinking, *Damn, that guy who drove me here is right! This place rules!*

I pick up the biggest stick I can find—it's more of a log, really—and walk to the water's edge. It's getting toward evening, the time of day when the grass turns gold. The common driftwood in my hands glows—a talisman to this royal moment.

The happiest man in Raupunga.

Holding it up, I scream, "Big! Heeead!" again and again.

He's so far off that I can't tell if he's moving away from me or coming toward me. Finally, his flapping tongue and flying drool come into view. I break out in goosebumps. He's a missile, a canine cannonball, and I'm the target. I sidestep just in time, matador-like, save my knees, and toss the stick into the swirling currents of the ocean. Big Head crashes into the froth and brings it back on cue.

Over and over I toss the stick and wrestle with him. He snarls and attacks with more force than I've ever seen. He sounds ferocious, but his bark-filled grin tells a different story—he's having the time of his life. When I can barely see, I jerk the mutilated stick from him and give his head a rub.

"Are you the greatest stick killer ever?" I ask.

The hole inside me has mended.

On the way back, Big Head thanks me by vomiting a mixture of sand, saltwater, and decayed marine mammal onto Lonna's door and carpet. Reluctantly, I take him back home to his chain. I don't want to overstep my boundaries.

When I arrive home, I pull around back and pick the last of the oranges. They're a bit tart but, like the autumn grapes, their location (my backyard) and their price (free) give them all the sweetness I need. Baetis, increasingly plump, darts from beneath the house, her belly rubbing the slick ground. She follows me around as I fill a bucket with water and find a rag. I rub her ginger spot before she sulks off to wait for the evening fire.

Dipping the rag in the bucket and wiping dog barf off the door of the van, I am the happiest man in Raupunga.

CHAPTER
11

USE YOUR HEAD

I STACK ENOUGH FIREWOOD on my arm to get us through the morning. Not that we really need a fire, mind you. It's spring. The trees are decorated in bright green buds, the grass in our rugby field is brushing against our shins and, actually, it's pretty warm outside. But I'm a sucker for ambience, and I love the crackling of wood in our classroom.

The days of blank walls, perfectly polished desktops, and empty journals are long gone. The room has become our studio, ground zero for our most creative projects. The kids *still* talk about *Three Billy Goats Gruff*. Just yesterday, Hiri asked, "Remember when I fell off the table, Mistah Chnn?" Which was followed by the ever-present question, "When are we going to do another play? The goat play was sweet as, Mistah Chnn!"

Our next great accomplishment was the Rainbow Fish mosaic. *The Rainbow Fish* has always been one of the kids' favorite books—or maybe it's just one of *my* favorites. In any case, it's about a fish with brilliantly colored scales and his decision to share his rainbow with other fish that have bland, normal scales. The project had many steps: we colored pieces of paper with crayons, markers, and paint; tore the colored paper into tiny pieces; and, little by little, glued a detailed recap of the story onto the wall. The whole process connects me to my mantra of *just change the blade*. Not only did it give the children a sense of accomplishment but it let me teach them the components of a story, such as setting, character, problem, and solution. If only we could find the time to put the finishing touches on it. Paintings, drawings, and student-published books also fill the room. It's my work, their work, *our* work—documentation of my life for almost a year.

I drop the wood at the stove's edge and swing the door open. In no time at all, I've got a fire roaring away. I write the day's schedule on the board, waiting for the sound of the expanding stove and exhaust pipe. This is the last fire. Soon, this classroom, these kids, Raupunga itself, will be just a memory for me. I'm going to miss this cast-iron stove with the glass door. It takes up an entire corner of the room. During the winter, its warmth was essential to our spirits. If a few children were absent, there would only be four or five of us in the room. We'd spread out on the carpet close to the stove and work away, adjusting our distance as needed. Now the fire begins to do its work. The heat causes some of our paintings to flutter and wave. One falls to the ground just as Arataki enters the room.

"Mistah Chnn! It's not cold!" she says in a scolding voice.

"I know. I know. I just like the fire."

"You're funny, Mistah Chnn."

"I know that too."

I've wanted to give Arataki a huge hug since her Nan passed a few weeks ago, but I don't think it's appropriate, even though I've shared hugs with my students in the past. I did, however, attend the *tangi*, a Maori funeral. The most memorable part for me was when the casket was carried out of the *marae*, a Maori place for worship. The entire community lined the path, and their sobs mixed with cold wind as the men broke out into the haka. I couldn't help myself, and once again my tears flowed, tears for Arataki, tears for everyone I've lost, and simple tears for the beautiful ceremony. I'd later learn the gestures and words for the haka, which symbolizes releasing a boat back into the waters—letting go. The pride of this small community shone in that moment, and I felt privileged to be a part of it.

Arataki sets her backpack down and starts tidying up the room—without being told, of course. She has exceeded all my expectations. She reads with reckless abandon now, and as she gained confidence, we began to focus on building her comprehension and vocabulary. Children can get so intent on decoding the words, I've noticed, that they fail to understand most of what they read. I remember when one of my students read a book called *Where Is My Hat?* It's a simple story about a boy looking for his lost hat. My student had decoded the words perfectly but understood nothing. When I asked him where the boy in the story looked for his hat, he replied, "There was a hat in the story?" Kind of like me when I read Shakespeare.

Hiri arrives and helps Arataki straighten the desks and wipe the board. Not for the first time, I wonder how they will turn out. What will they do with their lives? Will they be teen mothers? Will they go on to study after high school? Will they finish high school? Will they end up with gang members? I sigh, frowning at my bias. Who am I to judge whether or not being a teen mother is a good or bad thing? As Arataki moves from desk to desk, I find myself thinking out loud—it's a line from my dad—"Just be a good human and be happy."

"What'd you say, Mistah Chnn?" asks Hiri.

I smile. "Oh, nothing. Thanks for making the classroom nice. You girls are cool, you know that?"

They giggle and go about their business.

Morning news is the biggest it has ever been. With the twins and Will, another recent arrival, I've got eight students. I want them to develop their oral language skills, but some days we just sit for too long. With those days in mind, I've implemented a one-minute-per-person rule. Today, though, there is a lot of news, so I allow each student to say his or her piece. Even Will, who is shy and usually passes, shares something.

"Yesterday my brothers were doing the haka," he says. "They showed me. I like the haka."

I raise my hand and he points at me. "That's awesome, Will! I'm glad you shared with us," I encourage him. "Does anyone else have a question or something they want to say?"

"Can you show us?" asks Kea.

Will shrinks into the carpet, folds his arms, and doesn't answer. Time for some damage control.

"You know, it was nice for Will to share," I say. "Don't you think, class? Let's give him a big hand and move on. Good job, Will."

I give Will a nod and smile as he straightens up again, ready to listen to the next person's news.

"Now I'll go next. *Ata marie*, class," I begin, using the Maori phrase for "good morning." "Yesterday I took Big Head to the beach again. We ran and ran and ran. He likes it down there, because there are lots of sticks for him. It's more fun going to the beach with Big Head than by myself. Does anyone have any questions?"

"Is Big Head your dog, Mistah Chnn?" Hiri asks.

Taking a deep breath, I reply, "Nah, we're just hanging out. I don't give him any food, and he doesn't stay at my house. We just hang out." As I'm speaking, I realize that I sound like a lovestruck guy who can't quite admit that he's got a new girlfriend.

In truth, I'd love nothing better than to give the rascal a flea bath and let him in the house at night. Our sorties to the beach have become more frequent. Soon, I plan on asking if he can road-trip with me for the weekend—a big step and a risky one. Who knows what's going to happen when I go back home to the States. I'm not about to give up our fun: the boxing at the beach, the racing, and the vaulting over sand berms. It's a privilege to watch the greatest stick killer of all time, Big Head, in action.

Sure, when he's not with me, he's either chained to a tree or roaming around getting into trouble. And yes, he'd probably love for me to be his dad. But the fact remains: he's not mine. I take another big breath and finish my report. "Big Head is a good boy."

The pitter-patter of feet above our heads puts a halt to the morning news. Straining our necks, we follow the footsteps across the ceiling. They stop directly above the woodstove. Then a liquid begins to drip from a crack in the ceiling.

"Mistah Chnn!" Kea yells. "The ceiling is peeing!"

Laughter fills the classroom. He's right. Australian possums have invaded the school attic before, but this time they've gone too far. I've mentioned the footsteps to a few people, but all I've gotten are smiles and laughs. Not wanting to come off as a greenhorn making a big deal about a few oversized rodents, I've shrugged it off too. But this is unacceptable. No animal is going to piss on our classroom. I borrow traps and set them up on the roof. It becomes the new reality show at school.

The patient trapper always prevails. I've opted for traps— boxes with a spring-loaded mechanism—instead of poison; the last thing we want is for it to sneak away and die, leaving us with a decomposing animal in the attic. The possum has a choice of entering the box from the open end or through the top. So far they've been elusive, eating the apples leading up to the trap but cleverly staying away from the ones inside. To-day, though, I have a good feeling: I'm going to find something in the trap. Getting up to the roof becomes one of my favorite parts of the morning. I run and grab a low overhang, swinging my body forward, and then, on the backswing, throw my legs up and over the roof's ledge. Down in the yard, bouncing balls come to a halt, heads turn, and gossip ceases in anticipation of the daily possum report.

"Did we get one?" the boys shout.

"We got one!"

A possum's rear is sticking out of the top of the trap. I feel a little bad about being responsible for its demise. I know all the arguments against the possum, of course. It's an invasive species wreaking havoc on native animals, causing property damage and unsanitary conditions, blah, blah, blah. But it's also a living being just trying to survive. Carefully, I ease the tension off the metal bar and pull the lifeless possum out. I hold it up for the boys to see.

"What are you going to do with it?" asks Mick.

"Don't know. Maybe I'll make a hat out of its fur and let Big Head eat the rest."

"The meat is good for dogs, Mistah Chnn," he answers enthusiastically, offering to show me how to skin it after school.

"It's a deal."

When school ends, Mick comes by to skin the possum. Big Head is there too, because we are going to the beach later. He paces back and forth, sniffing the air and eyeing the possum with great interest. I can imagine what he's thinking, *C'mon, give it to me now. I don't mind the hair!*

Mick tells me that he and his sister will be moving away soon. You hear a lot about how uprooting a child can be harmful, but that wasn't my experience. Although I lost the ability to speak Chinese when we left Chicago's Chinatown, I gained a lot of confidence by learning to adapt to a different environment. Away from Raupunga, Mick might not feel the pressure to join a gang.

He takes the knife, makes a long, sweeping cut, and says, "It's always better to skin them right away when they're warm. Skin comes off easier."

He flicks his hair out of the way with bloody hands. His face is a picture of concentration, lines of care and determination etched sharply into his red-smudged cheeks. It occurs to me that Mick will do just fine in life. I help hold the body of the possum while Mick pulls on the skin. It makes a sound like heavy corduroy being torn.

"Is it okay to give Big Head the guts?" I ask.

"Should be sweet as, Mistah Chnn."

I hang the skin on the clothesline while Big Head tears into the carcass, ripping and swallowing large chunks at a time. In less than a minute, he's devoured the entire carcass, bones and all. He hops into Lonna, ready to work off the meal at the beach, panting through his wide, blood-rimmed mouth. *Thanks, Dad,* he might as well be saying.

In response, I sing: "I'm not your dad but maybe.... Glad you liked the possum. Big Head! Big Head! Big Head...is a good boy!"

After the beach I drop Big Head off as usual, but it's getting harder and harder to leave him there. Buddhists teach that attachment is the source of all pain and suffering, and I agree. But playing with Big Head just makes me too happy to give him up. Vulnerability—love is about vulnerability, about how much you're willing to risk in the face of inevitable loss. It's an investment in my soul.

When I arrive at school the next day, some of the boys are on the roof checking the traps. They just couldn't wait for me to get there.

"Hey! You know you're not supposed to be up there!" I yell, but my curiosity gets the better of me. "Any luck?"

"Nah," one of them responds. "We need more apples."

"All right, you might as well stay up there. I'll toss some up. Just drop a few pieces in. Keep your hands away from the trap and do not reset it!"

I probably don't need to tell them anything. I'm sure they're thinking, *C'mon, Mistah Chnn, we know how to do this.*

Today is a big day. It's our first official kapa haka rehearsal. After lunch we pile into five cars and head down to Mohaka School, which is perched on a hillside overlooking the ocean about ten minutes away. Forty or so children attend Mohaka and, unlike Raupunga, it hasn't had much staff turnover. The result, not surprisingly, is a little more respect and stability. This year the schools will perform Maori traditional song and dance together

Nance and Chel, the kapa haka teachers, greet us upon arrival. Nance teaches at the school and plays guitar, and according to the whispers, she is a lesbian. It makes me wonder how easy and open her life is here in the countryside. The Maori were greatly influenced by Christian missionaries, and most people still hold some pretty conservative views. For a moment, I envision Nance checking out San Francisco, a global hub for gay and lesbian life. Chel's broad shoulders and hardened face add up to one thing: the real deal. If kids get out of line, Chel only has to give them a look. If she has to open her mouth, then they're really in for it. We could use her around Raupunga. She's genuinely intimidating. Her physical presence matches her voice, and I've heard that both she and Nance play women's rugby. This may be a macho society, but in many ways the women in Raupunga and Mohaka reign too.

I jokingly state my observations to an older woman standing near me. "The ladies call the shots around here, eh?"

Her wrinkles deepen. "Yes. The women here are strong." Then, leaning toward me, she asks, "Have you heard the story about Te Kooti?"

Te Kooti, I learn, was a feared Maori warrior. He attacked the Mohaka Pa—a Maori fortress—with his followers in the 1860s. Mohaka's warriors were off on their own forays, leaving the children, a handful of older men, and the women to defend the pa. Against overwhelming odds, they managed to hold off Te Kooti until help arrived. The women in Raupunga and Mohaka still draw strength and pride from this piece of history. As the woman finishes the story, chills course through my body. All of this happened on the land where we are standing—where the boys will soon be performing.

The kapa haka performance has several acts. My favorite

is the actual haka, in which the boys take center stage. Traditionally, the haka was a war dance, with the aim of taunting the enemy and pumping fearlessness into the warriors. The boys get into it with foot-stamping, loud chants, and the famous *pukana*, a cutting glare that involves stretching your tongue out. In regard to pukanas, I think you either have it or you don't. Age has nothing to do with it. One boy who can't be a day over eight looks so fierce that it's kind of scary, all that ancestral energy coursing through his body. I tried my pukana out in front of the mirror (with no one around of course), but I just looked silly. Better for me to stick with the Bruce Lee stare.

The children from Mohaka, who clearly know the routine, shift back and forth on their feet from boredom while Chel and Nance go over a few directions with the Raupunga kids. The insecurity of the RPG kids is palpable, especially in the boys, who stand with slumped shoulders, trying to look cool despite their ignorance. It's something I'm still dealing with at age thirty, but I've come to realize that the more comfortable you are with feeling like an idiot, the easier it is for you to learn new things.

Kahu looks particularly bummed out. Last year he was *kaia*, the leader of the haka. Still, he's putting some effort into the performance by getting the group going with a call-and-response. Watching him, I realize that I should have asked Chel and Nance to choose two kaias so Kahu could share the responsibility. He's got potential, and he's smart, but I worry about him constantly. Actually, he reminds me of myself a little. He's someone I'd want in the boat when running a river of challenges. Studying and school, though, just don't interest him. Again, kind of like me.

Intelligence and good grades can go hand in hand, but more often than not they don't. You could say that making time to study, not partying the night before an exam, and actually going to class are smart habits to live by. By those standards I was a dumbass in college. By the time I reached my senior year, school and studying had begun to hurt. I'm talking physical pain. I'd sit down to study and my body would ache. It was torture. My teachers certainly didn't help. Most of my geology professors were research scientists who couldn't have cared less about their students. With no inspiration from them, I cultivated a passion for rock climbing and developed a terrible case of senioritis, planting myself squarely in the average range. C grades suited me fine. I knew I wouldn't pursue further studies in geology or a job in the field. I also knew my diploma wouldn't say average.

In fact, instead of thinking of myself as an underachiever, I considered my study-time-to-grade ratio to be above average. Not to say I didn't stress at times. Halfway through one chemistry exam, I realized I was in trouble. To even have a chance at passing, I needed to solve at least one more problem. Dozens of formulas, numbers, and graphs rattled around in my head, the product of an all-nighter. Cramming information is a lot like tossing clothes in a hamper. The end product has no rhyme or reason—it just takes up space. I began to despair, but after much page flipping I found a problem I could solve. All I needed were a few atomic weights to plug into the formula.

I stared at the large periodic table at the front of the lecture hall. For the life of me, I couldn't remember the symbol for potassium. I knew it was a tricky one, that it didn't begin with *P*. I raised my hand.

"I need the atomic weight for potassium but can't remember the symbol," I said to the teaching assistant.

"I'm sorry," he responded, "but I can't help you with that."

I put my head on the table. *Think, think, think!*

Suddenly, I knew exactly what to do. I waited for a different assistant to get close, made sure the other assistant was out of earshot, and raised my hand again.

"Hi, I was up late cramming for the test and my contacts

wouldn't go in this morning. These glasses are an old prescription from high school. Could *you* read the atomic weight of potassium for me?"

"Sure, no problem," came the sweet, unknowing reply.

I needed every bit of the curve to pass the test. However, being ill-prepared forced me to be quick-witted. As Dad would say, "Smart man, smart man."

The boys stamp their feet loudly, chanting words of power and respect. The haka is about tormenting your foe, about accepting the challenge of battle, so it's shirts off for the boys. Some of them even scratch themselves across the chest hard enough to draw blood. I watch them and contemplate their futures. All the boys standing before me are smart. All of them have potential. All of them will be men soon. But what kind of men will they be? Will they use their intelligence or let it go to waste? Again, I realize that I'm viewing their lives through the prism of my upbringing, of my values.

The kids have at least two practices a week, so our third term revolves around kapa haka. The ease with which the children learn song and dance both amazes and saddens me. At so many American schools, music, art, and dance have been replaced with scripted lessons designed to show progress on bar graphs. Academic testing may be poisoning early education in America, but here in New Zealand, I won't spend a minute of my time giving standardized tests. There are none. Sure, I'll run assessments, but nothing like the testing marathons back home.

The kapa haka experience is refreshing. Quickly, the unsure looks and out-of-sync movements give way to a crisp unity. No longer are the older children bored; feelings of satisfaction and self-worth shine through in their voices and postures. One act has the boys dancing *with* the girls, no doubt causing some sleepless nights. Before I know it, all the boys seem to be thinking, *Hey, hand-holding isn't so bad!* I, too, am ready for bigger things.

It's Friday afternoon, and I'm packed for a weekend in Gisborne. But first I have to pick up a friend.

"Kia ora, Mistah Chnn," Arataki's Grandpa booms from his doorway.

"Howzit?" I say, asking if I can take Big Head for the weekend. His answer surprises me.

"Sure, why not? And keep him down at your house if you want—bugger keeps howling at night."

"You sure?"

"Yeah, he has more fun with you, anyway."

"All right, just let me know when you want him back."

I walk around the house and he's there, waiting for me. His tail wags, and the energy seems to travel right through his body, all the way to the tip of his flapping tongue. I kneel and give his head a rub; he returns the favor with a few licks.

"All right," I whisper. "No more chain for a few days."

And off we go. He hops into Lonna's front seat like he's been doing it for years. As we pass the turnoff to the beach, he runs to the back of the van, staring out the window, pacing back and forth and rocking the van with his seventy-pound body. Then he jumps back up to the front seat. Then down and to the back. And again.

I slap the seat, trying to get him to stay put. He obeys, and I rub his head. The groove between his eyes isn't as deep as Toughy's, but he still likes to have it rubbed.

He's a good boy, a pleaser, but he needs to learn a few commands. I can't have him flipping out in the van while I negotiate the roads they call "highways" around here.

The road north of Raupunga skirts a tall cliff, and part of it washed out during the last storm. A single orange cone is all the warning you get. In America, there would be signs for miles leading up to the washout—or it'd just be closed altogether. Big Head sneezes and curls up deeper in the passenger seat. I coast by the orange cone, peering through the saliva-coated window. The wide Mohaka River Valley, green with the spring rains, commands my attention. With Big Head in here and that view out there, I couldn't ask for anything more.

The season isn't the only thing that's changing. Besides the borrowed dog and the hair I've begun growing back, I've decided to take a break from teaching when I return to America. The give-it-a-go attitude here has spurred me to prioritize my creative aspirations. Dreams of making movies or writing a book, ideas for carvings and paintings fill my head, keeping me awake at night. When I return to San Francisco, I plan to tutor and substitute teach part-time, while I edit video and write. And maybe, just maybe, I'll land my first real date with Lori. She moved on to a rebound relationship with an outdoorsy guy, but it sounds like she's finally done with him, which is good news. I'd hate to have to let loose the RPG when I return. I'd never start a fight, mind you, but manly thoughts persist.

A bright moon illuminates my way as I descend toward Gisborne. I've come to love this coastal city; it feels like my vacation home on the weekends. There's good food to be had, the surfing is excellent, I have friends here, and a few of the business owners know me. The man at the bakery always says the same thing, "Wazzup, mate? Survived another week in Raupunga, did ya?"

After witnessing white elitist attitudes and segregation at several other schools, Gisborne gives me hope in humanity again. Out of all the places I've visited in New Zealand, this one emanates the best vibe when it comes to equality. When I made my rounds to different schools here, I noticed a fairly even distribution of Maoris. Of course, some schools had more than others, but the main thing was that Maori culture seemed to be validated, even if the school's majority was Pakeha.

Gisborne has the honor of being the first place where Captain Cook landed, which resulted in the first interaction between the Europeans and the Maoris. I think this piece of history fuels acceptance on both sides. Not just tolerance, but acceptance. I tolerate mosquitoes and long lines at the grocer's, but I try to respect and accept other cultures, nationalities, and the different lifestyles people choose. So do they.

Big Head has never been to Gisborne, so he rams his nose through the crack in the window. For the first time, I'll be feeding him, so I stop and pick up a bag of standard dry dog food. In the evening, he sticks his nose into the bowl of kibble, then steps back, shakes his head a few times, and fixes me with those dark Lab eyes, his forehead wrinkled in confusion.

I stir the kibble. "It's food, boy."

He sniffs it again and backs away. His eyes droop, and he cocks his head. *But where's the blood, Dad?* He seems to ask.

Then I get it. He's never had dry dog food, never eaten anything but the real deal, and never in his life will he sink so low as to eat stuff that looks like goat droppings. He's used to liver, beef ribs, wild goat, and buckets of lamb hearts.

And with that we hop in Lonna and charge off to the store for some red meat, extra bloody. I can feel Toughy watching over us, thinking, *Hey! You made me eat those pellets!*

Real food always got Toughy in trouble. He'd gorge himself, get the runs, and make a mess. Worst of all, he'd lose his mind and growl at me, his dad, when I tried to take a marrow-filled bone away.

Grandmothers spoil their grandchildren. That's their job. When I moved to San Francisco, my sister and I were both a long way from having children, so my mom did the next best thing: she spoiled Toughy. We couldn't have a dog when I was a kid because my mom had a debilitating allergy to dogs, but that illness suddenly disappeared when I got Toughy. For his part, he learned quickly that Grandma's presence meant table scraps and better-than-usual garbage-can booty. His favorite time was Thanksgiving. Turkey was a narcotic to him.

Whenever Toughy raided the garbage, I'd scold him and put him in the bathroom for a few minutes. One Thanksgiving weekend, my family and I came home after a movie and found something was wrong. Toughy hadn't come to the door to greet us and was nowhere to be found. His work, however, was everywhere. We had forgotten to take the garbage out, and now a long trail of refuse was strewn across the kitchen floor, the turkey carcass devoured and every greasy bit of paper licked clean or eaten. Even when I called him, he didn't show. Just as we were about to panic, I peeked in the bathroom. There he was: fat, satisfied, and already punishing himself. Mom doubled over with laughter. Clearly, he had weighed the consequences and decided to go for it. If only I could've taught him to clean up his mess too.

Big Head curls his stinky self into the passenger seat, spent from a weekend at the beach. I'm sure he's introduced a new and particularly invasive species into Lonna's ecosystem: fleas. They join the clouds of hovering fruit flies, the result of a forgotten piece of fruit (probably a lemon) that rolled into a far corner. Fortunately, spiders have taken up residence in both corners of the dashboard, which helps keep the fly population in check. The fleas, though, are too much even for me. I add *Buy flea stuff* to my to-do list. Nonpoisonous spiders are cool. A few flies, cool. Fleas sucking my blood? Too much.

Big Head has never been in the house, and I wonder how Baetis will take it. I haven't seen much of her lately; I can only guess that she's busy setting up a nest somewhere for the birth. She's almost as wide as she is long now; it should happen any day. Luckily, her private entrance allows her to come and go without passing through the kitchen, where Big Head will be sleeping.

Time for a lecture. "Listen, buddy. You can't harass Baetis, all right? First of all, she'll kick your butt. And second, well, it's just not cool! Know what I'm saying? Big Head! Big Head! Big Head is a good boy!"

He lifts his head and licks his nose, appearing to understand. *Sure, whatever you want*, he seems to say. *Now where's that meat?*

The weekend felt just like old times. Surf, hang out with good friends, and curl up at the end of the day next to a mass of snoring fur. He's not my mass of snoring fur, I know, but I've taken to calling him a yellow-Lab-on-loan. He's got the van ride down by now, so I feel comfortable keeping the windows open without worrying about him jumping ship. He lifts his head for a second to catch a breeze as we cruise around some wide sweeping turns outside of Gisborne. Only another half hour to the Morere Hot Springs, my resting point.

I've got the hour-and-a-half drive between Gisborne and Raupunga down to a science. I rock up to the hot springs just thirty to forty-five minutes before closing. Sometimes the man charges me an entrance fee, and sometimes he doesn't. The short hike to the tubs takes me by fern trees and native bushes so green that they all seem battery operated. If I'm feeling down, the experience picks me up. If I'm already doing well, it buffs me to a shine. Today, I will shine.

A light sprinkle has begun to fall by the time I pull into the parking lot. The spring rain still has a little chill to it, but I change into shorts and go shirtless anyway. Big Head wakes suddenly. I grab both of his cheeks and give them a pull. "Sorry, boy. No pup-pups allowed. Be good! No chewing!"

Soon, I'm running barefoot up the trail, my body covered in goosebumps. Between my footsteps I hear the rain making tiny sounds when it hits the dense foliage, and a lower, more muffled noise when it lands on the soft earth beneath my feet. A crack of thunder, and the sky opens up. Now there is only the rain. I see the small stream near the tubs before I hear it. After a gradual bend, it tumbles out of thick bush into the clearing by the soaking pools. I slow to a deliberate walk and wade, knee-deep, into the frigid currents. I'm shivering but not cold. In fact, I feel incredible, connected to home, to family, and to Toughy. The class has just completed a science unit on the water cycle, and it's got me thinking.

The water in the stream, the water on my back, the water matting my hair and the water finding its way into the corners of my mouth: somewhere, sometime, we've met before. It's touched those I care about, flowed through the valley near Toughy's grave, and lapped the shores of my favorite California surf breaks. The world is not so big after all.

I'm surprised to see other people soaking in the pools. One of them, I learn, is a stone carver. I've been wanting to learn more about carving, so I don't think our meeting is a coincidence. His name is Matanuku, and he tells me he is a master greenstone carver. He agrees to teach me. With his high cheekbones and large eyes, he radiates intensity; he'll be a great teacher, I'm sure. I towel off and promise to meet him in a few weeks at his place.

It's still raining, but for the moment I'm impervious to cold and all negativity. Even the discovery of Big Head's chewing exploits back at the van can't upset me for too long. Expensive fly-tying material is scattered across the van; my homemade fishing net, with the handle crafted from the same walnut as Toughy's grave marker, now bears Big Head's teeth marks. I salvage the usable feathers and fur and put the rest in a small pile. Then, pointing at the pile and the net, I say, "No! No! Bad!" Big Head hangs his head and drops his tail. My lips tighten, and I rub behind his ears. He'll learn.

He curls up in the back of the van with his rear toward me.

Usually the turn of the key is a signal for him to settle down in the passenger seat. I call for him to take up the co-pilot position, but he just sighs.

"C'mon, boy. You know Dad isn't mad anymore."

Did he say 'Dad'?

He rises and shakes. Puffs of hair swirl off his body and fall to the sleeping platform. He eyes me, stretching, and hops into the front seat. He can't stay mad at me either, it seems.

We make our way home through the dark, rain battering the windshield. It reminds me of the night I broke down near Raupunga but now, one year later, things are totally different: Lonna is running sweet as, I'm no longer hurting so badly inside, I've got goals on the horizon, I love a cat and a cat loves me, and now there's a dog next to me—Biggus Headis!

Dog names always morph into an endless array of nicknames. They're used frequently, so saying them one hundred different ways makes sense. Toughy's "Latin" name was Toughis Doggis, so Big Head will be Biggus Headis. Baetis's name is in real Latin—baetis are a family of mayflies that trout love to eat. I play with Big Head's name all the way back home.

"Biggus Headis! Biggus Headis? Biggus Header is the bestest doggus in the whole wide world! Who's the bestest puppis? Biggus Headisss!"

In front of the house, I straighten up and grab his cheek.

"Really, boy. Don't mess with Baetis. This can be your home, but you have to listen."

I look up and down the road, making sure there are no cars or trucks coming, and call for Baetis, but she's nowhere to be found. As always, I look over the fence, bracing for a crumpled ball of gray fur in the road. Fortunately, the road is empty. We enter the house and are greeted with a familiar meow from the living room. When she comes out to meet us, her back arches and I see more of her teeth than I've ever seen. Then she tiptoes backward, never taking her eyes off the intruder. Only when she's back in the living room does she break her gaze from Big Head. She looks at me as if to say, *How could you?*

Big Head, meanwhile, growls a little but never lunges or barks. It's a good start.

I walk Big Head around to the kitchen, closing the French doors to the living room. I give him a blanket, some water, and some bloody meat—a five-star hotel compared to the tree and chain. The antagonists square up on opposite sides of the glass doors. Big Head presses his nose to the glass, stamping his front paws. Baetis swats at the glass and hisses, reminding me of newly licensed teenagers who flip people off and drive away. Big Head sulks away and collapses onto the blanket, apparently disgusted that he has to share me, his *dad,* with anyone else.

I thought I was the only one.

Baetis takes it one step further. She leaves the glass doors, shuns my head rub, and walks over to a pile of clothes. A glare that would melt glass and a squat let me know how she feels. She leaves a brown "present" on my clothes, then prances over to the fireplace.

I don't approve of that thing, she seems to say. *And will you hurry up with the fire?*

The weeks tick by with Big Head a part of my daily life until it's the last day of the term. Only one more term to go and my time in Raupunga will be done. As I pour myself a bowl of cereal, Big Head watches with great interest. As much as I enjoy watching him devour giant hunks of meat, I've been slowly weaning him off of blood. Recently, we overdid it. I'd tossed him a huge steak that he promptly downed. As I laughed at his carnivorous ways, his eyes crossed, and his body convulsed until the steak came back up—in the exact shape it had gone down. The shape of a steak, I concluded, is unnatural. An animal would never find a piece of meat with perfect right-angle cuts in the wild; animals only tear off what they can swallow. Ground beef is a safer choice, and I can mix it with regular dog food.

For the sake of my pocketbook, I hope he'll take to the straight kibble soon. Today, there are no worries as I run into a generous parent at the school. The man likes me, as his kids are happy and doing well in my class. It's a good thing, because he's one of the more formidable men around, a true tank. He shows his appreciation by giving me a bucket of beef livers for Big Head.

I toss one of the gelatinous masses near some flax plants. Big Head tears into it, bloody goo hanging over the rim of his mouth. A grotesque sight to us humans, but glorious to his mate, Memphis, who is standing patiently in the hopes that Big Head will share.

I encourage Big Head to be kind. "C'mon, share a little with Memphis."

Big Head glares at Memphis, causing his much smaller friend to cower and shuffle away. Memphis tries not to make eye contact but can't keep his nose from pointing in the general direction of the decadence. *C'mon, mate! Just let me smell it.* Big Head responds with a lunge and an aggressive bark, his jaws snapping just inches from Memphis's terrified face. A second later, Big Head gives Memphis a lick. *All is good, mate, but you still can't have my liver.*

I laugh and think back to an incident in junior high. Youth and competition for food and girls must account for the majority of skirmishes in canines and humans alike.

In sixth grade, my friend Scott wouldn't give me another piece of gum, so I took some out of my mouth (gum I'd gotten from him minutes earlier) and stuck it in his hair. He fumbled with his sandy blond hair, staring at me in disbelief before he retaliated with his own gum. The convenience store was still in sight, and both of us had enough money in our pockets to buy eight packs of gum if we wanted. Of course, gum wasn't the issue. Hormones and the instinct to elevate myself in the pecking order took over, so I clocked him, breaking his nose in the process. Twenty years later, I gave the best man's speech at his wedding. Just like Memphis and Bighead: no hard feelings. What's the saying? Boys will be boys.

I give Memphis a piece of liver and tie Big Head to the van. Then Ms. Kenton pulls up, and I notice a heap of white canvas sacks in the back of her truck. Time for meat bananas. The sacks hold dozens of freshly detached country delicacies. Docking season is here.

Docking is the task of hacking, chopping, slicing, or otherwise removing the tail from a lamb. As everyone knows, an animal's tail, given its geographic position, inevitably collects some dirty stuff. This can breed disease, so the solution is to simply remove it. It's safer for the animal and results in perfect meat bananas, a classic Kiwi treat I've come to enjoy.

Most folks might not think fatty vertebrae cooked over a fire sounds good; but because of my Chinese heritage, I have fond memories of sucking the skin, fat, and tendons from chicken feet during dim sum, surrounded by my extended family. When I was invited to a neighbor's for some lamb tails earlier in the year, I minced scallions, cilantro, and ginger, mixed it with soy sauce and a dash of sesame oil and brought it over for a dipping sauce. "Grandpa's secret sauce," I explained. Today I'm caught off guard, so I'll have to make do with lemon and salt.

There's work to be done if we're going to enjoy the treats at lunchtime. We'll need to set up the metal grate from Kea's house, dig a hole at the edge of the rugby field, and haul some wood from the woodpile. Kea, who has just arrived at school, is only too happy to run home to fetch the grate. First, he lets everyone know—with a scream—that we're having lamb tails. Instantly, the school is buzzing with excitement: there is something on the schedule besides plain old school. There are questions:

"Where's a shovel, Mistah Chnn?"

"Should I start the fire? Do you have some matches?"

"Can I get some wood, Mistah Chnn."

"Where are the lamb tails?"

"Should I go get some lemons from our tree!"

"Should I unload the lamb tails?"

"Are we having them now? Can we have them now?"

And answers:

"Whoa, whoa! The shovel is in the shed. Dig the hole where we had lamb tails last time. Remember the wood on top of the woodpile is still green, so dig down to get some of the dry stuff. The lamb tails are in those sacks. Yes, sure, go get a few lemons. Leave them in the sacks for now. No, we're not having them now. We'll light the fire toward the end of morning tea. Got all that?"

I sigh, watching the boys go about the preparations. Lately, instead of depressing myself with negative images, I've tried to envision a positive future for Kahu. He's an artist storyboarding movies or pumping out imaginative comic books. His hand moves independent of his mind, the creative spirit purposeful but without restriction. His face is grown-up, confident, and very content. There is no fear. He's a member of Black Power, but he has also become *more* than that.

Kea returns with the metal grate just as the bell rings, rushing in through the gate with Memphis close behind. I watch the two of them, boy and dog, with pride. Kea has grown physically and has improved in all areas of academics. When we were studying the five senses, I asked the children to draw and write about what they saw on their way to school. Kea drew the gate to the school, writing, "I see a gate, and then I am at school." Memphis has grown too and has no doubt tried to spread his genes around town. No one in the peaceful countryside neuters dogs.

Kea tosses the grate near the firewood and freshly dug hole. Big Head cocks his head toward the lamb tails, lifts his nose, and barks in excitement.

"You just had beef livers! Let's not get greedy. Now get in," I say, pointing to the back of the van.

Big Head hops into the back of Lonna and lies down. With Lonna's back hatch open, Big Head has the choice of lying underneath the van or taking what I call a balcony seat on the sleeping platform inside the van. Memphis sniffs the grate, investigates the hole, and leaves his mark on the firewood before joining Big Head to wait for lunch. Dogs love meat bananas even more than kids do.

Big Head has started to chase sheep, so it's leash time for him. Chasing sheep is a capital crime around here—a felony punishable by gunshot. Cole, the owner of the cows we once rounded up, gave me an ultimatum: "I know you love that dog, mate, but if he chases my sheep again, I'm gonna shoot him." Country folk will tell you it's hard to get stock-chasing dogs to stop once they start. One method is to tie a piece of meat around the dog's neck until it turns rancid and nasty. Another is to allow him to chase sheep but let the herding dogs rough him up. Neither method appeals to me. It'll be strict supervision for my borrowed dog.

The morning dissolves into lunchtime and, before I know it, the distinct aroma of well-cooked meat bananas fills the air. The first round is done. Blackened fur and skin peel away to reveal ghostly-white, steaming, fat-covered vertebrae. Lemons and a salt shaker make the rounds as we circle the fire, shifting according to the Aotearoa breeze. Thick smoke from burning hair wafts over waving grass and into swaying trees. Branches packed with spring-green leaves absorb the smoke, which in any case contains much more than carbon monoxide. Our smiles, our laughter, our indulgent slurping and sucking, even the obvious pleasure that Memphis and Big Head take in the proceedings—they can all be traced back to that small, fiery

We're mates for now, but when they bust out those lamb tails, you'd best stay out of my way.

hole with the metal grate. My clothes smell like they are so full of joy that I might just have to burn them too.

I video the whole operation, just in case I forget what an al dente lamb tail looks and sounds like. Some of the boys can't help but flash a few gang signs at the camera. The atmosphere has been calm, no incidents to speak of. How long it'll last, I don't know. The nicer weather means more parties and greater chances that the Mongrel Mob and Black Power will cross paths. Even the boys—who aren't actually prospects yet, technically speaking—seem to be looking for trouble.

I pass a posse of them on my way home. Some of them walk with that American gangsta shuffle, their pants around their knees. There's a copycat quality to the newer generation of gang types here, so different from their elders. I can see how the old-school Black Power guys bonded through a need for brotherhood, through their need to survive and thrive. It wasn't purely image-based or inspired by Hollywood's idea of what a gang member should be. I'll bet there's a bit of kids-these-days talk when the older generation of Mangu Kaha get together.

As I ponder the gang culture, I glance in my rearview mirror. One of the boys skips a rock toward me. I hear it bounce against Lonna's underside. Clenching my teeth, I get out to take a look and scream, "Use your head, man!" Sometimes I just feel like a big kid, but right now I know I am a grown-up (at least in one sense), a real, conscious adult who thinks before he acts. How many times did Dad say those exact words to me after I did something stupid? Hadn't I tossed rocks at I-Gaw during a brotherly-love scuffle?

"Come here!" I yell to them.

They saunter up to the van, oozing a whatcha-gonna-do-about-it? attitude, their pants down around their ankles now.

Changing my tone, I say, "That just wasn't very smart." Then, softening even more, I add, "Use your head, man. Just use your head."

Ian, a stocky boy, repeats my admonition a couple of times. "Use your head, man! Use your head, man!" he mocks.

Something in his eyes, though, tells me that maybe my words will register someday. Hopefully, before he causes himself or others harm.

With that, I lighten up a little more, allowing myself a slight grin. "That's right," I answer, ignoring the mockery. "You got it."

It takes awhile for lessons to hit home sometimes—if they ever do. For me, the idea that actions have consequences didn't become clear until I was sixteen, when my friends and I almost blinded a man. It was a cold winter day, short on daylight but with plenty of time for trouble. The streets were wet, so we couldn't skateboard. We were sick of skating in the basement, so we grabbed some BB guns to play commando. Everything was fair game: pie plates, cans, the gas meter, the lighted Santa on a neighbor's house, light poles, even one another. Then, peeking over the top of our backyard fence, I saw the commuter bus turning onto our street.

Two words: "The bus!"

Then: dive roles, strategic positions, and a volley of .177-caliber projectiles. After a few high fives, we parted ways for dinner. Later that evening a policeman, knocked at the door. My dad answered.

"Good evening, sir. Some boys must have been playing with air guns in this area. Do you have any air guns in the house?" the officer asked.

"No, I won't let my son have one. What happened?"

Someone shot a BB gun at the commuter bus, shattering the windows, the officer reported. A man on the bus ended up with glass shards in his eyes. "Thanks for your time," he said, turning to leave. "If you hear of anything, here's my card."

We were dead to rights. My friend's mom had seen us leave the house with his BB guns, but it didn't matter. The shame I felt was too great, so I would have admitted to the shooting regardless. My parents justifiably canceled my driver's education class, and I waited an extra year for the privilege of driving. We never heard from the man. What if he had sued my parents? Even worse, what if I had deprived him of seeing his children grow up? All because I didn't use my head.

I grew up in a good home with stable parents and not an ounce of violent influence. If I could come that close to seriously hurting someone, what are the chances that these boys will end up in jail or seriously harm—or even kill—someone? Many of them have no male role model nor anyone who has ever set boundaries or expectations for them outside of school. Add in the gang influence and it's easy to see why I'm concerned. They're still standing there as I pull away, chanting, "Use your head, man! Hey, man! Use your head!" All I can do is hope.

Farther down the road, I run into Mr. Tay—the man who pulled my résumé from the trash earlier in the year. As usual, a thinly rolled cigarette hangs from the corner of his mouth. He gives me the classic country head-nod. He's so relaxed that it's a little unsettling, making me think of the Chinese proverb, "Beware the patient man's fury." Maybe it's his stoic face or the way he walks, as if he's surveying his kingdom, watching over every acre of it. I don't know. I told him a few weeks back that he reminds me of Sean Connery in the movie *Highlander*. He smiles a little more when he sees me now.

He tells me that his son, who attends the school, really enjoys my science lessons. "We can't talk you into staying, can we?" he asks.

"I've thought about it," I say, "but I miss my family and my mates. It just doesn't feel right to stay. It's been incredible, though," I add. "And all because you rescued my résumé."

"Sweet as. Seemed like the thing to do."

As I drive off, I realize that the word *mate* has become an essential part of my vocabulary, replacing *dude*.

I pull up to my house, and my heart sinks a bit at the state of the lawn. It's reached the flop-over stage; it's so long that it can no longer hold up its own weight. *Catch goat to eat lawn* is on my to-do list, but I've just been too busy. Besides, the tall grass gives Baetis a nice place to hide and hunt. She is ready to burst any day. I had to take another slat out of the shuttered window so she could fit through her entrance. I fill a bucket with cat food and toss some ground beef in a bowl for her. She prances up to the meat and digs in. I watch her eat, and I get the chills. We've already been through a lot together. And now she's going to make me a granddaddy.

"Don't eat it all at once, girl," I say. "And please, be careful crossing the road."

I'm heading down to Wellington for a city-fix, and the van is packed with surfboards and fishing gear for stops along the way. The only thing I need to add before leaving is the crazy yellow Lab, *Mahunganui*. That's Maori, I've learned, for "Big Head."

He bangs up against the passenger window as I fishtail Lonna around the house in a weak attempt at taming the lawn. Blades of grass tear away, joining the growing bundle already stuck in Lonna's bumper, some of it kindling-dry, it's been there for so long. I really do need that goat.

Then, pausing in the driveway, I look over at Maka's place and at the outhouse smeared with fresh graffiti. I watch some kids playing on the hillside near the school. Inhaling deeply, I think about calling I-Gaw. Big Head postures up in his seat, his nose pressing against the windshield. He's ready to move on, just like his dad.

CHAPTER
12

SHORT BUT FUN

THE INCOMING TIDE EXTENDS the reach of the ocean, bit by bit. Foaming chaos recedes, leaving saturated sand, rock, and wood, a montage of Earth's building blocks. I follow Big Head down the beach, watching his paw prints set and disappear. The sand is his canvas. I have one wish: that he and I will leave our trail on the other side of the Pacific. Two weeks on the road have cemented our bond. I *am* his dad. We walked city streets, forded rushing streams, and wandered deserted beaches. Soon, I'll need to know if he's my dog or not. For now, we race down the beach, sand spitting as we pass, sea spray covering our legs, we swirl, swerve, and spin our way back to Lonna. At the campsite, Big Head settles in to watch me cook, his hind legs sticking straight out like a human in a recliner. Sand spatters dot his face, and water drips from the edges of his jaw.

I advise him, "Listen, buddy, I'm hungry too. You could do something to help, you know."

He is unmoved by my request. I slice and dice, showing off my culinary skills to no one but the smelly mutt at my side; we eat, watching the waves change and rearrange as they hit the shore. Afterward, Big Head licks the dishes clean, and I pour coffee for the road. There's work to be done. We point the van toward home.

It's Sunday afternoon, the day before the start of the fourth and final term of the school year. I enter my classroom and gag at the stench. After retreating and gulping a few deep breaths of air, I calmly reenter the room—not as a teacher, but as a bomb-squad specialist. With deft hands, I open all the windows, weaving crisply through the maze of desks and chairs as if my life depended on it. I'm back out the door with plenty of breath to spare. The strong breeze should make it tolerable in a few minutes.

In the meantime, I decide to check the status of the pool. The days are getting warmer, and it's time to divert Kea's household water again. The gate is locked, but I hop the fence, mimicking RPG's beer-guzzling teens. The generator is humming away behind the fence, and there are still a few beer bottles left by the benches. I look for the night bather's bar of soap, but it's long gone, dissolved by the winter rains. Three feet of stagnant water rests in the bottom of the pool, and the cracks don't look any worse than they did at the beginning of the year. With the chlorine diluted by rainwater and dissipated by time, I had considered trapping freshwater eels down at the river and raising them in the pool as a fresh source of protein for the winter months. It could have been a science project and a lesson on entrepreneurship. Who knows? We could have raised and sold eels to sushi restaurants all over the country. The boys would have loved it, but there just isn't enough time in the day. I'd best get to planning and cleaning if I want to be ready for the first week.

Back in the classroom, I search everywhere for the source of the smell but come up empty. It's not too bad with the windows open, though, so I turn on the computer, hoping for an email from Lori. Much to my delight, there's a message from her. Looks like the rebound guy is definitely out of the picture.

And just in time: I've only got a couple months left until I go home.

Time for the planning. Deep breath. First, the long-range plan. With kapa haka practice twice a week, two kapa haka festivals, and an extended field trip to Wellington, New Zealand's capital, the term is sure to be busy. We'll work on literacy through leveled reading, which allows the kids to work at their own pace; we'll do a few book projects; and we'll work on producing our new play, *Maui and the Sun*. After planning for literacy, I page through the New Zealand math standards looking for ideas.

With math, I've discovered, there's no way to avoid teaching exact skill sets. The older children will concentrate on money, which will be a good way to introduce them to place values and equations using larger numbers. The little guys will learn about shapes, comparison words (*larger, smaller, more than, etc.*) and simple rote counting. Feeling good about my big-picture plan for the weeks to come, I close my planner, lock the windows to avoid inviting theft, and head home to see if Baetis is around.

She wasn't around when Big Head and I got home from the trip, but her food was almost gone and the kitchen floor was dotted with paw prints. I know she's hunkered down somewhere nursing her little ones. She's there when I pull up to the house, pacing back and forth on the front steps, her belly stretched and sagging. Her nipples are red and swollen, evidence of a successful delivery.

"You did it, girl!" I shout.

Watery eyed, I stroke her ginger spot and run my hand down the length of her body. She pushes against my hand for a few strokes before dashing into the kitchen. Twirling around and meowing frantically, she makes her demands known.

Give me something besides this wretched dry food!

I respect her decision to keep the kittens away. A mother, regardless of species, needs a little privacy. Matriarchal pride and trust radiate from her eyes; she will bring them home soon, I'm sure.

The following morning, I wake earlier than usual as the classroom needs time to air out and there's photocopying to be done. I look at Big Head and growl, "Biiii—iig Head!" His powerful Labrador tail turns over and over, thumping the wooden floor. He yawns and stretches a couple times while crossing the room. Before I can hit the snooze, he's at the foot of my bed unleashing a barrage of good-morning licks.

"All right, all right! I'll get up, but no outside for you until we get to school."

The road, that death trap, has me terrified that Big Head will get hit. I feel bad about restricting his roaming, but I'd be devastated if something happened to him. Then there's the sheep-chasing habit. Over the break he pinned down a full-grown sheep. He would have killed it if I hadn't gotten over there in time. If a herder catches him in the act, he's as good as dead. Strangely, though, I was secretly proud of him—that's a tough dog. I scolded him, realizing that once I become a father, I'll feel the same way about my kids if they whup some ass—call it man stuff.

I hear a meow and run to see if the kittens are here. Nope. It's just Baetis demanding more food. When she leaves, I follow. With her tiny paws, she picks her way across piles of dried grass, her distended belly swaying from side to side. Upon reaching Arataki's fence, she turns to look at me.

Don't worry, Pops, she seems to say. *I've got it covered.*

And she's gone, up and over the fence to tend to her family.

Then I realize, surveying my yard, that someone mowed my lawn while I was gone. Sweet as.

When I arrive at school, a handful of kids and Ms. Kenton are already there. As it turns out, I've forgotten about the time change and, instead of being really early, I'm merely right on time. It's been like that lately—even when I pull bonehead moves, it all works out.

Our first day is a fun one. I decide to forgo our routine and do an intense book study all day. We read various picture books, discuss the characters, act out parts of the story, write and draw new endings, and make clay sculptures of the characters. All this helps with comprehension and gives the stories a deeper meaning to students, but it requires a lot of energy.

At the end of the day, the kids file out and I slump into a chair, my knees flopping to the sides and my back arching over the painfully small backrest. I love my class, but right now, I love them more because they're gone for the day. Clay animal sculptures stare at me from the table in front of me. I rock forward and grab a few, arranging them so they square off against each other. A red horse with blue hooves shifts back and forth in one hand, and a pink pig with yellow eyes, in another.

"Hey! Stop eating my hay!" the horse yells.

"I'll eat your hay if I want," replies the pig.

"Listen, you swine! No one talks to me that way!"

Snout meets hooves, and the horse tumbles off the table with the pig looking over the edge.

"Take that! Don't mess with the Bacon!"

Maybe one day, I'll grow up. I push the kid chair back, stand, and stretch. I look around like a kid who's sick of all his old toys, and then my eyes light up. Clumps of unused colored clay lie scattered on the tables, and I gather matching colors, rolling them into balls and squeezing them until they are soft and sticky. I spot a small circle on the board and, without warning, send a clay ball across the room. Slap! The ball sticks dead center in the circle. Then a chair and a file cabinet absorb a dose of my arm's power and accuracy. Maybe I should have been a pitcher instead of a teacher. I turn to my classroom door, half expecting to see Lori or another teacher walk in to see about the ruckus.

In San Francisco, my hyper ways often spilled into the hallway during lunch or after school. Most of my colleagues would shake their heads as I left footprints on the wall, cartwheeled down the hall, or juggled various items. After a while, though, I'd literally rope some of them into my antics. One time, I brought a jump rope into the hallway, the kind with plastic beads threaded onto the rope. As I skipped and jumped down the hall, the rhythmic clicking sound of the plastic on the floor brought out a few teachers, including Lori. Soon, we were all trying our hand with two ropes—double-dutch style. With other teachers there, Lori and I could relax and enjoy each other's company without the pressure of it feeling like a date.

I took one end of the rope as she tried to read the rhythm of the ropes. We smiled at each other but quickly turned away. Lori threaded herself into the ropes, her hair bobbed, her feet flashed, and I cheered for her, "It's a record for Ms. Lori!"

I, on the other hand, was terrible at double dutch and could barely jump into the swinging maelstrom, so I suggested jumping a single rope while in a handstand. (I'd seen it done in a circus performance and needed to try it.) With a few years of gymnastics in my past, I was able to hold a steady handstand but couldn't get any lift for the rope to pass under my palms. Next thing I knew, Lori had grabbed hold of my ankles to give me a lift while other teachers turned the rope. The rope passed under my hands and her feet. Nothing mattered other than the fact that Lori was touching me!

Next, it was her turn. She smiled, sweat dripping down her face. I imagined it would have been the same look she'd have given me after we'd hiked to the top of a mountain—hand in hand. Lori tightened her pigtails, seemingly making a production of it—by then, she knew I liked her hair in pigtails—and tucked her shirt in before she dove forward with her hands outstretched. I allowed her pants to slip down her leg for a better grip on her ankles. Now I was actually touching her skin! One teacher, who knew my feelings for Lori, blushed as if she were rooting for us to be together.

And then the bell rang, ending our fun. I lowered Lori, and our eyes met.

I wanted to say, "Look at how much fun we had in the hallway. Imagine what we could do on real date."

As I pick the clay off the board and file cabinet, I wonder what will happen with Lori when I return. One teacher at our school told me, "Timing, Ryan. Timing is everything." The truth is, if we had gotten together, I wouldn't be in Raupunga.

The next day, I notice a large brown smudge on the ceiling above the woodstove, more or less, where the possum urinated. It also looks like the ceiling is drooping a little. I've found the source of the smell. Something, probably possums, died in the attic. My chest tightens: I'm a killer of babies. We caught adult possums, so the brown splotch on the ceiling is most likely the remains of their litter. I tell the children about our blunder, but they have little sympathy. Australian possums are so invasive, so disliked, that the government puts out a bounty on them. A man from the New Zealand Fish and Game Council visited the school and distributed anti-possum literature, including a sticker that read *Possum Busters*. Theoretically, a kid could put himself through college by killing and skinning possums and catching and selling wild goats. No paper routes in these parts.

I tell Ernie, the father of the twins, about the puddle, and he makes a nasty foray into the attic after school. Later, when I see him, he hangs his head. "Ahh, bro," he says. "Ahh, bro..." I was right about the puddle.

Soon, the smell is completely gone, the pool is filled, and we bask in summer. The day of the first kapa haka festival arrives. The whole community pitches in with transportation and preparation. Women I've never seen before primp and fuss over every strand of hair; even the boys get some black lipstick. Beaded skirts click and sway, and the children mill about practicing their pukanas, those intense expressions that often include an outstretched tongue.

The amphitheatre is large and packed with over five hundred people. A local radio station has wired the stage with microphones and is airing the performances live. Children from more than a dozen schools are waiting to perform. As the junior class takes the stage, some of the older kids—joined by a few RPG community members—break into a haka right in the middle of the audience. No other school has done this, and I have never seen this particular haka. Later, I learn it was to let everyone know, "Hey! We are Ngati Pahauwera! Pay attention! This is what we are about!" One line in the haka details the tribal boundaries of Ngati Pahauwera—and its theft at the hands of white settlers. The boys rise from a chest-pounding kneel, raise both arms above their heads, slap their thighs, and throw a right fist, all while bellowing in unison.

"*Pahauwera! Maungaharuru! Ki uta! Tangi tu kit e moana!*"

Imagine if you attended a grammar school play in the States and a bunch of Native American kids suddenly started screaming a song about white people stealing their land. Someone would probably call the FBI and arrests would be made in the interest of national security.

The older children take the stage, and they're oozing self-worth. I wish I could bottle it and feed it to the boys on a daily basis. Their voices carry over the crowd's chatter and, at this distance, they appear to move as one, something I couldn't appreciate in the confines of the practice room. As they march off-stage, I notice that many of the boys are shaking, bloody crisscross scratches mark their chests from one of the actions. It gives me the chills. I'm beginning to understand the hearts and minds of the people whose land I've been living on.

After seeing so many people from Raupunga and the surrounding communities together at one time, I realize that, besides living in the area, most of them have no ties to the gangs. It's like my mom once told me: "Most of the time, people

Girls in Full Dress.

only remember when you screw up. They remember the bad things—not the good things." She was right, as usual. Invariably, when I've talked with people from neighboring towns, they've been less than complimentary about Raupunga:

"Why would you want to live there?"

"Lock the doors. They'll go shopping in your house when you aren't there."

And, my favorite: "I hope you have a good machete."

Lately, I've enlisted Mom's maxim in RPG's defense, and I refuse to let a few negative incidents shape my impression of Raupunga. Sure, I'll remember the madness, but I'll also remember returning home to find that someone had stacked firewood on my doorstep or that someone had left buckets of lamb hearts for Big Head. My bone-carving session with Rangi and the hook-shaped carving he gave me for my birthday will always bring a smile. And then there's goat busting, running with Kea to look for the foal, heading a roundup, the haka, and the children's laughter—those are the memories that will stay with me forever. This community could have easily shut me out, treated me like the outsider I am, but instead I've come to consider Raupunga my home away from home.

Nevertheless, there's no doubt of Black Power's influence on the kids. I can't help but wonder if there will be another all-on incident before I leave. As it turns out, I don't have to wonder for too long.

§

A few weeks later, I arrive home to see a man in a black leather jacket arranging tires against the corrugated metal fence of Arataki's house next door. The skies are gray and a steady drizzle has soaked through the man's flimsy hood, but he continues his work, his dripping face, stoic. He gets up on his tiptoes to adjust a tire, offering me a better look at his jacket. He's patched. Rangi isn't there, but Black Power members and prospects are congregating at his house. A kid with a blue bandana wrestles another tire onto a stack. I wouldn't be surprised if they started filling the tires with sand or dirt. Tonight, without a doubt, is a sleep-at-the-beach night.

"Heading to the beach to sleep!" I yell. "This is crazy!"

The man, whom I've met before, laughs and shakes his fist. Arataki is inside the house, probably, doing her homework. Just like normal.

This time, it was no accidental killing. It was a battle. A Black Power member died from a gunshot and Maka, the first man I met in Raupunga, lies in a coma—stabbed with a screwdriver. Like last time, the action took place in Wairoa, thirty minutes to the north.

About fifty people were involved in the brawl. For some reason—or lack thereof—the powers that be scheduled back-to-back court dates for Black Power and Mongrel Mob members. The result? Lots of red and blue colors in close proximity—all the reason in the world to start swinging, stabbing, and shooting. Police broke it up with pepper spray, and the Armed Offenders Squad flooded Wairoa. A Black Power member was fatally shot as he tried to escape the mêlée. Police have locked down the towns of Wairoa and Frasertown, and Rangi is stuck in Frasertown. No word on when he'll be allowed to come home. The man behind the fence, I'd guess, was probably tapped to watch over Arataki and her family in Rangi's absence.

Once again, the peaceful country is on hold.

I turn to Big Head and say, "You're a lucky boy. We're sleeping at the beach tonight."

I give him a couple of left hooks, and he growls, gnawing at my hand and shifting his head so I can reach his ears. I sigh and look at his toothy grin. I've been trying not to think about leaving Raupunga, but with only two months left in New Zealand, I'm starting to get anxious. How will I bring Baetis back? Is Big Head mine? He's flea-free now, and Baetis has stopped hissing at him. As I pull out of the driveway, I say a little prayer: "Please, he has to be mine."

Arataki's patched protector raises his fist again as I drive by. I'd let that guy stand guard for me any day. It makes me wonder. What would *I* do if Rangi's house was being attacked? Would I take up arms to defend it? What would I be able to do against guns? The thought of something happening to Arataki sickens me. If I heard screams, I'd have to act. Helping my neighbors fight off Mongrel Mob would have nothing to do with gangs. It would, however, have everything to do with love, which makes me think about something I'd read while perusing gang articles online: "Unity, identity, loyalty and reward are normal characteristics that are admired, but when associated with gangs they become distorted," Walter Miller and Malcolm Klein wrote in a study of gang culture.

I couldn't agree more. Maka was shot months ago while he sat in a car eating fish and chips. Did the shooter think he was being loyal to his colors? Did he feel like he'd gain the respect

Black Power man standing guard (behind fence).

of his people for shooting Maka? Where is the line? When does massive pride cross over into *distortion*? The Black Power guys stacking tires behind the fence brim with unity and loyalty. Isn't America simply showing pride and unity when it invades another nation? Or is my own government distorted? It's overwhelming. I need the beach—and a lung-searing run with Big Head.

When we head back to RPG the next morning, I learn that the police stopped carloads of Mongrel Mob members from passing through town. It's easy to picture how that might have gone down: the Mob, drunk and seeking revenge, would slow-roll through Raupunga, guns in hand, their laughter turning to anger, fingers moving to the triggers. They have an idea of where some Black Power members live, so they take a few potshots at the houses. Juiced with adrenaline, they start firing randomly at all the houses, even the peaceful white house with the blue trim—mine. The idea of it gives me the shivers, but there's nothing I can do about it. I turn on the hose and give my garden some love. My chard and bok choy wave to and fro in the morning breeze; I pick a few weeds and stretch, ready for another day in RPG.

The day passes without incident, but nighttime could be another story. After school, I pack for another night at the beach and make a hasty search for the kittens. I notice a few large plastic bags hidden under my house. Turning my head would be the wise thing to do, but wise and Mr. Chin don't always jibe. One bag, which weighs next to nothing, makes a crunching sound when I inspect it. I smile, squeezing it gently; the telltale aroma of marijuana wafts through the tightly tied top. The other bag is full of clothes, which puzzles me. I back out and look around. Seeing no one, I grab both bags and hurry inside. The crunchy bag holds more weed than I've ever seen in one place. There's enough in there, I figure, to put me in the realm of dealer, enough to land me in jail, enough to fund a year of travels, and more than enough to make me cackle madly. It'd be just like the TV show "Cops." As they cuff me and drag me off to jail, I'd shout into the camera, "It's not mine! I found it under my house!"

In the other bag, I find a Black Power leather jacket, a vest, and a couple of Black Power caps. I take pictures of the gang attire but, out of respect and fear, resist trying on any of the garments. Who knows what happens to unpatched people who pose in the real deal? Obviously, someone is afraid of having his house raided and needed to ditch the evidence. What better place to stash it than the teacher's house?

After two nights at the beach, I decide to sleep at the river instead. Vineyards line the roads north of Raupunga, many of them extending right down to the river's edge. One vineyard nestles into a grand, sweeping bend under a two-hundred-foot cliff which rises to the plateau above. After hard rains, fresh deposits of driftwood and pumice line the shore. I like to toss the stick for Big Head here. The sound of the river bounces off the cliff face, a perfect lullaby. Bedtime, though is hours away— I've got to prepare for a title fight. Big Head, already my archrival in boxing and wrestling, has challenged me to a stick fight.

Toss it under the teacher's house!

In the New Zealand spirit, I've made my own monopod out of plywood and a tree branch, which doubles as the staff I wield against Big Head, the greatest stick destroyer of all time. Our battle royale takes place on the grassy flat at the edge of the river, our private coliseum. "In this corner," the announcer booms, "weighing in at seventy-five pounds, Big Heeead, the merciless Stick Destroyer!"

He wastes no time, hurling his body into combat; I dodge and weave, twirling my staff behind my back and over my head, prodding and thrusting at his vulnerable areas. He leaps and lunges, relentless in his attack. Our battle ends like all the others, breathless with the joy of play.

A pickup pulls up to camp as I'm picking burrs out of Big Head's coat. It turns out to be the manager of the vineyards, Paul, who lives down the road. So impressive is his great, grizzly beard that I fear it could act as a sail and carry his scrawny body away. We talk gangs.

"Armed Offenders stopped me," he says with a chuckle, stroking the gray monster on his chin. "Thought I might be part of a gang—me!"

I see what he means. With his amiable grin and delicate spectacles balanced on the bridge of his fifty-something nose, he's the living embodiment of the word *nonthreatening*. We talk about the river and, as it turns out, he's a fly fisher. I tell him I've been sleeping at the beach to avoid potential crossfire and that I plan on sleeping here tonight. Okay with him, he says, so long as we head out fishing the next day.

We go out the next evening during the magic hour, a term fly fisherman use for the last hour of light, when insects hatch, trout feed, and the waning sun transforms the river's surface into a moving palette of golds and reds. I wade out into the river, watching the current reroute around my legs. Crimson swirls collect downstream from me, gradually flowing back into the main current.

Mayflies fill the air, their movements ordered and classy

in the way of organisms perfectly adapted to their environment. They dip repeatedly onto the river's slick surface, lay-
ing eggs to ensure the birth of the next generation. Trout rise
to feed, but not on the egg-laying mayflies. They're feeding
on something else, on some type of insect that's right below
the surface. The seasoned fly fisher, with his well-trained eye,
watches the *way* the trout feed, the character of their rise out
of the water. If the trout were feeding on the mayflies, their
rise would be splashy and aggressive. These trout are casually
sipping something, leaving just a hint of disturbance.

So I pick my fly accordingly, feeling purposeful. More trout
begin to feed, their snouts and dorsal fins barely breaking the
surface. I target the nearest dimple in the water and promptly
hook a rainbow trout. It leaps several times, peeling line from
the rod and through my fingertips. I guide the trout into the
net and marvel at the irony: over a century ago, the ancestors
of this rainbow trout were imported from Sonoma Creek, just
north of my home in San Francisco. As I release the fish, I
notice the fresh teeth marks on the net's walnut handle from
Big Head's latest chewing exploits. It triggers a rush of images: Toughy's gravesite, my arrival in New Zealand, the fate-
ful breakdown in Raupunga, the barefooted interview, my
encounter with Paul. In an instant, everything that brought
me to this time and place plays out on the river's mirrored
surface.

People fly-fish for all sorts of reasons. One of them is to escape from reality. I wouldn't call it escapism, exactly, because
I know there is no such thing as forgetting my problems. But
standing in a trout stream reminds me that everything is as it's
supposed to be. Bubbles form, rise, and disappear seamlessly,
and the intimate relationship between insects and trout plays
its chords. Life and death flow in unison. Sinking or swimming, it's all part of being. And that's easy to forget—so I go
fishing as often as I can.

An ageless bellow of laughter echoes off the canyon walls,

breaking my gaze from the river's surface. I slosh to the bank and run to find Paul landing a nice trout. We high-five like we're old friends except, of course, we're not. We just met yesterday, and all because it wasn't safe to sleep at my house. Later that evening, we dine with his wife and share fly-tying secrets. They insist I take their spare bedroom for the night. Everything happens for a reason.

The next morning I receive word of a miracle: Maka has come out of his coma. Rangi is back home, no doubt happy to see the latest work on the fence. The police have dismantled their roadblocks; the tangi (Maori funeral) for the dead Black Power man is over, his assailants behind bars. This all-on chapter, it seems, is done.

It's been an eventful week, even for the people of Raupunga. Now it's time for Baetis to add to the week's events. I still haven't seen her kittens, so I scour the neighborhood, crawling under the house again and poking my head into the many car bodies dotting the area. No luck. Her ravenous appetite and long nipples, though, reassure me. It's been well over a month, so her kittens must be charging around by now, mini-feline bundles of energy.

While she eats, I make a nest in my surfboard bag with a piece of foam and a few old shirts. Then I carry her to the back room and show her what I've done.

"This is for your family," I tell her. "Don't worry about Big Head. This is your room. Bring the kitties here, okay? Bring them here," I urge her, patting the nest and her head at the same time.

She kneads the foam for a second and darts off.

"Bring 'em back!" I yell as her rump disappears out the window.

The next morning I hear the plank bouncing under her weight. I look for her in the kitchen, expecting her to stroll in as usual, demanding food and a head rub, but she never appears. Instead, her steps fade away to the back room where I made the nest. Soon, a high-pitched meow shoots down the hall and I scramble to meet my grandkitties.

There are two of them; a ginger kitten and a tabby resembling Baetis lie curled up in my surfboard bag. I wonder if some of the litter was lost to predators or if these two were the only ones to survive the birth. Baetis uncurls for a second as if she wants me to get a better look, and the kittens lose their hold on her nipples, beginning to whimper. I collapse to the floor and embrace them all. We lie like that for a while, one big happy family.

Once the feeding is finished, I stroke the kittens more vigorously. They push into my hand, unalarmed. The tabby is especially spunky and swats at my finger. The ginger kitten, however, wobbles away precariously. Her large forehead and widely spaced eyes are sure signs that something isn't right. My first thought is that she'll have to be put to sleep, but then I remember the rule I made when Toughy was dying: when he can no longer have fun, then it's time. As if she knows what I'm thinking, the ginger kitten rears up on her hind legs, boxing at Baetis's tail. She swings a right hook, then a left, and then topples over into the clothing pile, her momentum rolling her right back into suckling position as if that's what she intended to do all along. As I laugh, my skin erupts in goosebumps; I gaze down at her for a few long seconds before I turn away from the nest.

"As long as you're having fun," I say with a sigh.

Big Head barks away in the other room, apparently jealous. I chuckle and rub his head extra hard. It's getting busy around here.

The kittens provided a temporary distraction, but now I'm back to fussing over the latest incident. Despite the return to normalcy, I'm having trouble sleeping. I keep working it over in my head, trying to figure out where I stand on gang culture. There's something gnawing at me, a new feeling that I can't yet articulate. But something in me is changing.

Good job Momma!

Big Head and I roll toward the school, never taking Lonna out of first gear. I imagine the land around me as it must have been centuries ago, without houses, without railroad tracks, without the outhouse covered in graffiti. I see the land with just the pa, the Maori fortress, built by a proud people who have never been conquered. The school, remember, is built on an old pa sight. Kea's ancestors, in fact, donated the land for the school. Blood may have been spilled right here in the parking lot. My gaze shifts to the school's play structure, to the rugby field, and to the rolling hills beyond. The children don't just live on this land. For many, it is *their* land. I exhale and shake my head.

The cold, dew-soaked grass worms up between my bare toes. Then the grass dissolves into mud and I'm standing in the rice paddies in a village in China—*my* roots. What if I lived on the land where my ancestors had lived? What if my ancestors had fought battles to defend it? What if colonization had brought decimation and oppression to my people? What sort of pride would I have? I might be deeply angry, profoundly in need of a sense of identity. I'd probably need to belong, to feel like I owned something. Add in the economic woes, the broken families—would certain values of mine be *distorted*? I'd definitely be part of a gang if I grew up here.

I chain Big Head up for the day, a little wiser, maybe, and with a greater understanding of how the latest madness came to be.

Today we'll paint the props for our play, *Maui and the Sun*. Kea plays Maui, saving us all from eternal darkness. I've already written the script, so the kids recite their lines together, as a group. This strength-in-numbers approach takes some of the individual pressure off the children. Arataki wants to narrate again. It's a perfect role for her—being in charge and moving the performance along. One day, I'm sure, she'll take on that role in the community.

I've cut out a gigantic cardboard sun that will hang on a rope and pulley (high-tech, I know). I lay it on a large tarp along with orange, yellow, and red paint. The children take turns kneeling and brushing sunshine onto the tarp. For a while all is peaceful, with the children united by a common cause. The twins, their motor skills rapidly developing, swirl the paints around with their tiny hands. Arataki paints the shape of a *koru*, the Maori pattern that mimics an unraveling fern. I kneel with them, overwhelmed by a sort of early onset nostalgia. This will be our last production. I hope they will remember it—and remember me. Soon, though, the kids pop my bubble, reminding me that they live in a very different world.

"It's my turn!"

"No, I just started!"

"Move! I'm here now!"

Fairness may rule the minds of children, but it can ruin the lives of adults. The older I get, the more comfortable I am with the unfairness of life. As the children battle over who gets to paint a certain piece of cardboard, I see a hole in a door and, through that hole, a small bedroom with blue carpeting.

I-Gaw and I shared a bedroom until I was nine years old. A flimsy, hollow door was the entrance to our battleground. I knew it was hollow, because Dad lost his temper during one of our struggles and kung-fu chopped a hole in it. After he did it, I got on a chair to look into the hole, expecting to find something spectacular.

Every time I walked into that room, I saw that hole in the door, a reminder of something. Was it a reminder to learn to share? Did it remind me to respect my brother? Did I realize how fortunate I was to share a room with my only sibling at the time? I know this now, of course, but the only thing I knew at the time was that Dad—one of the most levelheaded men I've ever known—had a pretty mean backhand chop. We must have been really going at it to make him that angry.

Immediately inside, and to the right of the door, was our bunk bed, complete with roomy headboards perfect for securing our favorite Hot Wheels cars. My headboard housed my double-decker Hot Wheels suitcase (all of the cars were my favorites) and a fishing magazine. *Star Wars* sheets covered our mattresses. On the opposite wall sat my desk, a dresser that we shared, and I-Gaw's desk. The five drawers in the dresser were split evenly—no arguments.

The rest of the room, however, was nothing less than a turf war, ever-shifting property lines creased into carpet with toes or fingers. Some days required acrobatics. Keeping my feet on my bed, I'd reach across I-Gaw's property, put my hands down on my property, and open my dresser drawer. Similarly, exiting the room was always a project for one of us. Some days, I'd have to crawl out the back of my headboard and do a crotch-splitting jump into the hallway, with the springs on the bunks squeaking while the frame bounced against the wall. When I owned the front-door property, I-Gaw had to leap from his top bunk and angle it just right so he'd hit the hallway carpet. I protested when he put his feet on my headboard, but in the end his vote counted more than mine; he was my older and, more importantly, *bigger* brother. One time he calculated wrong and nailed his head on the doorjamb. I remember feeling bad but, hey, fair is fair.

Kea speaks up. "Here," he says, handing a brush to Rachel. "I don't want to do this. I want to paint my *mere*."

Suddenly, nobody wants to paint the sun. Instead, they all want to paint their cardboard meres, a close-combat weapon shaped like a small paddle that Maori warriors once used.

I restore order. "Listen up! I want Arataki and Hoera to finish painting the sun. The rest of you can paint your meres or practice your lines. Got it?"

After school, I set the props out in the sun to dry. Even after four years in the classroom, I'm still amazed at the instant quiet, the serenity that settles over a school within minutes of the children's departure. Big Head hops out of the van, knowing that the kids' absence means it's time to run. We'll hit the beach as usual, but first we'll pay a visit to Maka.

Ike is pacing back and forth on Maka's porch when we arrive. His head is shaved, and his black jacket is three sizes too big, but that's the style. He's a new face in the village, a cousin of a cousin—or something like that. He almost never walks in a straight line, waves his arms a lot, and talks to himself. I don't know if he's patched, but he loves flashing the Black Power fist, and he loves RPG. Like the kids, he calls me Mistah Chnn. Yesterday, he came by the school while I was teaching science to the older kids. Upon seeing a vacant seat, he sat right down. This amused everybody, but given the rumors I'd heard about him—an addiction to sniffing gasoline, his recent release from jail—I decided to play it cool.

"What's up, Ike?" I said, hoping he wouldn't create a scene. "We're learning about sound waves. You're welcome to join us. Just raise your hand like everybody else if you have something to say."

Poor Ike. All he wanted was a little attention, so he nodded, folded his hands, and sat up in his chair. His mostly toothless grin lasted only a second, giving way to a look of studious concentration. The kids laughed, and I continued with the lesson.

Now, as I make my way to Maka's door, Ike greets me like an old friend. "Mistah Chnn! Wuzz up? Black Power! Black Power!" he chimes out in a good-natured way.

"Hey, Ike. Learn anything yesterday?"

"Ahh, man, I wish yooz wuz my teacher when I wuz in school."

"Thanks, Ike. That makes me feel good. Maybe you can go back to schoo—"

Uninterested in my motivational ramblings, Ike jumps the railing and runs out to the side yard, swinging his arms in big circles. There's a black sheep tied to a stake, a gift to Maka from another family. Ike dances around it, one black sheep to another. Before I can get too deep into that line of thought, Maka appears at the door. It's been just over a year since I first met him at this very spot. He's moving a little slower than usual. A puncture wound and a coma will do that to a man, I guess, even one as tough as Maka.

"Yo, Maka, just wanted to see how you're doing, mate."

"It was a rough go, mate," he says, lifting his arm with a grimace.

"Crazy! You know, I have to get a few pics." I raise my hand as though I'm introducing him and shout: "The first man I met in RPG, ladies and gentlemen—shot, stabbed, and in and out of a coma during my time here."

The Tabby taking a break from playing with Ms. Ginger.

He begins to laugh, but then stops abruptly. Laughing hurts. I take a few shots of the small entry wound. There are still stitches sticking out of the divot, but it isn't all that impressive from the outside. Apparently, the screwdriver made it all the way to his lung. He's lucky to be alive.

Speaking of living, the ginger kitty—or Ms. Ginger, as I've started calling her—continues to amaze me. Her balance worsens by the day, but she persists at *living*, at doing everything normal kittens do, albeit a little clumsier. The kittens spend a lot of time romping in the garden. I weed and prune while Ms. Ginger ambles through crimson stalks of chard, unaware that a hunter is stalking her. Crouching low behind the deep green spinach, the tabby shuffles his paws, his tail whipping back and forth. Then he lunges, taking down his weaker sister. Together, they roll into the thyme and basil. Unable to restrain myself, I give them a misting from the hose. They dart in through the open door, continuing their escapades inside, and I capture the family on videotape. Ms. Ginger sways back and forth, contemplating a leap from a rock. Tiptoeing across the fireplace step, she wallops a twig, and prances over to Mom for her favorite activity: tail hunting. Baetis saunters away with Ms. Ginger in pursuit, falling, rolling, and stumbling, doing whatever she needs to do to move forward.

A few weeks later, the inevitable comes—a trip to the vet is finally in order. Ms. Ginger's neck muscles strain to support her head, and her tiny legs crumble under her weight. I carry her over to Baetis and the tabby for farewells. It makes me cry, but it inspires me too. Her existence was brief, but she had plenty of time for fun. She didn't know how long or how short her life would be and, come to think of it, none of us really do.

CHAPTER
13

THE BEST SANDWICH

I RAISE A SACK above my head and body-slam it to the ground. Big Head, not wanting to be left out, joins in the beating, his jaws locking onto the burlap sack while he holds it steady with his paws. I push him away, turn the sack upside down and shake it violently. Finally, the contents of the bag plop onto the walkway in a moldy brown pile. The concrete steams, and an earthy tang fills the air. My plants will love their new food.

As I split the rain-cemented sheep pellets into smaller pieces, the tabby kitten crouches under the bok choy and chard, the sun warming his fur and lending his blue eyes a green hue. I catch him searching for Ms. Ginger. Just a few days ago, she was bouncing off the colorful stalks as if they were pinball bumpers while he waited in ambush. Who would have thought a one-pound bundle of fur could make such an impact? I shoo the tabby away, working the fertilizer into the soil surrounding the thriving plants. Summer is exploding all around me, and I've been going shirtless, hanging out at the pool, getting sunburned, walking with bare feet on the hot pavement and, of course, working in the garden, which is yielding more than I could possibly eat.

I snap the largest stalks off the chard and pinch the seedpods off the top of the basil, rolling the last one in my fingers and savoring the smell. My great grandma, *Bok Bok*, (Chinese for "great grandma") would be proud of this garden. I can still see her face: lips pursed, eyes intent on the task but blank at the same time. She raises her shovel and yells at me because my errant football has crushed some of her plants. Bok Bok tended a garden in our backyard when we lived in Chicago's Chinatown. On the good days, she was merely glum; on the bad days, she was angry and glum. Her head hung low, and her feet skidded along the ground like some dehydrated survivor just staggering out of the desert. As a kid I never thought to ask why she was so melancholy.

Like many of my relatives, she never learned English. And unfortunately, my Chinese was never good enough to carry on a real conversation with her. Needless to say, our communication lacked details. As I've gotten older, I've learned to appreciate the hard work my ancestors did, and I've tried to learn more about them through my parents. Bok Bok's husband, I discovered, left her for another woman. Culturally, he was not in the wrong, and Bok Bok blamed herself for not being a good enough wife. Even her peers shamed her. By the time I entered the picture, she was consumed by self-pity and had chosen to sleep under the stairs at my grandpa's house. If only I had the wisdom and communication skills when she was alive to tell her, "You are a great woman who still has a loving family. Forget that guy!"

The garden was her escape, a slice of satisfaction in a world where smiles were hard to come by. Her life taught me that regret and self-pity, though normal, can destroy a person. I know now to allow those feelings but not to dwell on them. She's been gone for over a decade. My garden in Raupunga, in this land far from Chicago and far from our roots in China, grows in memory of her.

The tabby resumes his position under the canopy of leaves, unbothered by the musky smell of the compost. He burrows into the new layer of soil, carving out an indentation to fit his body. Satisfied with his work, he yawns and rests his chin on a large and fibrous chunk of cow dung, utterly at peace. I need some of that relaxation too; it's time to hit the hot springs.

Upon seeing my overnight backpack, Big Head jumps into the van, excited for the trip. I'm excited too, but as I'm locking up the house the reality of my impending departure dawns on me: I won't be around to pick the new crop of oranges and lemons, and I won't have time for a pet goat. Once I leave, it could be many years, possibly decades, before I return to Raupunga. By then, the children will have their own children, and maybe my white house with the blue trim will be gone. Over in the passenger seat Big Head sighs heavily. Perhaps he too knows that his time here might be limited. Probably not. Soon, his head begins to sway with the curving road, flecks of drool dropping down to the hair-covered plaid seat. I, on the other hand, am feeling far from my usual laid-back self. I've got a lot on my mind.

Thankfully, the parking lot is empty; I could use the solo time. As I trudge up the winding path, I contemplate the offer I've received to stay on for another two quarters. No matter how hard I try, I can't envision another six months in Raupunga. It just doesn't feel right. It's time to go home. Soon I come upon the tumbling stream and, beyond that, the bathhouse. The steam wafting off the top of the pools welcomes me back, like Mom calling me to come in the house at the end of the day. I slip into the tub, hoping to turn off my mind, but even the soothing water can't rinse away the anxiety. There's the logistical flotsam associated with moving: How will I ship my belongings home? How much should I sell Lonna for, and who will buy her? I need to close my bank account, cancel my utilities, clean both the classroom and the house before I leave town. But then there's the big stuff. Is Big Head mine? How will I get him and Baetis home? Are people mad at me because I'm not staying? They shouldn't be. I told them when I started that it was just for the year. It's all too much.

I exit the hot pool abruptly, trying to outrun my worries. A dunk in the cold stream, with its jolting, body-wide tingle, brings me back to the moment. I can feel the sand and organic matter swirling through the water, brushing my skin. My serenity doesn't last long. Within a few minutes, I'm back to planning, making mental notes to bring my camera next time, my mind awash in dozens of pictures and video shots I wish to capture before my departure. I'm overscheduled, pushed to the max, so what do I do? Add something else to the schedule, of course.

Those who know me would expect nothing else. How can I pass up an invitation to visit Matanuku and Linda, both of whom teach carving and weaving classes? My pumice carving has come a long way, and I'm eager to try my hand at a more substantial medium. As it turns out, they're hosting a weekend class, and they live just across from the hot springs, a streamside slice of New Zealand's best.

When I pull up to their property, two alpacas are glaring back at me. Actually, they couldn't care less about me, but they stamp and snort at Big Head, letting him know who's in charge around here. Next to a relatively new barn stand a couple modest houses and a church-like building with large windows. Some open doors invite me in, and I stroll over for a look, the alpacas following my every move. Inside, everything is covered with a fine layer of dust, and large pieces of sandstone line the tables. All the sandstone pieces, I notice, have depressions in them. Without thinking, I step forward and slide my fingers along the nearest one. It is cool to the touch but feels alive at the same time. A car crunches gravel; Linda and Matanuku have arrived.

Linda tells me where to stand and to stay still while Matanuku prepares a ritual to welcome me onto their land. He stands tall, holding a *taiaha*, a Maori weapon that looks like a combination of a spear and a long sword. My eyes widen at this display, but I resist fidgeting. The purpose of so many

Maori rituals, I've learned, is to test your mettle, to look into your being. As Matanuku grunts and swings the taiaha with controlled snapping movements, his eyes turn glassy, nearly popping from his skull. His swipes and jabs are passing within a foot of my face, but I stand true and even half consider grabbing the weapon from him. With one final grunt, he turns his back and kicks dirt behind him, a signal for me to follow him.

Matanuku wants me to *feel* the stone changing shape, so I am not allowed to use any power tools or even modern files. I use the ancient method of rubbing my piece of *pounamu* (the Maori word for "greenstone") on wet sandstone. I lose myself in the process; the rhythmic scouring sounds have a presence much like the flowing waters of a river. Over the course of the weekend, my rectangular piece of stone takes on a teardrop shape. I use nothing but my hands, water, and a stone. "Allow a shape to reveal itself," Matanuku tells me. Greenstone is one of the hardest stones on earth; it was used for making knives in ancient times. Shaping a hard stone with a softer stone for many hours calms both my breath and my mind.

All that stone rubbing burns a lot of calories, so Matanuku and Linda prepare a *hangi*, a Maori method of preparing food. They dig a deep pit and heat rocks over a large fire, where they then place food-laden baskets. Then they cover the baskets with leaves, wet burlap, and soil for a few hours to allow the earth's sweetness to permeate the meat and vegetables. The hot stones hold the heat and slowly bake the food; they are aptly named hangi stones. They are sometimes used for decades, but they must be chosen carefully; they can explode when heated. Large pieces of iron, such as railroad ties, can be substituted for the stones.

I watch the process carefully, making mental notes so I can prepare a hangi for my friends on the beach in San Francisco. Big Head watches from the back of the van and lifts his nose when I finally sit down with a plate of wild boar, cabbage, and *kumara* (Maori sweet potato). The meat falls apart in my mouth, and the kumara tastes like candy. Between bites, I rub my tear-drop-shaped greenstone, turning it over and over between my fingers. Force and strength have their place, but persistence, consistency, and a freeness of spirit can shape a stone. I add this practice to my growing bank of wisdom, right alongside *just change the blade.* This weekend was just what I needed.

On the way home, I notice long lines of waves stacked to the horizon. In surf lingo, it's pumping. As I pull up to a beach to check the conditions, gales rock Lonna from side to side. Balls of sea foam roll along the windswept sand, disappearing as fast as the crashing waves can replenish them. The grass on the adjacent hills lies flat from the wind, swirling and swaying like strings of algae in a river. Clouds race along the sky, chasing their shadows across the ocean. As Big Head and I step out of Lonna, a strong gust rips the door handle out of my hand, and the door narrowly misses Big Head's tail. Unaware of the close call, he charges head-on into the rushing air, biting at one stick, then another, and pawing at every log within reach. I lean into the wind, watching the sloppy waves crash against the steeply angled beach.

The conditions are too raw for surfable waves today, but tomorrow could be the day I've been waiting for. Often, the same storm that created the waves makes for unfavorable conditions at the beach because of the wind. Tomorrow the storm will have moved on, but its energy will live in the waves. Maybe, just maybe, they will roll over the right sandbar at the right angle during the right tide. And I'll be there to ride them. For months, I've been watching a long curving sandbar build steadily at the mouth of the Mohaka River. If it survives this storm, it could produce surfable waves. My mind is filled with anticipation of what could be, of what can be, and of how things mostly aren't but occasionally are. So I will get up at five thirty tomorrow to check on the waves at Mohaka, a place I've visited daily for almost a year. What a shame if I'm not there when the ocean wants to dance.

I notice a wall of rain in the eastern sky and the sun striving to find a hole in the clouds. I scream for Big Head to follow me up a steep hill. Seizing the moment and catching it just right consumes me in many different ways. Sometimes a good hatch of insects on a stream lasts only ten minutes, during which time the trout feed ravenously and often selectively. Not only do you have to be there with the right fly, but you also have to make the right casts. And, of course, there's the fresh powder I seek on my snowboard, the untracked, chest-deep fluff. I've also started trying to catch rainbows.

After studying the clouds' movements, the location of the sun, and the size of the raindrops, I try to position myself in the right place to watch a rainbow materialize. When I hit it just right, the clouds part, a rainbow pastes itself to the center of my vision, and I'm reminded all over again of the brevity of beauty. It's not quite as exhilarating as tucking myself inside the tube of a wave, but I'll take it. The rainbow eludes me today, as a formidable bank of dark storm clouds obstructs the sun just when the wall of rain is in the perfect place. Perhaps I'll fare better tomorrow.

Between the carving, the wind, and the prospects of a morning surf at Mohaka, I've managed to bury my anxiety about leaving. As the Kiwis say, I'm sorted. We roll into my driveway just as darkness falls.

Big Head strolls into the house and collapses under the table, resting his head on a dustpan. He ignores Baetis and the tabby, seeming to understand that they are part of the family and harassing them will get him in trouble. Despite his occasional attempts to kill sheep, he's a pleaser. Baetis and the tabby join me in bed. Wishing to bring the whole family together, I call Big Head over. With heavy paws he crosses the room and rests his chin on the edge of the bed. Baetis rises to her feet to place herself between him and the tabby.

"It's okay, girl. He's going to be your brother," I say without even thinking.

Lowering herself into a crouched position, she pushes her head and body into my hand. She kneads the sheets, readying her claws for action, but she doesn't hiss or bare her teeth. If she could speak, I'm certain she'd scold me: *First the house, now the bed!* I sit up and invite Big Head onto the other side of the bed while continuing to rub Baetis's head. He jumps up, sighs, and sprawls onto his side. Sandwiched between my smelly dog on one side and my first cat and grandkitty on the other, I slip into a deep sleep right away.

I awaken to hisses, yelps, barking, and a sharp pain on my cheek: my kids are fighting! Furious, I shoo Baetis and the tabby away and yell, "Off, boy! Get off!" Big Head drops his head and reluctantly steps down. Taking one step away from the futon, he looks over his shoulder, forehead wrinkled and eyes drooping.

Everything about him says, *Dad, it's not my fault.*

My guess is that Big Head shifted in his sleep and Baetis, the protective-mother-warrior, feeling threatened, unleashed her claws. My face was caught in the crossfire. Luckily, the scratch on my cheek isn't very deep, and she didn't get my eye. Not wanting to play favorites, I scold both of them one more time before turning the lights out.

I don't remember them returning to bed, but when my alarm sounds, I'm sandwiched once again between my yellow Lab and two cats.

There's still a faint glow on the horizon as we leave the house. The trees, leaves, and every blade of grass sit idly in the morning chill. Just as I predicted, the wind does not affect the waves this morning. I have no inkling what tide works best for surfing the Mohaka River mouth and no idea if the sandbar survived the storm. All I can do is go check it. Big Head paces back and forth, seemingly in disbelief that we are going to the beach so early. Once he feels the washboard rumble from the dirt road, he stands to attention, ready to burst through the door.

Sharks lurk in the shallows of my mind. There isn't a soul in sight. Even the hills, normally dotted with sheep, are bare. No one would hear my screams. At the river mouth, a plume of silty freshwater cuts into the ocean's deep blue. Sharks, I know, often use the transition from clear to murky water as ambush points. My heart rises to my throat. I hate crowded surf spots, but this morning I wouldn't mind sharing the odds and giving the sharks a *choice*. A set of waves appear and the glassy ocean leaps to attention. A decent wave breaks over the sandbar. The ocean has sent me gifts to ride; besides, I could use a shower.

"Listen, boy, I'm going surfing. You stay with the van. Let someone know what happened to Mr. Chin if he gets eaten." I'm only half-kidding. Big Head cocks his head, unused to the length of my instructions: *Hey, Pops*, he might as well be saying, *if it's anything besides "come here," "sit down," or "good boy," I don't understand what the hell you're talking about!*

I quickly slip on my dank wetsuit, giddy as a kid on his birthday, and splash into the river, letting the heavy current push me out to sea. Even if I wanted to turn around, I couldn't. With miles of beach on either side of the river, though, I know I can eventually make my way back to shore. The first rays of the sun blast over the horizon, covering the hills in gold and making the water glimmer. I'm out past the swirling currents, paddling effortlessly, my board slicing through the mirrored surface.

A set of waves approaches, the biggest I've seen, and I stroke hard, getting in position to drop into one. The "drop" is the crucial point at which a surfer stands and slides down the face of a cresting wave. I execute the drop and experience Mohaka like never before, weaving up and down a perfectly peeling head-high wave. The wave has traveled many miles and here, at the end of its life, we share some time. All worries of sharks are gone now; I paddle harder and catch one more wave of equal quality before calling it quits. I will have the patience of an angel at school today.

In the classroom, even the children can sense something different about me.

"Mistah Chnn, why are you smiling so much?" Kea asks.

"I surfed Mohaka Beach this morning. It was awesome!"

"I didn't know you could surf there."

"Sometimes it just comes together, Kea."

"Did anyone see you? I want to watch you surf. That'd be mean as!"

In some ways I would have loved a witness, but some memories aren't meant to be shared. Any recollection other than the one in my head might take away from the sacredness of what transpired this morning.

"No, it was just me," I answer. "But maybe I'll let you know next time."

Kea surfs through the room, sliding his hand up and down an imaginary wave. Then he sits at his cluttered desk, opens his journal, and begins work on a drawing of a horse. I watch his determined face, his hand moving in short controlled strokes, while all around him the class chatters quietly. I squeeze my lips together as tears well up; I'm going to miss these little guys. As much as I find myself contemplating the children's futures these days, I've made a conscious choice to be vague in my images. Their futures are theirs to determine, not mine. Improving their reading and instilling a love of learning, however, can't hurt. *Maui and the Sun* is ready for its debut.

I ask them to form a circle on the rug. "Quickly, quickly!"

"Look, Mistah Chnn," Kea calls out. "I'm moving quickly, but I'm not running."

"That's the one," I reply, nodding.

The twins bounce in unison over to the rug, their pigtails swaying in perfect opposites. Finally, I've gotten a handle on the art of teaching different ages at the same time. Rachel, the class's first new entrant, has taken on a sort of leadership role by showing the new kids what she's learned. I smile as she stops at the shapes poster to demonstrate her geometry prowess.

"This is a square," she explains, her large brown eyes twinkling. "And this is a circle."

"That's a circle too," chimes Will, pointing at a poster Rachel made months ago.

He's right, so I say, "Hey, Will, maybe tomorrow you guys can make your own shapes posters."

Kapa haka transformed Rachel from a shy five-year-old to one brimming with confidence. I explain the plan for the rest of the day, which will culminate in the class performing *Maui and the Sun* for the senior class.

"Aww, do we have to, Mistah Chnn?" Arataki complains.

"It'll be good practice," I respond. "There will be even more people on graduation night in the audience. Think about how hard you have worked on this. Look at the props, the sun, and the other paintings. You guys don't even need your note cards anymore because you know your lines."

"Maybe we should give ourselves a round of applause," she suggests.

And with that, the circle disintegrates in a fit of clapping and giggling. We regroup by the door and make our way to the Whanau Room for rehearsal. The class has four five-year-olds now, and the play serves up perfect doses of oral language practice, art, collaborative skills and, most importantly, the joy of a good story.

The afternoon presents a challenge different from the paddle out this morning. I take a deep breath, prepping my patience for the boys. Since the last all-on event, they've been gripped by gang fever. One of the boys bleached RPG onto the back of his head, and despite our efforts to keep Black Power's raised-fist sign off school grounds, the boys flash it to each other and doodle it on their desks and notebooks. Fighting gangs, I realize, isn't so different from fighting terrorism. You can't beat an ideology simply by telling people it's no good. You have to give them more opportunities, alternative choices.

Jude, a stocky and brash boy, struts across the room, bragging about the money he will make once he is patched.

"Bro," he crows while holding his crotch, "I'm gonna have me a flash car with flash rims. Huh, Mistah Chnn?"

"Yeah, sure, Jude."

What can I say? This is just like when I experimented with being mean in middle school. There's no stopping the boys' involvement with gangs. The extent of their involvement, though, remains to be seen. The gang—like a church or any community group, I've realized—provides support in times of need. What they say about families holds true with gangs: twice the happiness and half the pain. That said, the communal aspects of gang life often seem to take a backseat to the business opportunities. As Jude's comment shows, the dynamics of gangs are changing as drugs and money become increasingly big factors. As Ross Kemp noted in his seminal documentary, *Ross Kemp on Gangs*, "When money takes over, loyalty, honor and respect can go out the window." I believe it. Money can do disturbing things to good people.

So who knows what will happen? Renegade-maverick attitudes can be good. If everyone followed protocol, this world would be a boring place, and nothing would ever change. Since it's my last time with the older kids, I decide to give them a little sermon.

"Hey, guys, everyone over here. Mr. Chin has something to say," I begin, trying to be as matter-of-fact as possible. The boys slowly make their way to the middle of the room, some of them rolling their eyes. "Well, sometimes it wasn't easy, but I've enjoyed my time with you older students," I begin, locking eyes with Kahu for a second. "You guys were amazing with the haka—I mean, really cool stuff. I learned a thing or two about pride and what it means to be Maori. And you know that feeling you had after you performed? You can repeat that feeling by accomplishing other goals. I can't tell you what to do, but I really hope you go on to a university. You know, check out something new. Whatever you do, just be a good human and be happy. My dad told me that in high school. Oh, yeah, and one more thing," I say, pausing to look at each boy in the room. "Use your head, man!"

"Use your head, man!" a few of the boys repeat in unison. They might forget everything else I just said, but I'm confident they'll remember that.

I've said my piece. I step back, and the boys return to their car-pimping fantasies.

Later at the beach, with coarse sand massaging my feet and Big Head frolicking in the waves, I find myself repeating Dad's words. *Just be a good human.* It's such a simple mantra, yet so easy to forget while pursuing individual dreams. My grandpa taught my father this way of living through example.

Grandpa's generosity saved him from persecution when the Communists took over. After World War II, people all over China pointed fingers and sought retribution. If you treated people badly, then you were a target when Mao took power. My great grandparents, on my mom's side, were hauled off to labor camps for treating their subordinates poorly.

It's easy to imagine a caravan of government cars parading down the narrow muddy streets of the villages. Some people looked out barred windows, around corners, and through cracked doors. For many, this was the day they'd been awaiting to even the score. Officials in perfectly pressed coats stepped out of their cars, straightened their hats, and waited for information. The rich, and those in power, were the first to go.

Grandpa, however, had nothing to worry about even though he was a wealthy man. He'd summoned doctors when neighbors were ill and treated everyone with respect; no one turned him in. His caring and contagious smile saved him and our family. Just another reminder of karma and to treat people how you want to be treated.

With so little time left, a sense of urgency has come over me. I've doubled my collection of pumice, sticks, and logs in recent days, soaking my favorites in a bleach mixture and drying them out in the oven. My plan calls for bringing a couple boxes of sticks and stones back with me. The long summer days allow me to visit both the beach and the big bend in the river where I met Paul, owner of the bushiest beard in the world. Today, I decide to scour the river first, partly to see if Big Head will remember his encounter with "the monster."

On our last visit, the monster—an electric fence—shocked him. I could empathize, as an electric fence stunned me earlier in the year. While fishing one weekend, I crossed a seemingly vacant field when, suddenly, a large bull appeared over a rise. We locked eyes in a classic high-noon stare.

"Just passing through," I assured him as I eased toward a fence line. "You the man."

In response, he snorted and stamped. I swear I could feel the tremors despite the soft grass under my thick-soled wading boots. My cautious slink toward the fence quickly became a full sprint, and I tossed my fly rod over as I ran. I grabbed the top of a post with my left hand, stepped onto the lower wire, gripped the top wire with my right hand and immediately toppled backwards onto the ground—victim of a two-hundred-and-twenty-volt shock. I felt limp and a little dazed, but there was no time for pain. I popped up, grabbed the top of the wooden post with both hands, and flung myself over. The experience left me so out of sorts that I considered gripping the fence with my other hand to restore my equilibrium.

When Big Head had his run-in, he yelped and howled like I'd never heard before, and he shivered the whole way home. He doesn't know about electrical currents, of course; all he knows is that something near the river caused him extreme pain. As we rumble down the narrow track leading to the river's bend, he stiffens up as if he were a child entering a doctor's office for vaccinations. I can't help but laugh.

"Who's afraid of the monster?" I chide. "Big Head! Big Head is afraid of the monster!"

By now, there's a doomed feeling in the van, a sense of impending disaster heightened by the gray sky, the muddy river, the slow thumping sound of Lonna's tires on the washboard road, and Big Head's increased panting.

I fling the door open and run toward the electric fence. Normally, Big Head would be leading the charge or at least glued to my heels. Today he just sits there next to the van, like the lone kid who watches his friends enter the abandoned house, too afraid to join them. The scaredy-cat.

Trying to downplay his fear, he gives me a ho-hum look. *You go on, Dad. I don't feel like playing today.*

I hop the fence and call to him. He can't take it: Dad down by the river, all those sticks begging to be chewed. He charges full-speed for the bank, bouncing through the tall grass, ready to meet his tormentor.

"You can do it, boy!" I yell.

Then he pulls up short, his eyes fixed on the one-eighth-inch galvanized wire. He scans the length of the wire, looking for a weakness, but sees nothing to inspire confidence. He doubles back to the van to regroup as I continue my encouragement. A few moments later, he explodes through the grass, threading his body under the wire and gliding down to the river.

And then he lets loose: sand is flung, sticks are mutilated, and large quantities of drool are produced. I can't wait for him to meet my friends and their dogs. He will race Po the Chesapeake Bay retriever, wrestle with Nanuk the great white

Samoan, maybe romance Cocoa the boxer. Big Head's Kiwi accent is sure to impress the females. And Lori, of course, will love him. In her last e-mail, she offered to let me stay with her until I find a place—another reason I want to get home as soon as possible.

But I'm getting ahead of myself. *Easy, Chin. The dog's not really yours, and you don't know what's up with Lori. She'd offer up her place to any of her friends.*

By now, Big Head has his confidence back; he leaps over the fence one way and immediately dives back under it the other way. After repeating the routine several times, he stops and sits just inches from it.

I've got you figured out, he seems to say. And now it's time to hit the beach.

The unusually heavy spring rains have swollen the river, bringing fresh driftwood down to the beach. I've been gathering logs so big lately that Lonna creaks and groans when I load them into her belly. We wander the beach for hours on end. I pick up a piece of driftwood, knowing it has a story.

Before humans lived in New Zealand, the moa, a now-extinct giant bird, dropped seeds into the dirt. One of these seeds had the perfect location; sunlight squeezed through the forest canopy to nurture its young leaves for most of each day. As the centuries passed, its roots reached deeper and deeper, and the tree became the giant of the forest. It was healthy in appearance but rotting from the inside.

One winter, a giant storm with hurricane-force winds churned into New Zealand. The giant tree resisted, pushed back, but the wind was too much, and it toppled to the ground. The same storm created a flood and altered the river channel. The tree was swept away, but the root ball stayed buried in the riverbank. After another century, the root ball succumbed to the pull of the river, which polished it, buried it, and swept it away, then drew it back, and pushed it away again and again. The root ball has finally reached the ocean, and I stand over it. I smile and bring it home with me.

As we drive back, I get to thinking about *my* story: My great grandma tortured by Communists; my great grandpa forbidden from buying property in the United States; my grandpa forced to change his name to enter America; my mom and aunt, who were starved in labor camps in China; my dad who nearly drowned as a boy; and, most of all, my family's grueling work of forging a future as immigrants in America. It's dizzying. Every trial and triumph, the saga of my ancestors, lives in me and is as much a part of this story as Toughy and San Francisco, and Big Head, Baetis, and Raupunga.

In my front yard, I wrestle the polished driftwood into place among my other beach relics. What do you do with driftwood? You make a driftwood sculpture, of course. This new piece is of a lighter color than the rest—a nice contrast. I fuss with the placement, spinning, turning, and flipping it around until I'm satisfied. So lost am I in my project that I don't notice my visitor until she speaks.

"Howzit, Mistah Chnn?" says Nica, Big Head's owner, propping her arms against my fence.

My chest tightens. She could only be here for one reason.

"Mistah Chnn," she says with a smile, "we reckon Big Head would be gutted without you. You should take him."

Upon hearing his name, Big Head lifts his snout from a bucket of beef livers. He looks at Nica for a second, decides it's of no importance, and dives back into his dinner.

Whew. I had a hunch that something like this might happen, but I couldn't let myself get too comfortable with the idea. "You don't know how much that means to me," I reply. "Maybe I can do something for you guys."

"My yard can use some work. How about you make one of these sculptures at my place?" She points to the driftwood sculpture.

The deal done, Nica meanders back toward the school, and I stand rooted, almost in shock, at the beauty that this tiny New Zealand town has brought into my life.

"Did you hear that, boy? I'm your papa!"

Big Head, now finished with his meal, lifts his head from the sleeping platform in Lonna, his mouth rimmed with blood, his breath reeking of liver. I grab his cheeks and put my forehead to his.

"That's it, Mr. Liver Breath. You're going home with me."

He yawns and licks my face in reply. I turn to work on the driftwood sculpture, my eyes filling with tears. Baetis charges around the corner of the house, the tabby right on her tail.

I tilt my head back and look up to the drifting Aotearoa clouds. I punch the air and hoot, "Big Head! Yeah! Big Head!"

In honor of the great news, I prepare a meaty feast for us. Soon, the smell of roast chicken fills the house. The tabby and Baetis lie curled up on the futon; Big Head opts for the prime real estate under the kitchen table. Usually, I share just a leg, neck, and the gizzards with Baetis and Big Head, but tonight we will eat the entire chicken together as a family, in celebration. I rest the steaming dish on a stump in the living room. Baetis rubs against my shin, and the tabby copies her moves. Both of them weave in and out of my legs, meowing and purring in perfect synchronicity. Hearing the commotion, Big Head beelines over to my side, knocking down a few chairs in the process.

"Listen, guys, you're officially brother and sister now, so just chill out, all right?" I dig into the juicy meat with my hands, pry an entire breast out and wave it around until it cools. Big Head—suddenly strangely patient—sits back on his rear; Baetis and the tabby follow suit. They are all sitting so close to me that I could hug them all in one loving swoop. I split the chicken inches from their faces, feeding them and thanking them for all they've done.

"See?" I say. "It's all good. Sharing's not so bad, huh, Big Head?"

There are no fights at bedtime, not with so many full stomachs.

The next morning I call a pet mover. I explain my situation, the logistics of which have been keeping me up at night.

The man on the other end of the line hears me out and says, "We can help you, mate."

"But here's the thing. I live in California and won't be back there for a couple weeks. Can you keep them here, and I'll ring you when I'm ready?"

"Like I said, mate, we can get it sorted."

"Oh yeah, and you'll need to pick them up too. I'm selling my van and have no way of getting them to Auckland."

The man sighs as though I'm bothering him. "No worries. Just call me a few days before you need them to be picked up."

"Can you give me an estimate?"

Big sigh. "Um, let's see. Pickup, kennel, flight, um…say around fifteen hundred?"

Simple as that. No deposit. No paperwork.

Not bad. With the exchange rate, airfare for my new family will cost around nine hundred dollars. I'll miss the easy flow here in New Zealand. I can only imagine the hassle I'd go through in the States: What kind of dog? Does it have its shots? Do you have a fax machine? You need to sign pages one, three, and eight and send the papers back with payment in full before the end of the business day. What? You want us to pick them up? That's extra. Wait! Did you say you don't have a place to live yet? We can't take the pets without a shipping address. And on it would go.

The tabby kitten will be going to live with Andy. Baetis's mom—the Tabby's grandma—Indian, has gone missing, so Andy is in sore need of another cat. He's stoked to take the spunky rascal and has already named him Dude. Andy thought it would be appropriate since his usage of the word has skyrocketed since meeting me.

There's another task on my list that's been nagging at me—something I must do regardless of how immature it is. I would never forgive myself if I didn't try jumping the high point in the barbed wire fence behind the school. It's the same fence a *kid* had cleared easily during our goat hunt. I jog toward the fence telling myself to just go and do it. No warm ups, no scoping it out, just cruise out there, leap it, and cross it off the list. Simple enough.

I realize I've failed as soon as I leave the ground. The rusty barbed wire catches my right shin and knee, and I roll over the fence, trying to minimize the damage. In typical post-wipeout fashion I'm up in an instant, just in case anyone was watching. *Nothing to see here—move along!* I have no idea how Nick cleared that section of fence during our goat bust many months ago. Dark blood drips from my leg, but it's just a superficial wound. At least now I can cross *Try jumping the high part of the fence* off my list. Maybe if I had written, "Jump the high part of the fence," the outcome would have been different. As Yoda from *Star Wars* once said, "Do, or do not. There is no try."

One by one, my tasks fall into the done category, and the end-of-school ceremony arrives. *Maui and the Sun* provides some entertainment between speeches and awards, but the kids come down with stage fright. In rehearsal yesterday, Kea waved his great weapon at the sun and bellowed his lines. Today, he raises his hand and murmurs as though he's requesting a soda at a fast-food joint. Oh well.

Manu a member on the board of trustees, recounts the story of my cover letter, handwritten on scraggly notebook paper. "Oh, and look! He's a teacher!" he says, recalling his reaction to my job application. Everyone laughs at this. The guy they took a chance on a year ago has turned out okay, it seems.

He presents me with a fishhook he has carved out of wood and bone. In Maori culture, it symbolizes safety and is thought to bring good fortune. Indeed, looking back at the most transformational year of my life, to say I feel fortunate would be an understatement. There's someone else I need to say goodbye to as well. Although Angie's back problems kept her away from Raupunga for the last half of the school year, I haven't lost touch with her.

Do or do not.

The sheep scatter when I unlatch the gate to her front yard. The sound of an ATV augments the typical countryside hymn of *baaa*s to which I've grown accustomed. Angie's partner, Huck, is rounding up the sheep for shearing, and they mill about nervously in a paddock near a large barn. Their moans have a desperate quality to them because they *know* that it's time for pain and suffering. I hold the video camera out the window, catching a few close-ups of their concerned faces for a video piece I'll later title *Herded*, a stream-of-consciousness commentary on our lives in the paddock, herded by various aspects of Western living. I know the comparison has been made before, but it's a good way to try out a few images and ideas that have been rattling around in my head. "Those sheep have the same expression as most people on a commuter train," I say to Angie when she appears on the porch.

"Yup, you're just lucky you like your job," she says with a wink. "I mean, what's not to like about teaching at Raupunga?"

Angie knows as well as I do that it's time for me to leave, but she cannot hide her sadness. She has watched over me and helped me to thrive. In some ways, I think she sees me as the son she never had. As for me, just knowing she was there gave me confidence.

We sit at her kitchen table over a cup of tea and slices of toast slathered with a half inch of butter—New Zealand's most popular sandwich. We relive the year's events, punctuating our stories with exclamations of, "Only in Raupunga!"

She asks what I plan to do when I return home.

In reply, I sketch out a few of the options I've been considering: substitute teach for money, edit video, write some, and generally follow my creative whims. New horizons, in other words.

"That's the one," she says with a big smile. "You'd be wasting your talents staying in the classroom."

And with that, we hug a tearful goodbye. She was right. Libras and Aquarians *do* jibe.

The last fun activity on the list is to go fishing with Tim. He's only eleven, but I've never treated him like he was a kid. He's simply my fishing mate, there to share in the glee of catching a fish or to laugh at me when I slip and fall. I find him in his loose gravel driveway, waiting for me with his chest puffed out, a proud young man standing next to his latest pile of skinned Australian possums. They're so freshly skinned that they don't even smell.

"I've packed us some rabbit sandwiches," he says, beaming.

"Got a rabbit along with the possums, huh?"

"Oh...yup. Got the rabbit a few days ago, and my dad and I shot the possums last night."

Apparently, he's feeling a little celebratory as well, but I'm not to be outdone, so I nod and tell him, "I've brought aluminum foil, salt, butter, and lemons. You know? So we can cook a trout streamside."

"Sweet as."

Karen and Jenny, Tim's mom and sister, meander up from the barn, their faces dressed in countryside smiles. Jenny has a handful of woven flax flowers. I comment on their beauty, and she stands a little taller before telling me she taught herself how to weave. Even after a year, I'm still amazed at New Zealanders' willingness to create, to try, to give it a go. She has a few unwoven pieces of flax; I think of Lori and ask, "Hey, can you teach me?"

I drive extra slowly on the way to the river, savoring every bump in the road, licking the lollipop instead of biting down on it. There are a lot of memories: the straightaway where a jackrabbit would sometimes race Lonna; the bend where a double rainbow arched over me; the small rise where we always surprised a few goats feeding from the land; and the clear-cuts where I gathered my winter firewood. Along the way, Tim gives me the latest tally on animals he's killed. I listen hungrily; I've heard it all before, but this time I can't get enough.

The river is high from the late-season rains, and cottony white clouds dot the deep blue sky. Each step I take on the river, I know, will be my last for a long time. Big Head follows in my footsteps, leaving our prints in the soft mud along the bank. This is our last day in New Zealand together; the pet movers will pick him and Baetis up tomorrow. Tim walks on ahead, the squishing of the mud beneath his feet audible above the river's gurgle, and Big Head cools off with a swim and a roll on the bank. I turn to look back at the tracks we've laid. The next rain will erase them, but they will live for an eternity in my head.

The trout come easily today and—solemnly, joyfully—we prepare our riverside lunch. We gather sticks for the fire, clean the fish, and reduce the fire to coals. Meanwhile, the

Big Head taking in Aotearoa one last time.

river strums her finest tune for two fishing buddies on their last outing.

After a few mouthfuls of baked trout, I unwrap Tim's sandwich, the foil flapping in the breeze. Chunks of meat and hair poke through the squished white bread. I take a tentative bite, watching a thin line of bubbles in the river. My mind drifts. I see my family and Toughy and a piece of bone-shaped walnut. Finally, I see a blue house with white trim. Big Head sits back on his haunches, as though he's waiting for a mimosa at brunch, and considers the rabbit hair sticking to my lips. I pat his head.

"Mate," I say to Tim through a mouthful of food. "This is the best hairy rabbit sandwich I've ever had."

CHAPTER
14

UNION

TWO WEEKS LATER I'M standing in Lori's apartment, and for a second, it's awkward. "Umm, well," I mumble, motioning to the living room floor, "I can sleep here."

"What? No," Lori says firmly, shaking her head. Then she points to her bedroom, "You're sleeping in here with *me*."

Hours earlier I had shown up at her door with a handful of fresh flax. "What's that for?" she asked.

"Flowers," I replied casually.

Turns out, she hadn't received a gift of flowers from a man in over a decade. I sat at her dining room table, hands flashing, strips of flax flapping, and heart fluttering, happy to have something to concentrate on besides our nervous chatter. With each woven flower, I stamped my presence on the moment—a moment four years in the making.

After the flowers, we sat on her balcony staring out at the city for a while and making small talk about the grandeur of San Francisco and California in general. Her hair, her petite frame, and her smile hadn't changed in the time I'd been away. In fact, her cuteness seemed to increase each minute in the waning sunlight. I could barely look her in the eyes, so I sneaked glances of her when she wasn't looking. Even though we were both nervous, everything also felt oddly familiar.

As the sun dipped, she announced she was going to take a

shower. Alone at her kitchen table, I weaved another flower and savored the sound of the running water, the blow-dryer, and the opening and closing of the medicine cabinet. Lori is older than me by a few years, but like me, she passes for much younger. When she emerged from the steamy bathroom in fitted black jeans and a tight polyester shirt, all I could say was, "Oh...umm...can I use the bathroom now?"

Our first date included dinner, margaritas, and a walk around Lake Merrit in Oakland, a walk bursting with romantic places for a first kiss. We stood at the edge of the lake, the city skyline glittering on the water. Then we planted ourselves on the swings at the lakeside park, dragging our feet through the sand and sneaking brief looks at each other. Neither of us said anything about it, but we knew the wait was over. Instead, we reviewed our history.

"When did you first start teaching?" she asked. "Five years ago. That's when I first saw you."

"Oh, yeah. That's right." She dug her heels extra hard into the sand. "I can't believe it's been two years since the *letter*."

"Neither can I. We hung out a lot, but those weren't real dates." I laughed. Then I stopped abruptly with mock concern. "*This* is a real date, isn't it?"

She smiled, stopped swinging, and replied, "Yes."

It seemed as though every duck, goose, and seagull stopped whatever they were doing, their surface wakes fading into the glassiness as they waited for us to lock lips. But the buildup to the moment was too much, especially with us reviewing our past and what seemed like destiny. Nerves got the best of us; we finished our walk with no kissing.

But now, here in her bedroom, there's no stopping us. I slip under the covers, streetlights shining weakly through the curtains and illuminating her face. My arms are stone, as if locked in place. I'm petrified, unable to believe this is actually happening after imagining it for so long. Then Lori wiggles easily into my embrace. At last, we kiss.

As the Kiwis would say, "That's the one."

My alarm sounds all too early; I'd like to spend the rest of the day in bed with Lori, but a couple of special animals landed on American soil last night. Baetis and Big Head are being driven up from Los Angeles at this very moment. I kiss Lori goodbye and tiptoe out of her apartment. Outside, I let loose, leaping over an imaginary barbed wire fence, the streets of Oakland dissolving into a green field full of stampeding cows. No hill is too steep, no bush too high, and I bound and spin as if I am goat busting with the boys. I'm always amazed by the energy I have after the first night with a new girl—or in this case, *the* girl.

I get to the meeting place first, and the parking lot is empty. A heavy marine layer is blocking out the sun this morning, but nothing can quell the joy that courses through me. Soon, a white van with the words *Pet Taxi* stenciled on its side pulls around the corner. In the back, Big Head rears up on his hind legs, and we lock eyes through the side window. It's hard to say who is happier, dog or man.

"Big Head!" I bellow. "What are you doing, boy? Big Head!"

He bounds out of the van, jumps on me, and runs around and around, his hindquarters moving faster than the rest of his body. Somehow he knows exactly where to go: he leaps into my van, his new doghouse on wheels. Baetis, meanwhile, glares at me through the wire mesh of her kennel. Her look says, *What the heck? Where am I?*

An hour later, we pull up to our new home. I knew the city would be too overwhelming after a year in the country, so I rented a thirty-three foot trailer nestled in the redwoods south of San Francisco. The sun begins penetrating the marine layer in the treetops, and its rays filter through the canopy of giant redwoods towering over us, greeting us as we arrive.

Baetis stretches and takes in her new surroundings. Her belly is a little swollen, so I kneel down to investigate. Yep. She got busy again before she left. Looks like more than one

Kiwi kitty got off the plane last night. I was going to have her spayed before I left, but I didn't want the added stress on her. One more litter and her momma days will be over. Baetis rolls over onto her back. At full arch she pauses and presses her paw into my hand, a gesture I interpret as, *Good to see you, Pops. So this is America?* I rub her head, telling her about the window ramp I'll build for her. I also tell her to be careful, because there are different kinds of animals around here. The landlord's small black Lab comes racing down the driveway, tail wagging, drool flying—and obviously enamored of the new dog with the exotic accent. Turning around slowly, she lets Big Head—who still has his goods—get a good whiff of her behind. Right then, I decide to let Big Head spread his Kiwi genes just once before being neutered.

This story will go on.

chapter 15

WITHOUT RAIN
THERE CAN BE NO RAINBOWS

S NOWBANKS BLOCK THE ROAD, the last of winter desperately hanging on under the sheltering evergreens. We plow through these holdouts, determined to make it to one of my favorite camps. In the meadow to our left, last year's grass lies matted to the ground; tips of this year's grass, a bright vibrant green, are just beginning to poke through. Waterfalls swollen with runoff cascade down the steep bank on the right side of the road, sprinkling us as we rumble by. Early wildflowers honor us with a dash of color. As we pull up to the spot, I feel something leave me. I've just completed one orbit of my life.

Leaving Holly, my trusty old Astrovan, at the dirt road, we hop a fence and descend into a familiar valley. We're mostly quiet, our eyes on the snowcapped peaks, on the aspens swaying in the wind, on each other. Smiles and tears come and go. Big Head, totally unaware of the gravity of this trip, crashes through the tender young growth, kicking bursts of sage into the air where its scent mixes with the pines that surround us. Lori at my side, her hair in pigtails, makes smaller and shallower footprints next to mine. We come to a small rise that overlooks the valley and its meandering stream. The stream's chorus sings loud and clear, "Welcome back."

At the edge of a grove of trees, a piece of bone-shaped walnut lies on its side. With trembling lips and a heaving chest,

Welcome back.

I flip it over and read the engraving. The ground is wet, soaking my pants as I kneel. The sand that blankets Toughy's grave has sunk, and clumps of grass crowd into his space. Two years have passed—a hiccup in time for this valley but an epoch of change for me. Today, there is no need for a pick and shovel, no need to beg my dog to eat, no need to catch my smile.

As we hike out, I look down, concentrating on my feet. The ground underneath the dead grass is still very soft, so each step makes a *crunch-squish* sound.

Crunch-squish, Toughy died. Crunch-squish, I followed my dreams. Crunch-squish, Big Head is here now. Crunch-squish, I-Gaw passed thirteen years ago. Crunch-squish, Lori—the girl I love—squeezes my hand.

Mena Kore E heke mai te ua, Ehara te Kopere.
"Without rain there can be no rainbows."

EPILOGUE

My Chinese name is Gin Fu, meaning "wealth." My life is rich with family, friends, experiences and, of course, memories.

I FOUND GOOD HOMES for all of Big Head's puppies and Baetis's kittens. Then it was time for their Kiwi-gene-spreading days to end, so Big Head was neutered and Baetis spayed. Baetis enjoys following Big Head and me on walks. They can be found cuddling together in Lori's and my bed, on the rug, or in the sunny areas around our yard.

With the advent of Facebook, I've been able to keep in touch with the people I knew in Raupunga. In March 2011, I learned that a few of the "boys"—as I called them back then—are in jail and another has sustained injuries from gunshots. The news saddens me, but I still believe they can make a positive impact in Raupunga. It is never too late to make changes.

A new orbit came into my life on April 4, 2010: my son. Lori and I look forward to teaching him the value of stories and memories.

I like to think of this project as a memory built of memories. As I wrote and revised the manuscript—and spent thousands of hours editing video—the memories I chose to share grew richer, became more meaningful. I've heard that happiness is a skill that must be practiced every day. Appreciating and learning from memories is also a skill.

To say this was the hardest project I've ever taken on would be an understatement. At times the work stressed my relationship with Lori to the breaking point. Somehow though, I understood that my challenges were part of a journey that would eventually make a great memory. I recognize now more than ever that the love I give and accept, the choices I make, and the experiences I create today will be my memories tomorrow.

TO THE PEOPLE OF NGATI PAHAUWERA

IT'S BEEN ALMOST A decade since you took a chance on hiring me. With all my heart, I thank you again for one of the most transformational and memorable years of my life. Not a day goes by that I don't think about the children and the *haka*. It was never my intention to write a book or edit videos about my experiences with you, but if there's one thing that I learned from living in New Zealand, it's that creativity is inherent and not something to ignore. This story had to be shared.

When I lived in Raupunga, I strived to be open and respectful. The difference between your upbringing and history and mine is so vast that it would have been easy to pass judgment on each other. We had a beautiful year together because of our respect for one another. As I wrote the book, respect was still a top priority of mine. Names have been changed to protect privacy, and although the gang culture added flavor to the story, I took great care not to sensationalize the events that took place, or the lifestyle that some of Raupunga's residents choose to live.

I look forward to bringing my *whanau* to visit someday. I want my children to feel the pride of the Maori people, to run on the sands of Mohaka beach, and to experience the haka.

Tu Meke!
Mr. Chin

CREDITS

WHEN I STARTED WRITING this book, I promised myself to appreciate the process no matter how long or frustrating it turned out to be. I knew I had a good story to share, but I also knew I needed help in honing my writing. So over the course of four and a half years, I worked with three different editors.

Chris Smith, my surfing friend, was the first to review my writing. As a magazine writer and editor, he had little tolerance for tangents. Chris's edits put a clamp on my overwriting tendencies.

The problem with memoir is having too much material to work with, so it's difficult to determine what will be poignant to the reader. Ali McCart was the next person to pound away at the delete button while reviewing my manuscript. Her keen sense of a story's flow helped me choose and restructure information in a way that I could never have done myself. Thirty pages were deleted after her initial edit. Then, over the course of a year and a half, I wrote another thirty pages in expanded scenes, new scenes, and added detail where she felt the story was lacking.

When it came time to proofread the manuscript, I was contacted by S. Evan Stubblefield, a colleague from my teaching days. Together, we found a balance between my surfer-dude lingo and proper grammar.

Chris Smith
Writer, photographer, editor
www.ca-smith.net

Ali McCart
Indigo Editing & Publications
www.indigoediting.com

S. Evan Stubblefield, MA
Copywriter, editor
www.simhawrites.com

Brett Neiman
Cover design
www.brettneiman.com
www.simpletonmusic.net

Vinnie Kinsella
Interior design
Vinnie Kinsella Publishing Services
www.vinniekinsella.com

Digital Bindery
E-book and multimedia e-book design
www.digitalbindery.com

Leigh Brooks
Web site design
www.leighbrooks.com

Shirak Agresta
Animated Title Page for Enhanced Edition

Bob Richardson
Video Sweetening for Enhanced Edition
www.sqwarellc.com

ACKNOWLEDGMENTS

IN JANUARY OF 2007, I walked into a writing class at Portland Community College. A woman looked at me sternly and said, "Okay, tell us. What is your book idea?"

Despite the pressure of being put on the spot in front of the class, I managed to let my story spill out, "My dog died, my brother passed, a beautiful Maori village, crazy gang stuff, new dog, first cat, and then—there's this girl that I love..."

The woman replied, "If you don't write that book, I will write it for you!"

That woman is Julie Fast. She is a published author and an expert in bipolar disorder and depression. She is challenged by those illnesses herself, so she is a constant inspiration. Her book *Get it Done When You're Depressed* has a home at my writing desk because writing a book and feeling depressed go together! Really, I've never been so insecure about what I was *doing* until I started writing. I can say with confidence that this project would never have been started, let alone completed, had it not been for Julie's unwavering enthusiasm and support. Thank you, Julie. More information about Julie can be found at www.juliefast.com.

This project would not have been possible without my family. Mom and Dad, though separated now, will be together in my heart for the rest of my days. No matter what I have done in my life, as long as I am passionate, they have supported me. Thank you, Mom and Dad, for everything. And to my sister, Eileen, thank you for never judging my meandering ways. I love you all.

Working on a project of this magnitude is hard enough without the demands of growing a relationship and a family. Thank you to Lori and my son for creating balance in my life. Without you, this project would mean nothing.

ABOUT THE AUTHOR

RYAN CHIN LIVES WITH his wife and son in Portland, Oregon. His love of fly-fishing and surfing connects him to rivers, and the ocean. Time with waves and currents reminds him to pursue those silly little streams of thought that run rampant in his head. He believes a person can never have enough reminders. Sharing his experiences through writing and filmmaking helps remind him of lessons he's already learned.

CPSIA information can be obtained at www.ICGtesting.com
Printed in the USA
BVOW071434121111

275928BV00001B/2/P